ADVENTURE CARAVANNING WITH DOGS

TO HEL IN A HOUND CART

JACQUELINE MARY LAMBERT

Copyright & Disclaimer

First Paperback Edition 2022

Book Design and Formatting by Debbie Purse

This is a work of creative nonfiction. The events and conversations in this book have been set down to the best of the author's ability, although some names and details may have been changed to protect the privacy of individuals.

All information, advice and tips in this book are based on the author's personal experience and do not constitute legal advice.

While every effort is made to ensure its veracity, there are no representations or warranties, express or implied, about the completeness, accuracy, reliability, suitability or availability with respect to the information, products or services contained in this book for any purpose. Any use of this information is at your own risk.

ISBN (paperback): 978-1-7396222-1-3

ISBN (ebook): 978-1-7396222-0-6

Contact:

Facebook: www.facebook.com/JacquelineLambertAuthor

Amazon: www.amazon.com/author/jacquelinelambert

Goodreads: www.goodreads.com/author/show/18672478.Jacqueline_Lambert

Bookbub: www.bookbub.com/profile/jacqueline-lambert

Blog: www.WorldWideWalkies.com

Adventure Caravanning With Dogs

To Hel In A Hound Cart

Journey To The Centre Of Europe

Jacqueline Lambert

I would like to dedicate this book to all those around the globe who suffered as a consequence of the 2020 coronavirus pandemic.

PART I

SPAIN AGAIN

Map of our Trip

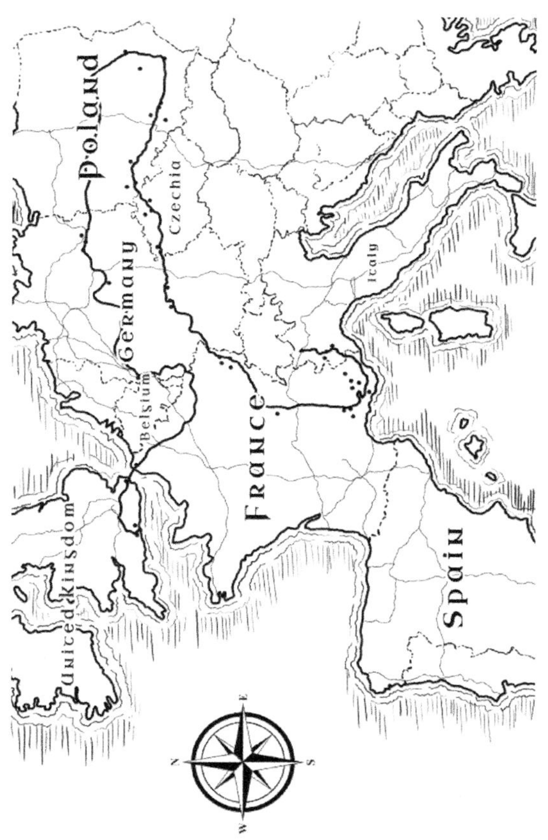

1

LEAVING LOCKDOWN: A BIT OF A SCRAPE

Good luck is in the eye of the beholder...

If we got there, it would be third time lucky.

Twice before, my husband Mark and I had planned to tow Caravan Kismet ('Fate') from England to Spain with The Fab Four – our quartet of loveable Cavapoos (a cross between a Cavalier King Charles Spaniel and a Poodle).

Our first attempt got as far as... the French side of the English Channel. Expiring in Brittany's 35°C (95°F) heat, we couldn't face heading south into Iberian temperatures reported to be over 50°C (122°F), so we turned left and went to Romania.

The previous September, two days before we were due to board the ferry to Spain, our tenant gave notice. We postponed our crossing to sort out a re-let, which would restore the income that funds our travails. I mean travels. The delay meant no time to nip through Spain before our planned ski season in northern Italy.

The unexpected seems to follow us around. Our

friends call us the Ca-Lamberti. They often utter phrases such as, “It could only happen to you two...”

Yet, what happened next came right out of left field. We were ambushed by a global pandemic.

Overnight, we were locked down in northern Italy, the epicentre of Europe’s number one coronavirus hotspot. It was impossible to return to Britain. As full-time nomads, with our home rented out and every campsite closed, we literally had nowhere to go.

We were stuck in Italy until restrictions lifted at the end of June. After eight months in one place, including four months under one of the strictest coronavirus lockdowns in the world, we were desperate to leave. The UK was still off limits. It was locked down, its borders closed, and we still had nowhere to go. Our options prompted a lively discussion,

“We could still go on a road trip,” Mark said. “A caravan is the perfect socially distanced way to travel. It’s transport, ensuite hotel, and restaurant all in one.”

I considered the infection risk to ourselves and others. Since we’d spent the pandemic isolated in a mountain village with a population of fewer than ten, I concluded,

“We obviously don’t have coronavirus. If we stay in the caravan and avoid contact as far as possible, we’re less likely to catch it. Europe is opening its borders, and I reckon businesses who have been closed all these months might appreciate our tourist euros.”

Satisfied it was both legal and safe to travel, all we needed was a destination. Since we’d lost three months in lockdown, we no longer had time to execute our original plan to tour Poland and the Baltics, so Mark suggested,

"What about Spain?"

Seconds after Mark and I sat down together for our first night inside our home-on-wheels, we heard the familiar machine gun rattle of torrential rain hammering on our roof.

The caravan was pristine; cleansed to a sheen in readiness for our expedition. Then, our little bog monster, Ruby, took a last spa bath in her favourite muddy ditch, just outside the door. She sneaked in looking like a drowned rat and smelling much worse. Once inside, she shook over everything, including Mark's laptop, then hid behind a curtain.

Welcome back to adventure caravanning with dogs!

Despite this rather moist re-introduction to mobile living, we were happy to be on the road again. Well, not exactly on the road. We were parked up on a piece of waste ground next to the apartment we'd rented for the winter, but would be on the road again early the following day.

On that perfect bluebird morning, who knew that, for the second time in our caravanning career, a lorry would drive us up the wall?

Less than an hour into our trip is where you find us gazing at Caravan Kismet wedged hard against the retaining wall of a hairpin bend, after the reckless truck ran us off the road.

We were in a dilemma. If we moved either forward or

backwards, the rough rock would tear the caravan open like a sardine tin. As we wondered how to get ourselves out of this predicament, traffic continued to build up and cause a further hazard on the precarious mountain road.

"If we let the opposite tyre down, would that bring her away from the wall sufficiently to move her?" Mark suggested. It didn't look hopeful, and that would just add a flat tyre to our woes.

"What if one of us jammed ourselves against the embankment and pushed with our legs? 'Legging it', you know, like canal barge pilots. They lie on the deck of their boat and walk them through tunnels?"

It was way too dangerous. I was grasping at straws.

Our eternal confidence that 'There's always a solution' was looking more misplaced than ever, when, out of nowhere, a flock of angels appeared, clad in orange overalls.

Several workmen wearing tangerine-coloured hi-vis clothing spilled out of a nearby house. They got stuck straight in by managing the traffic.

In rapid Italian, one workman indicated he would do something. I wasn't altogether sure what until his mini-digger clanked up the tarmac on its caterpillar tracks. He tied an industrial-sized cam strap to Kismet's chassis. Expansive gesturing suggested he would use the digger to pull the caravan away from the wall.

I was sceptical. Since the top was wedged, I didn't think pulling the bottom would do the trick. Besides, I was worried that it might twist Kismet's undercarriage, but I lacked the Italian and sign language vocabulary to object.

Amid the kerfuffle, a gathering crowd was urging

Mark to move forward. We've had bad experiences in the past with people trying to take over when we're manoeuvring the caravan in tricky situations, so Mark only ever listens to me. As the mini-digger tugged, like a sudden ray of light from Heaven, a gap opened up between Kismet and the embankment.

"Mark. Drive forward. Now," I yelled,

It was a matter of millimetres, but there was just enough clearance for Mark to pull away and swing around the bend.

Mindful of not adding to the traffic jam we'd created, I bandied a few swift but heartfelt "*Grazie mille*"s to the workmen and onlookers as I vaulted back into our van, Big Blue's cab. Then, two rather shaken road trippers continued on their way.

"Let's go to Conad," I said. Our not-so-local supermarket in Pont St. Martin was nearby. "We can take five, grab a coffee, and assess the damage."

With few shops in the mountain villages, a regular two-hour round trip to Conad had punctuated every one of our ski seasons. We knew that, besides having a café, the supermarket car park was large enough to accommodate Kismet and Big Blue's twelve-metre (40 ft) majesty.

Dings and scrapes to a beloved vehicle are always distressing, but as we ran our hands down Kismet's sides, we couldn't quite comprehend the extent of the damage.

"All I can find is a gash on the plastic trim above the wheel arch, and a graze along the Perspex bedroom window. Obviously, they won't be cheap to repair, but they're both replaceable."

A closer examination led me to say, "I think we can probably live with it. The trim is just decorative. It's not functional, and the scratch on the window is right in the bottom corner, out of the main field of view."

As we rationalised the incident, we agreed we would take scrapes and scratches over the other possible outcomes. Those involved losing our home. Or our lives.

We consoled ourselves with a palate-searing coffee, deep breathing, and a slice each of our favourite fruit flan. Mark berated himself for being careless, but I asked him,

"What else could you have done? Perhaps if we'd stopped to buy vegetables in Gressoney St. Jean, we wouldn't have met an impatient lorry on the apex of a blind hairpin. And if you had not been such a gentleman, you wouldn't have pulled over so far, trying to solve the problem the lorry driver caused. But if you hadn't got out of his way, the truck might have hit us head on, or peeled off our entire left side."

Even so, I bemoaned our bad luck a little.

"I said, 'Rabbit. Rabbit. Rabbit.' on the first of June. It was the first thing I said. I haven't remembered to do that in ages, and I was really pleased, with it being the month we depart on our travels. It was supposed to bring us good luck."

Mark was quite sanguine. "Maybe it did," he said. "What if the workmen hadn't been there?"

"True..."

"In the midst of the calamity, even the best possible outcome looked terrible. Those workmen got us out of a sticky situation really quickly and with minimal damage. Considering the circumstances, you could say that your 'rabbit' worked some magic. I'd say that if anything, we have been extremely lucky."

The plan had been a scenic drive on A-roads through the Aosta Valley to our destination, Paesana, in Piedmont. Instead, we picked up the *autostrada* and paid the tolls. Now, all we wanted was to get there, settle in, and calm down.

Without thinking, I pushed the giant red button at the toll booth for a ticket, then recoiled with horror as I realised I had potentially touched coronavirus. We had no hand sanitising gel; it was the one thing we could not buy in Italy. For the rest of the journey, I sat with my contaminated hand aloft, as though delivering a blessing. I tried not to touch anything; Mark, myself, dogs, water bottles, door handles – all much easier said than done. It was a timely demonstration of how easy it was to spread the virus. I vowed to root out my gloves next time, or place a tissue over my button-pressing finger.

We found the campsite in Paesana easily. The Italians are a friendly bunch, but the owner welcomed us with a level of excitement that Ruby might lavish on a previously undiscovered mud puddle. A return to some normality, albeit with face masks and socially distant two-metre gaps, was a brave new world for us all. Throughout lockdown, I had never left Staffal, so checking in was my first experience of wearing a face mask. Besides steaming up my glasses, I felt as though someone was trying to chloroform me.

Manoeuvring was tight. Kismet's tail caught on a pitch marker. Another tiny scrape, but nothing compared to the earlier incident.

While Mark prepped the caravan, I took the pups for

a walk. Despite the relief that we were still here to enjoy the remains of the day, I felt fractured. My flimsy cloak of composure was in tatters. I needed to chill.

I found a footpath along the River Po. The air almost dripped with the scent of honeysuckle, and the pooches splashed and played in the clear water. For travelling, I had worn my long hair in practical plaits, but as I walked through meadows on the banks of the Po, a bee got caught in my tightly tethered mane, right next to my scalp.

It was just one of those days.

"What did you think of the river walk?" Mark asked when I got back, peering at my semi-untethered locks.

I relayed the bee incident, along with my initial impressions,

"It's not exactly the pristine nature of Monte Rosa. There was so much trash on the riverside path, and groups of teenagers hanging around."

The truth is, Paesana is incredibly pretty, surrounded by bosomy green hills, with smart, rambling villas peeping out through curtains of lush green vegetation. There were footpaths everywhere, and field upon field of fruit trees and crops in the valley proved it was a major part of Italy's food basket. But it was civilisation – and after four months of total isolation, I was simply not accustomed to it. In addition, I had realised an uneasy truth. It was impractical to dodge all human contact and avoid touching everything.

I recalled the astronauts on the doomed Apollo 13 space mission. To return to Earth, the crew had to abandon the sanctuary of the lunar module, Aquarius, which had acted as their life raft. It was a move fraught with danger and uncertainty. No one knew whether their damaged mother ship would survive re-entry into Earth's atmosphere. Abandoning the refuge of our apartment in a deserted ski village during such uncertain times, I felt much the same.

It was not the most promising start to our Spanish Stroll. Possibly, all I needed was wine and a good night's sleep. I hoped things might look better the next day for our proposed investigation of the stunning nearby hill town of Saluzzo.

I thought of the day four years ago, when we first moved into our caravan full-time. Within half an hour of collecting Kismet from storage, we had our first adventure. It was most definitely an adventure, as defined by Yvon Chouinard, because something went very wrong.

A flatbed lorry speeding around a blind corner on the wrong side of a narrow country lane nearly ghosted us. It was carrying a static caravan.

The Universe certainly has a sense of humour.

At least I could console myself that on previous form, if we survived a near-death experience within the first hour of a trip, the rest should be plain sailing. Shouldn't it?

2

HILL TOWNS AND CLOUD FORESTS – SALUZZO AND PIAN MUNÈ

The Paramount Pyramid, Oompah Parties on the Po, plus the Charms of the Chub

Saluzzo was primarily a conveniently located stopover to break the journey, but Mark and I anticipated our visit eagerly.

Founded in 1,000 AD, Saluzzo is one of the best-preserved medieval towns in the Italian region of Piedmont. It occupies a striking hilltop position, with the perfect pyramidal peak of Monviso, 'The Stone King', in the background. Saluzzo takes its name from the Salluvii, one tribe who first settled in the area, while *Il Re di Pietra* – The Stone King, is allegedly the mountain upon which Paramount Pictures modelled their logo.

Yet, orbiting the ugly, industrial areas on the outskirts, searching in vain for somewhere to park, left us underwhelmed. Just after we gave up and set off back towards the campsite, the one-way system deposited us at the parking in Piazza Garibaldi. Part of the lower town, it was in a perfect location right next to the *Cattedrale*, which had waited patiently for our arrival since 1481.

Saluzzo has a very understated atmosphere. On narrow, ancient avenues, cobbled with pebbles, we wandered up towards the hilltop castle. The street, *La Salita al Castello* – The Ascent to the Castle, took us past 15th-Century palazzos and the square, civic tower. The tower dates to 1462 and, following several additions and extensions, is now nearly 48 m (160 ft) tall. We gave the pups a drink from the Drancia fountain, whose carved relief was smoothed and eroded with time. The blank imposing bricks of the castle walls befitted its use as a prison up until 1992.

The old town's buildings were run down and crumbling, although there were cranes everywhere; evidence of money being spent on renovation. There was very little there and for us, Saluzzo had none of the charm of the lovely hill villages of Vézelay and Mirmande that we had visited in France. Maybe because it was an authentic, working city, rather than a manicured tourist trap, carefully designed to impress.

It was 25°C (77°F) and cloudy, which cut out our view towards Monviso, but made a tour of the town with our four pups bearable. Since coming down from the mountains, the heat had been oppressive. Like stepping into a sauna. We ambled back past the 12th-Century church of St. Giovanni and the Casa Cavassa, a museum in the former residence of Galeazzo Cavassa and his son Francesco, vicars to the Marquis of Saluzzo.

A stone carving of the Cavassa family crest above the

door particularly appealed to me. Heraldry often favours majestic animals, such as the eagle, bear, or unicorn. I imagined how the Cavassa choosing-a-coat-of-arms conversation might have gone,

"Hey Dad, shall we opt for a lion rampant? An eagle *épandre*? Or a what about a stag salient?"

"No, son, I think we should have a fish."

"What, you mean something big and impressive, like a marlin? Or fierce, like a shark or piranha. Or maybe we could go for clever and playful, like a dolphin."

"C'mon Fran. You know a dolphin is not a fish. It's a marsupial. I was thinking more along the lines of a *chavasson*?"

"A chub? That's not very imposing – and aren't they a coarse fish, renowned for being really easy to catch? Even without bait?"

"Yes, they are, but you will surely change your mind once I tell you my interesting fact about the chub.

"As you know, our family motto, '*Droit quoy quil soit*' is ambiguous. It can mean either 'Straight Ahead No Matter What' or 'Justice No Matter What', which the chub represents perfectly. It is well known both for its affinity for swimming upstream, as well as an unswerving commitment to fair play and due process."

"Wow, Dad. You're a genius. It's perfect. And *everyone* will get that – even an English person looking at it in five hundred years, by which time chub will also have become slang for an erection."

Another of Saluzzo's notable features is its excellent food. Back in the lower town, we stopped for *pranzo* – lunch at one of the many street cafés under the porticos.

When the coronavirus lockdown eased in Italy on Star Wars Day (May the Fourth be With You!) we could buy takeaway food or coffee to eat elsewhere. Now, the restrictions permitted drinking or dining at an establishment, albeit with outside seating only. Since we travel on a budget, we visit restaurants only occasionally. However, this was a rare privilege we'd been denied for months. At the end of June, this was our first meal out, sitting at a table, since mid-February. It felt like the most extravagant treat.

During his internet research, Mark tantalised me with a picture of a delicious-looking ground beef burger with octopus. I pressed him for details as I salivated on the street, but he had forgotten the name of the restaurant. In the eatery we chose at random, I settled for fresh grilled tuna with salad, followed by *panna cotta* and a coffee, all served by a friendly waiter wearing a face mask. While it was not an octopussy surf 'n' turf, it was a fine second choice. After four months of lockdown and near-total isolation, it was unbelievably exciting to be 'somewhere else' and 'out to lunch', with the congenial buzz of other people around. A pandemic certainly makes you re-evaluate how much you value simple pleasures.

Mark and I were tired when we got back, but not only from the heat and exercise. Our nights in Paesana were not restful. Like Quasimodo, the bells troubled us. We had exchanged distant clarions of cowbells in the Alps for a duo of campaniles in uncomfortably close proximity.

Our campsite was on the road to the Sainte Croce

church. I could not pinpoint the location of the Sainte's competing bell tower, but they each chimed every half hour and were out of sync just enough to leave very few minutes of the day – or night – chime free. 7 a.m. was a particular percussive highlight. The reverberating ad-lib of bongs, booms, wallops, clangs, clatters, peals and jingles from both belfries reminded me of the classic ten-minute 1970s drum solo by Cozy Powell. At least it got us 'up and at 'em' before the daytime heat kicked in. Since we had dropped to 600 m (2,000 ft) from an Alpine village at 1,800 m (6,000 ft), we were feeling the force of Italy's early summer heat.

Marked hiking paths surrounded Paesana, but perhaps because we like the views, or were missing the mountains of Monte Rosa, we headed up hairpins for the high ground. The primeval fantasy realm we found was unlike anything we had seen before in Europe. It reminded us more of humid cloud forest in Costa Rica or Hawai'i. Unfortunately, at the top, as in all the best cloud forests, mist obscured the views.

It was a relief to be out of the heat, though, and a nice change to walk somewhere where everything was not steeply uphill, as it had been for the last eight months in our vertiginous Monte Rosa valley. We strolled with the pups through the charming, mysterious woodland. Damp, mossy and deserted, it was filled with magical wooden animal carvings. The path led to a beautiful waterfall, whose white water looked almost luminous against the dark primordial shades of emerald. If we'd seen elves and faeries dancing in the spray, we wouldn't have been surprised.

In winter, Pian Munè is a small ski resort, so we took

advantage of the mountain refuge to treat ourselves to only our second post-walk coffee and cake since lock-down ended. So close to the French border, the service couldn't have been more Gallic if a militant baguette-wielding *gilet jaune* had hurled our snack at us. With a dismissive wave of her hand and without looking up from her iPad, the boss shooed us away from the unoccupied, shady tables on the wooden terrace in front of the restaurant.

"You can't sit there. That is for lunch. Go over there."

Our clothes clung to us like clammy shower curtains as we dripped with perspiration in full sun. Mark told me,

"On my way inside to order, she snapped at me, 'You will be fined if you don't wear a face mask.'"

Had Mark not already paid, I would have voted to leave immediately and deny her the business, although the excellent coffee and fruit flan made up for the couldn't-care-less attitude. The local blueberries from the abundant fruit orchards of Cuneo (pronounced Koon-yo) were almost the size of damsons.

Back at the caravan that afternoon, a violent thunder-storm split the skies and made us rejoice that The Bells had forced us out early for our walk. We had met the two ladies camped opposite while they were out walking their dog and felt sorry for them braving the torrential rain in a tent. In more normal circumstances, we would have invited them over to sit in our caravan. Unfortunately, in such blighted times, social distancing prevented such random friendly encounters, which are so integral to the pleasure of touring.

It was not just The Bells that gave us another sleepless night, though. The campsite seemed popular for parties, although the ridiculous oompah karaoke did stop on the button of 10 p.m.

We knew that because, between them, the clocks chimed twenty.

3

TOWING THE GORGES DU VERDON – OUR MOST CHALLENGING DRIVE… EVER

While towing a caravan, we admire sheer drops that are measured in miles

"The Transfăgărășan was nothing compared to this!"

Mark was referring to the day we joined the Mile High Club – with Caravan Kismet in tow, you understand. The Transfăgărășan is Romania's second-highest mountain pass. It crosses the Carpathian Mountains at an altitude of 2,000 m (6,600 ft – or 1.25 miles) and features on a website that lists the world's most dangerous roads.

Kismet has conquered several mountain passes but none compared to the Gorges du Verdon, which caught us entirely by surprise.

'We drive past the gorge," Mark informed me before we set off. If only he'd got his facts straight…

When we looked it up later, the Gorges du Verdon also appears on the Dangerous Roads website. I am fairly sure that whoever described the drive as 'not for the fainthearted,' was probably referring to navigating it with a car – not in a 5 m (16 ft) van with a 7 m (23 ft) caravan in tow.

We hadn't given any thought to the route that led to our destination; our plan was simply to see the Gorges. Who would not be wooed by 'Europe's answer to the Grand Canyon'? (A title also appropriated by the nearby Ardèche, a little less deservingly, since Verdon is actually the second largest canyon IN THE WORLD!)

I say we, but secretly I wondered whether, following the hairpin-related tribulations on Day 1, Mark had decided to get back on the horse that bit him…

Our first worry was getting Kismet out of the campsite at Paesana. Space was so tight that our manoeuvre in had forced us to use the pitch opposite. Since we arrived, vehicles had filled every space around us. Luckily, our neighbour departed about 5 a.m., giving us one speculative route out; provided we could swing Kismet round without catching her bum on the hedge at the back and her towing gear on the electricity bollard at the front.

Getting others to help with your caravan is always fraught with problems. In sticky situations, everyone develops their own slightly unique vision of a solution. Even if you explicitly tell them your plan, you usually find that they know best. Not only that, moving a large vehicle such as a caravan is a super-macho show of strength, so people (more accurately, 'men') tend not to understand that you have to watch the back, front, and the top, all at the same time. They invariably launch straight into pushing as hard as they can with scant regard for anything approaching a plan. This was the very means by which we lost quite a few bits of Kismet's rear end in Romania.

So, with some trepidation and all fingers crossed, we delivered what we hoped were crystal clear instructions in a mixture of pidgin-Italian and English to the English-speaking wife of the Italian muscle we co-opted from next door. For once, it worked. We swivelled Kismet forty-five degrees, hitched, and drove off without even the hint of a problem.

Although it was eighty miles further, but only fifteen minutes longer than the scenic route through the mountains, we opted to take the *autostrada*. It followed the Côte d'Azur, which we thought would be a pleasant drive, and rather gentler on our van, Big Blue's overworked clutch.

A plethora of quaint terracotta-coloured hill villages invaded our coast-bound vistas. A tough, unyielding castle guarded each one. The town of Mondovi spilled down a typical Piedmont tump, like toffee-coloured sauce dripping down a green Christmas pudding. We passed into Liguria, which shared the same undulating, verdant landscapes as Piedmont and, judging by the number of castles, the same troubled past.

Then, we saw the sea. At Imperia, as we turned right along the coast, the ocean beyond that most Azur of Côtes was a distinct Mediterranean blue. The pink or white blooming oleander bushes planted along the *Autostrada dei Fiori* – the Motorway of the Flowers were a much more pleasing alternative to the UK's bloom of ragwort and rosebay willowherb. Instead of exhaust fumes, sweet, jasmine fragrances streamed in through Big

Blue's windows, left wide open to keep our cool. The twenty-seven degrees of heat reflecting off the concrete carriageway had defeated her air conditioning: a situation we soon discovered was permanent.

We crossed into France and flew past Nice and Monte Carlo before turning north through the centre of Cannes. As we passed through broad boulevards lined with palm trees, there was not a leaf out of place. Each of the ostentatious villas in the hills above boasted its own regimented lines of standard-issue cypress trees.

An expensive, Monaco-registered gangster-mobile with blacked-out windows summed up the obscene wealth and 'F-You' attitude of the place. He raced dangerously up our inside on a slip road then slewed straight across our nose into a line of traffic, leaving us with nowhere to go. Although far too busy and far too important to deliver it in person, the middle finger he flashed in our direction was implied.

Originally, we had planned to visit some pretty villages in the mountains above Nice, but we pushed on. Brash, busy, and brimming with their own self-importance, we decided none of these ill-mannered, modern-day coastal Gomorrahs was our kind of town. Money can't buy class. In fact, it usually buys the opposite.

The narrow hairpins of the D6085 wound a treacherous route away from the crassness on the coast into the magnificent, layered limestone mountains above Cannes and Grasse. The sheer number of motorbikes and classic, open-topped cars suggested the route must have been a designated 'scenic drive'. I noticed some mention of Napoléon on a sign, which showed I had something to look up.

"He probably crossed through here with his elephants," I smirked. Mark gave me a withering, sidelong glance. (He knew I knew it was Hannibal.)

Later, I discovered the road was actually the Route Napoléon from Cannes to Grenoble, which follows the marching route of Boney and his troops in 1815. After escaping exile on the Isle of Elba, he landed on the Côte d'Azur with his troops and set off to conquer Paris and overthrow King Louis XVIII. He succeeded, and his subsequent 'Hundred Day Campaign' went swimmingly. Until Waterloo...

They say a week's a long time in politics, but in a single day, French domination of Europe ended and Napoléon was exiled to St. Helena, where he ended his days. They dub Route Napoléon 'one of the best drives in France'. It also features on the website Dangerous Roads, so someday, we must conquer it with the caravan.

Our journey took us through several nature parks; the Parc Naturel Régional de Préalps Azur and the Parc Naturel Régional du Verdon. Near Escragnolles, we stopped for fuel. It was the only thing to do there, because sadly, they had cancelled their Donkey Festival due to COVID. A little further, we joined a Route de l'Histoire et des Legendes.

We hadn't booked a campsite, since few seemed to have websites, but we had one in mind, whose friendly owner had earned excellent reviews. There were dozens of sites in the area, so we were confident we would have no problem.

"We go past the Gorges," Mark told me as we started driving along a narrow lane that ran alongside a river. At Rougon, we happened upon a municipal campsite by the water that looked appealing, so we pulled hastily into a layby for a quick discussion.

"We're only eight miles from our proposed destination," Mark said.

"Ah, well, we might as well go on. We know that's here, so we can easily come back," I said. Famous last words.

The next eight miles were the most challenging of our entire caravanning career.

We had hairpins, overhangs, and sheer drops you could measure in miles (0.4 miles to be precise – or 0.7 km), with no safety barriers to speak of. In places, the road was wide enough for only one vehicle, and these sections often took us by surprise because they were hidden by blind corners. On a sunny Sunday, you could add to the mix crowds of motorcyclists with a death wish, huge A-class motorhomes taking advantage of their excellent, all-round visibility to admire the view, as opposed to watching the road – and a British caravan causing chaos. Caravan-hating former *Top Gear* presenter Jeremy Clarkson would have been so proud.

I fear for the observational skills of the average driver, since we hardly travel incognito. A bright blue van, two metres high, with paddle boards on the roof, towing a seven-metre caravan. I always enjoy noting the point at which oncoming drivers spot us and slam on their brakes. Often, it's just a matter of feet from our bonnet. Even on a road that urged caution with every bend – and regardless of the unguarded sheer drop – drivers still hared recklessly around corners and tried to squeeze past us when there was no room. On at least three occasions, this caused gridlock. Rather than wait a millisecond to let us clear a bend, the oncoming cars chased each other nose-to-tail until nobody could move.

Curiously, the responsibility for reversing on a narrow mountain road appeared to fall squarely upon an articulated twelve-metre/forty-foot van and caravan combo, rather than a microscopic Renault 4.

Formula One racing driver, Sir Stirling Moss, famously said, "It is necessary to relax your muscles when you can. Relaxing your brain is fatal."

I felt like lecturing the other drivers. The Gorges du Verdon is no place to relax your brain.

Driver stupidity was the very reason that we failed to make it around the final junction en route to our campsite. As we positioned ourselves for a left turn, the rear of Caravan Kismet stretched back far enough to cork up the narrow village road in La Palud-sur-Verdon. With a spectacular lack of foresight and anticipation, a long snake of cars mindlessly followed each other until, bumper to bumper, about twenty cars blocked the road onto which we were obviously trying to turn. With a timely response, it would have taken a moment for someone to stop and let us go on our way, no reversing necessary. But impatience and lack of awareness denied us our route, so we couldn't unblock theirs.

Fortunately, regarding U-turns, Mark is as matter-of-fact as Britain's Conservative government. Let's call this one 'Let's Go For Herd Immunity And If Your Granny Dies You Will Just Have To Take It On The Chin,' which pretty well sums up their approach to the early stages of the pandemic. The unobservant, bovine drivers sitting in a line left us with no choice but to abandon our left turn (Herd Immunity) and continue straight on (with Lockdown and Social Distancing Which Has Already Proved Successful Throughout The Rest Of The World) to find somewhere to turn around our twelve-metre/forty foot length.

It was such a shame that, despite these caravan-dressage heroics, our proposed campsite turned out to be a scorched field with no shade, so we executed another *volte face*. We called this one 'Strict Quarantine For Travellers From Places Abroad, Which Mostly Have Lower Infection Rates Than Britain. And Bugger Social Distancing.' The latter was in celebration of the newsreel pictures of our home beach in Bournemouth on a sunny weekend during lockdown. It was crowded with half-a-million people, shoulder to shoulder, enjoying furlough, a scheme whereby the government paid them 80% of their salary to stay away from work.

We had spotted a shady municipal campsite just before the village of La Palud-sur-Verdon, and that is how we ended up in Camping Municipal Le Grand Canyon. There, for good measure, we did another U-turn on our policy of having a few days off the booze. We had a glass of wine and called it 'Chief Adviser to the PM, Dominic Cummings, Breaking Lockdown and Quarantine Rules By Driving Himself And His Wife from London to Durham While Both Showing Coronavirus Symptoms Then Having A Day Out In The Car To Test His Eyesight.'[1]

Well, if U-turns and rule breaking is good enough for the government, it's good enough for us.

Cheers!

[1] 'Dominic Cummings: What is the scandal about?' BBC News 26 May 2020: accessed online 15th February 2022 via www.bbc.com/news/uk-52811168

4

MOUSTIERS-SAINTE-MARIE AND SUP IN THE GORGES DU VERDON

We go to one of France's favourite villages – and head up the creek with a paddle!

The Gorges du Verdon is the most wonderful part of France that you've never heard of.

At least Mark and I hadn't and couldn't understand why; what, with it being the world's second largest canyon next to the Grand Canyon and all. Mark has seen the Grand Canyon, so he could offer a comparison,

"The Grand Canyon is so big it's almost impossible to take in. It's impressive, because it's huge and spectacular, but Verdon is truly beautiful."

We rose early with the intention of visiting Moustiers-Sainte-Marie – a worthy member of the very long list of 'Most Beautiful Villages in France'. Instead, exhausted after our hair-raising drive in, we opted for a chilled-out day in the shade around the caravan.

Since we were on the road for an extended tour, winter and summer, we had brought a huge amount of gear – ski stuff and four winter tyres, all our windsurfers and SUPs (Stand Up Paddleboards), plus bicycles, dog trailers, and a blow-up boat. This had forced us to be selective about what we included.

Our super-sized awning, the tent thing for the side of the caravan, occupies three large plastic storage boxes. It had been the first casualty of this thinning out, although Mark convinced me he had a solution. He committed to creating a significantly lighter awning from scratch, out of purest green. It sounded like one of the character Baldrick's cunning plans in the TV sitcom *Blackadder*. Yet, as good as his word, he fashioned a low-cost, compact, and lightweight awning using only a roll of PVC-coated polyester sheeting and stitch-on awning rail insert. The end result was far better than expected. It looked quite artistic, like those trendy sails that people drape over their patios, but in a much more 'Lambert' shade of lime green. It matched the fully surrounding windbreak, which was our latest innovation in Cavapoo Containment to stop our four pups from straying; particularly that Nosy Rosie, who has no qualms about popping in to visit unsuspecting neighbours inside their campervans.

With tremendous excitement, we treated ourselves to dinner out. The sweet little village of La Palud-sur-Verdon was a short walk away from our campsite along a shady footpath, where the dogs could run loose. We bought some walking maps in one shop, then made the waiter laugh out loud in the Styx restaurant,

"*Deux fish and chips, s'il vous plaît.*"

"Very English," he replied, even though I'd ordered

my two fish and chips in perfect French, with a Lancashire accent.

Well, there was no resisting it once we'd seen it on the menu, despite the array of local delicacies and the *plat du jour* – dish of the day; grilled pork with tarragon. After so long away from home, we were missing some staples of British cuisine, such as steak pudding, curry, and a roast. Battered hake and *pommes frites* with tartare sauce and a slice of lemon was the next best thing to a square of paper, filled with cod and chips from our local chippy. Laced with vinegar, sand, and a Bournemouth beachfront sunset, you can't beat it.

To a former professional beer-taster, the locally brewed Verdon ales also sounded interesting. I tried the white beer with *citron* – lemon – and bergamot. Mark chose amber ale with chestnut and gentian. They were both delicious, so we ordered another one each. I am not sure we would have enjoyed them quite so heartily had we known that the thimble-sized artisan bottles cost €7 each. Our drinks cost more than our overnight accommodation.

The following day, we arrived early at Moustiers-Sainte-Marie, whose ancient pastel-coloured buildings nestle into the arresting backdrop of a huge, limestone cliff and narrow gorge. Our early start paid off, since the huge cliff still shaded the village. Even at 8 a.m., when we took our fur family for their morning pee poo, the heat of a Provençale July was fierce. A pleasant walk up through quaint, narrow and, thankfully, shady streets joined the free car park on the main road with the village. Moustiers is an artisan kind of place, famous for ceramics and soap, created from the renowned, aromatic Provençale lavender. The factory for the famous L'Occitane products was in nearby Manosque, and in more normal times, offered free guided tours.

We walked up to the 12th-Century chapel of Notre-Dame-de-Beauvoir, which looked down upon the town's terracotta rooftops. Legends varied about the metal star strung on a chain across the gorge above the chapel. The main one suggested that, after being imprisoned by the Saracens, Baron Blacas promised to hang his star above Moustiers if he returned safely from the Crusades.

On the steps of the chapel, a little boy was passively aggressively refusing to have his photo taken. Every time his mum raised her camera, he stuck his water bottle in front of his face. I giggled as she rolled her eyes at me with a knowing but resigned look.

"Voulez-vous un photo avec un chien?" I asked him. "Do you want a photo with a dog?"

To the delight of his parents, he posed willingly with Lani next to him, face uncovered and beaming broadly into the lens.

Back in the village, we popped into the tourist office to ask the whereabouts of an ATM.

"*Credit Agricole,*" the man said, spattering the expansive Perspex protective screen with saliva.

At the ATM, a pleasant chap, dressed all in black, came over to say 'Hi' to The Fab Four.

"Where are you from? I'm from *Bourgogne*. Burgundy in English."

Somehow, I knew he was a biker. I guess the mane of wavy, grey hair above his all-black ensemble of T-shirt, shorts, and a leather waistcoat gave him away.

"I'm going canyoning this afternoon," he said. "I've wanted to do it for twenty years."

His enthusiasm was infectious.

"You've chosen the most incredible place to try canyoning," we said. "Enjoy!"

Luckily, hubs and I have already terrified ourselves with canyoning. For us it involved abseiling down through a thirty-foot waterfall, with the water pushing our feet off the sheer and slippery rock, cliff jumping, then a horrendous full body flush through a natural drainpipe in the rock. These days, we have to forgo such pleasures because of The Pawsome Foursome, although we wouldn't be without the love and joy they bring every day.

The summer season was not quite in full swing, perhaps because of the lockdown, so most of the cafés and restaurants in Moustiers-Sainte-Marie were closed. We decided to visit the reservoir, Sainte-Croix, for coffee and stopped at the town of Salles-du-Verdon. It was bursting with shops displaying inflatable flamingos and garish beachwear. Just as the bakery was closing for lunch, we scored a tasty Nutella muffin and coffee to enjoy at a shady table outside.

The town itself was set back from the lakeside, so, fortified with caffeine and chocolate, we walked down to the water's edge. While there were a few small gaps, sunbathers occupied most of the shoreline and we didn't feel it was polite to inundate them with a pack of wet, excited hounds. The Fab Four are very noisy when chasing sticks into the water and inevitably choose to shake themselves over an unsuspecting sun-warmed beach body.

We dunked the pups to cool them off, then returned to a car park we had sighted adjacent to the Pont du Galetas bridge, which spans the gorge where the River Verdon empties into the lake. Most of the lakeside car parks had height barriers to stop motorhomes from camping overnight on the shore. The surf boards on Big Blue's roof also prevented us from entering. This car park was free, had no height restraints, and was close enough to the beach to carry down our SUPs. It would have been rude not to.

The campsite had warned us to take care when launching or swimming in the gorges. The lake is the third biggest in France and was man made as part of a hydroelectric power scheme. This signals the potential for sudden and dramatic changes in water levels. Since the area around the Pont de Galetas was busy with pedalos, electric phut-phuts, and kayaks, which were for hire nearby, we figured we would be safe.

The majesty of the gorge causes involuntary sighs of awe to leave your body. In places, the limestone cliffs soar nearly 1,000 m (over 3,000 ft) above you. The colours are other-worldly. Daubs of orange streak the pale limestone, and the river achieves the most unfeasible shades of jade and swimming-pool turquoise. As we paddled upstream, we passed caves where swooping flocks of swallow-like crag martins nested. A shimmering, white pillar of water in freefall down the canyon walls contrasted with underlying mossy rocks. In places, we navigated beneath overhangs to enjoy a light, cooling sprinkle of water droplets, which imprisoned diamond flashes of sunlight as they fell.

With two dogs each, we left behind most of the boats

and went at least a mile upstream. Away from the crowds, we reached a point where the sheer rock walls gave way to an expanse of pebbly beach. The Fab Four and Mark swam, but the icy water literally stole your breath from your lungs. Even in the blazing summer heat, I couldn't face full immersion.

The current was too slack to offer much help against the wind that whipped sharply up the ravine on our return paddle. The downstream leg also passed with more incidents than our outbound journey.

At one point, when our boards came close, Rosie vaulted from Mark's to my board, so that I had a trio of pooches aboard. My balance is not great, so when I had a bit of a wobble, Rosie half jumped and half fell into the water. Instead of swimming back to me, she made a beeline for shore, if a sheer rocky cliff could pass for 'shore'. She scrambled up onto a rock ledge, so I scooted over to retrieve her. As we approached, Ruby shot me a look that demanded,

"Shall I go ashore? Are we going ashore? Rosie has gone ashore. Should I follow her?"

Of course, Ruby took matters into her own paws and leaped off. She swam over to join Rosie on the cliff, which was not helpful. In a reasonably shambolic fashion, Mark and I both paddled over and retrieved everyone. I picked up Ruby, while Mark collected Rosie, although somehow Lani abandoned my ship and left me alone with Ruby, so Mark had three dogs aboard – and his balance is worse than mine. A quality he was about to demonstrate in spectacular fashion.

The wind blew away my baseball cap. Although I'd tied it to my bikini, its tether had come loose. A chap in a pedalo graciously retrieved it and waved it aloft like a trophy.

"I'll fetch it," said Mark, ever the gentleman, but sometimes forgetful of Newton's third law of motion.

He threw the hat over to me – and the equal and opposite reaction was that his SUP tipped up, landing him and the rowdy three in the river. Our pups on SUPs, in their brightly coloured life-jackets, had attracted plenty of attention throughout our paddle. However, I'm sure their impromptu ducking with Mark will have been the most Instagrammable shot of them all. Sadly, we have no photographs ourselves. Mark had barred me from taking my camera on the basis he could never trust me not to get it wet. In different circumstances, I might have felt inclined to point out that I was the only one who didn't fall in.

But back on shore, the clear plastic dry bag I wear around my neck to carry Big Blue's key was so full of water, all it needed was a fairground goldfish. My camera would not have survived.

We had spotted a *8 à Huit* store in Salles and called in to get something for dinner. Luckily, we caught it when it was open. Despite the twelve-hour promise implicit in its name, *8 à Huit* spent much of its time closed, as it admitted on a sign sellotaped to the door. I might write and suggest they re-brand it *8 à Huit Sauf de 12h à 15.30h et Dimanche Après Midi* to reflect the three-and-a-half-hour lunchtime and Sunday afternoon closures.

The selection of fresh fruit and veg was great, and I bagged two superb, marinated pork chops from the *boucherie* opposite, but somehow, I lost my celeriac remoulade on the way home.

Later, Mark found my celeriac remoulade where I had placed it, on the shelf by my bed in the caravan. He called me a lemon; which by Mr. L's usual standards, was extremely polite.

To be honest, we were both lemons, because we both got the tops of our feet sunburnt on the SUPs. I had applied sunscreen; Mark never bothers, but despite being the type that binds to your skin, my shoes must have rubbed it off. I already had a blister from my trusty sandals, which had gone stiff after lengthy immersions in sea water the previous summer. Then, a half-litre glass bottle of Orangina fell out of the fridge and its edge landed right on my big toe. It felt like someone had hit my nail bed with a hammer. I voiced my equal and opposite reaction to that, and it was a lot stronger than "lemon", let me tell you.

They say, "No foot, no horse" and the same applies to humans. I had tried so hard to protect my feet, but with blisters, sunburn, and a bruised big toe, I couldn't wear any kind of footwear.

Luckily, ClimbOn cream, my wonder medicine, worked a treat overnight and took the heat out of the sunburn. The next day, we planned to stay off our feet anyway, and scare ourselves silly by driving the picturesque but vertiginous Route des Crêtes – the Crest/Ridge Road. I did not wish to be forced into my dad's shoe-based singularity – sporting sandals with socks. To show due respect, that very year, I sent Dad a pair of socks with sandals printed on for his Father's Day gift. I was incredulous when we spoke on his special day.

"What do you mean, you refuse to wear such a kind, thoughtful present?"

For years, I lambasted Dad about this footwear foible until I tried it for myself in New Zealand, to keep sand-flies at bay. As a backpacker, I travelled light. I had only sandals and hiking boots and it was too hot for boots. To my surprise, sandals with socks is unbelievably comfortable, but I can't possibly admit that to Dad...

The prospect of the drive made us both quite nervous, but Mark consoled me.

"The Route des Crêtes is not on the website Dangerous Roads – and we're doing it without the caravan."

What could possibly go wrong?

5

DRIVING THE ROUTE DES CRÊTES

Vultures and Voitures

With storms forecast, we battened down and gave up on our Route des Crêtes plan. Yet, despite distant thunder and light rain the previous evening, I awoke at 7 a.m. to a sky of powder-blue Provençale perfection.

"Shall we get up and go for the Route des Crêtes?" I asked Mark.

The D23; the Route des Crêtes or Crest Road, is a circular, panoramic drive, high above the Gorges du Verdon. It is another famous French balcony road, blasted into a sheer cliff face. Unlike the main road we'd taken to our campground with Caravan Kismet in tow, the Route des Crêtes was built purely for pleasure on what had been an old mule track. We were quite nervous about it anyway, regardless of the weather. Its high point is approximately 1,300 m (4,200 ft); not the best place to get caught in a storm on a narrow highway blessed with hairpins and dizzying drops.

Since the loop is only 23 km (14 miles) long, we estimated it would take an hour to drive. Even with our recent poor record of thunderstorm avoidance (storms had soused us several times on walks in Monte Rosa), we thought the weather gods would be pushing it to whip up a tempest out of nowhere in so short a time...

On our first evening and a few morning walks with the dogs, I met a smiley, friendly young chap sitting on a bench near the campsite. He loved the pups, particularly Rosie. He threw sticks for her, which she bounded along to retrieve with her usual irrepressible joy.

Sebastian worked morning and evening at our campsite. He had a dark, tanned and muscular physique.

"I love the area," he told me. "I climb and hike, but I work all hours to earn money to buy climbing equipment."

"Do you ever get a holiday?" I asked.

"Not for two years."

Sebastian gave me a few suggestions to make the best of the area.

"Drive the Route des Crêtes in the morning, so that it is not too hot, and visit Castellane. There is a market on Wednesdays."

As with most of the roads in the Gorges du Verdon, the drops on the Route des Crêtes are immense and the safety barriers, if indeed there are any, the height of a matchbox. We read that those with vertigo should travel anti-clockwise, since this direction hugged the mountainside, rather than the sheer drop side. This is not possible, since part of the route is one-way.

We made our preparations like a couple of convicts going to the scaffold. In case of overhangs and low tunnels, Mark removed the SUP boards from our roof rack. At the roadside a few hundred metres outside the campsite, he pulled over to clean the windscreen before setting off up hairpins. You can't be too careful.

"Are you sure we should do this?" I asked. The nerves had well and truly taken hold.

"It will be fine," he reassured me, which was ironic coming from him, considering what happened a short time later.

Even before we reached the initial *belvédère* ('beautiful view') designated view-point, we paused to admire the magnificence of the countryside laid out before us.

At the first stop, *Belvédère de Trescaire haut*, I walked to the edge of the cliff, clinging on to the security barrier like a sailor gripping the rails of his ship in a storm, my knees weak with trepidation. At its highest, the gorge is 700 m (nearly 2,300 ft – or 0.4 miles). From hundreds of feet above, it seemed odd to be looking down on the shiny, dark backs of crag martins, who flitted in huge posses around the gorge walls.

"Don't go near the edge," Mark warned. I could hear the tremble of raw fear in his voice.

Mark and I both wibble with heights and by the third *belvédère*, Mark was so shaken by the exposure at the view-points, he said,

"I won't get out to look. I don't want to lose my nerve for driving. Just take loads of photos and I can admire the views afterwards."

Back in our van, Big Blue, we proceeded without seat belts, so that we could make a hasty exit if we looked like going over the cliff. We'd heard the local legend of a Maserati that skidded over the edge. The occupants cheated death only because the car got caught up in the branches of a tree. If anything happened, Mark promised to get the dogs out first.

"What if our brakes fail?"

"I'll just run into the rock wall."

I was pleased that he joined me at *Belvédère du Pas de la Bau*. We knew that griffon vultures had been re-introduced into the area in 1999, the year we were married, but we did not expect to encounter a dozen of them circling in thermals above the gorge. Mark quickly lost confidence and went back to the dogs in the van. He left me with a,

"Be careful. Don't get carried away and forget where you are."

A friend of mine, an experienced rock climber, plunged himself into intensive care from Pillar Rock in the UK's Lake district. He momentarily forgot where he was, and stepped backwards to take a better photograph.

I could have stayed for hours to absorb the magnificence of these gigantic birds as they soared and wheeled, adding drama to an already dramatic landscape.

As we continued on to *Belvédère du Tilleul*, the magnified shadow of a vulture passed over Big Blue's roof and momentarily blotted out the sun. It felt like we'd been overflown by a pterodactyl. A primeval shiver rippled up our spines.

Unlike the other roads in the area, and bridges in most of France, the tunnels on this road-built-for-pleasure all had height and width markers. They were even less relevant than they might have been on the D952 into Palud-sur-Verdon, since the Route des Crêtes has plenty of stopping places where it would be possible to turn around. On the main road into the Gorges, U-turns were absolutely not an option. Once you started, you had to finish – and there was no signage to help.

In the narrow and precipitous one-way section, it was reassuring to know there was no chance of crazies approaching head on. Yet the Route des Crêtes saved the scariest until last. Replete with blind curves and the sort of drops that feature in a base jumper's wet dream, I said to Mark,

"I'm glad we're on the mountain side, not the OSS (Oh Sh** Side)!"

To keep Big Blue as far from the precipices as possible, he just stared resolutely ahead and hugged the rock wall.

It took about ninety minutes door-to-door, with stops at most of the fourteen *belvédères* and a quick call into the lovely bakery in Palud for fresh croissants for breakfast.

I felt so grateful to have experienced it, since it had seemed the impending storm might deny us the chance. It was a spectacular drive and well worth doing, but for us both, the highlight was the vultures. To see one would have been a privilege, but to witness so many together was just incredible.

We agreed that it had been nowhere near as terrifying as we expected, but it had been quiet, the weather perfect, and we had taken it at our own pace. A set of circumstances that would not coalesce when it came to towing our caravan out of the Gorges...

6

VERDON TO AVIGNON

We plan, the gods laugh...

Big Blue and Caravan Kismet were all packed up and ready to go right on schedule at 9 a.m.; all set to tackle the dodgy precipitous part of our route out of the gorge while it was traffic-free.

We had appointments in Avignon the following day, but it must have been a quiet day for the gods, who decided upon a little sport at our expense.

As Mark pulled off our pitch, I heard an ominous grinding noise from Caravan Kismet's wheels. I shouted to Mark to stop.

"I think the brakes have locked on."

Brake trouble.

Just the ticket when you're about to tow a caravan on one of the world's most dangerous balcony roads, with sheer drops measured in miles.

We stopped to check the obvious. The caravan hand-brake was off. We pulled forwards and reversed in an attempt to release the brakes, but both wheels continued to grind.

Like a terrier shooting down a rabbit hole, Mark disappeared beneath the caravan. I made myself useful with an internet search for anything obvious. A forum popped up immediately and suggested that failing to pull forward slightly after reversing a caravan can cause the brakes to lock.

We always de-compress the tow hitch after reversing. A lesson we learned the hard way on our very first day of caravanning, which delivered a practical demonstration of the effects of compression.

1. Either you can't disconnect the caravan from the tow ball, or;
2. If you do disengage, the hitch immediately shoots forwards with the power of Mike Tyson's jab to leave a lovely dent in the back of your car. A perfect and lasting *aide-mémoire* for next time.

Mark revealed that no reversing had taken place. Lately, rather than driving up ramps to level Kismet and jiggling forwards and backwards to line up the ALKO wheel lock with pinpoint accuracy, he simply jacked up the caravan, aligned the lock, then shoved a block under the wheel. A no-tears approach to levelling and locking.

I phoned our dealer, who suggested rocking the caravan backwards and forwards might release the brakes. Once again, we rocked and rolled; all to no avail.

Finally, we reached the dreaded point of last resort. Mark uttered the ominous phrase,

"You speak French. You'll have to phone a mechanic."

My heart plummeted like a caravan off a cliff.

Our last trip had taught me how to ask a campsite receptionist for jump leads – *les pinces*. I opened Google Translate and noted the phrase for 'caravan brakes locked on' – *freins de caravane bloqués,* and used my best French to explain our dilemma to the campground receptionist. She looked up a number for a mechanic, but refused to phone on my behalf. My pleas on the grounds of diminished vocabulary fell on deaf ears. Her compromise was that if I struggled, she would take over the call.

Then, Mark burst into reception.

"Hold fire. The breakaway cable looks tight." (The breakaway cable engages the caravan brakes should the caravan unhitch itself while towing.)

A taut breakaway cable applying the brakes was another early mistake in our caravanning career. Like the opening of a hydroelectric dam, relief flooded through me. I was convinced we had found the issue.

We hadn't.

Defeated, I trudged back to reception a second time to take on Practical French, Random Challenge #47: 'Get a Mobile Mechanic to Fix Locked Brakes on a Caravan at the Municipal Campsite in Padon.' I was in such a tizz that I even got the name of the town wrong – the campsite was in Palud-sur-Verdon.

I couldn't understand a word from the first garage. The receptionist took over the call and quickly relayed a succinct verdict. The mechanic's avalanche of impenetrable wordage basically meant,

"*Non* – No."

I got on better with the garage in Castellane, which

was just as well. Serving a customer, then fielding an incoming phone call occupied my receptionist friend throughout. I was on my own.

"*Trente minutes*," said the lady at the garage. Thirty minutes. Hope swelled in my heart.

"Thirty minutes until the mechanic comes?" I felt I might burst with excitement and relief.

Yet hope ebbed away like fluid from a severed brake cable when Madame clarified that *trente minutes* was not when the repairman would arrive to save our bacon. Thirty minutes was when I needed to call her back to get a price for the mechanic to come, because,

"*J'ai des choses à faire* – I have things to do."

I delved further to clarify the un-volunteered terms and conditions and discovered the price I would get in thirty minutes was for a technician to come to the campsite to give an estimate for the work.

"There is no way he can do the repair on that visit, and you must pay mileage for every fifty-kilometre round trip from Castellane to Palud."

"Is the mechanic available today?" I asked.

"*Non*."

"Even to do the estimate?"

"*Non*."

"It's Friday, so does your mechanic work on Saturdays?"

As predictable as night follows day, and trouble follows the Ca-Lamberti, the answer came,

"*Non*."

With a sinking heart, I agreed to ring for the price in half an hour. At least it would give me a chance to find an alternative to this obvious *pis aller* – last resort.

I relayed the excellent news to Mark's legs. He had been busy. He had a wheel off and was still scrabbling around beneath the caravan. Once again, I searched the internet in the vain hope of finding a better solution. By now, the witching hour of 10:30 a.m. had passed. Campsite reception was closed and locked, along with any further options to conscript my reluctant translator into our web of mechanical misery.

I resigned myself to an expensive and possibly lengthy delay to our travels. Normally, getting stuck somewhere as lovely as the Gorges du Verdon would be no hardship, but tribulations such as these only ever happen when you're on a deadline. We had long-standing and hard-won appointments to keep in Avignon the following afternoon.

Britain's imminent exit from the EU would invalidate The Fab Four's UK pet passports, so we'd arranged to see a vet to get them French passports. Also, with impeccable timing, on the first day of lockdown, I lost a filling. With dental surgeries closed throughout the pandemic, I had endured months with a cavity.

Unlike the garage personnel in Castellane, Avignon's vet and dentist worked on Saturdays.

I scrolled through the thoroughly British AA, RAC, and Red Pennant European recovery websites. The straightforward solution was clearly one that involved a transaction made in association with a native English speaker and an immense wad of cash. Then I heard a tremendous clang and a yelp. I leapt out of Big Blue,

"Are you okay?" I asked Mark's legs, convinced that Kismet had slipped off the jack and crushed him.

"I've fixed it," came the jubilant cry. "Come and look."

I squirmed underneath the caravan to join him and saw the system of levers that operate the caravan brakes.

"What did you do?" I asked, expecting some technical wizardry.

"I clobbered it with the torque wrench and it clunked back into place," Mark said.

So, while I challenged my French vocabulary in conversation with two mechanics and sought inventive solutions via the internet, simple brute force had won the day. It was the mechanical equivalent of turning it off and on again. I hugged him in relief.

With the wheel re-attached, I noticed a very distinctive sound as Mark drove Caravan Kismet forward.

Silence.

I called Madame to say I no longer needed her estimate for the estimate. Her deadpan reaction was hard to decipher. As a former salesperson, I know how infuriating it is to spend valuable time preparing a quote, only to be told, "Oh, I don't need it now," – or simply never hear from the customer again.

However, in that moment, I knew another payment had become due.

The torque wrench had spared us hundreds of euros and an interminable delay. The gods would exact their price.

Despite our forebodings, we executed the terrifying hairpins to Moustiers-Sainte-Marie without incident and continued on our way through the lavender fields of Valensole. Purely by accident, we had arrived in Provence at the optimum moment to see lavender, right in the middle of the brief season (between mid-June and mid-to-late July, depending on the year and the weather).

If you drive on the UK's A303, you summit a small hill near Amesbury and Stonehenge appears. I remember my thoughts the first time I saw it. *Is that Stonehenge? The world-famous ancient monument, just there by the side of the carriageway? It can't be...*

Then I realised; it was the real thing.

It was an 'Oh Wow!' moment.

The approach to Valensole was similar. We topped a rise and suddenly, our entire vista was extraordinary; filled with rippling waves of the most vivid shade of royal purple. The road cut straight through two magnificent fields of lavender, with hazy blue mountains as the backdrop on one side and a conveniently located Provençale farmhouse, built from golden stone to the other. We pulled over on the roadside and walked through neat rows of pillow-like lavender plants. The field was alive with white butterflies and the buzzing of bees. The scent was heavenly.

The route onwards to Puimoisson was jaw dropping, with a barrage of constantly changing vistas and scents. Yellow swathes of sunflowers smiled and bobbed their heads in front of a landscape blanketed in violet. Pink oceans of clary sage reminded me of someone sweating in a nylon shirt. Regimented lines of curry plants transported me back to Saturday nights in the famous Brick Lane curry houses, close to where I worked as a beer-taster in the East End of London. Along with the fresher aromas of aniseedy fennel and stands of pine trees, the chirruping sound of cicadas also drifted in through Big Blue's open windows, which was now her only functioning air-conditioning system.

It was beyond Apt (the commune *and* the adjective)

that the deities deployed the next surprise they had in store.

The Mistral.

In Languedoc dialect, *mistral* means 'masterly' and there was little doubt over who was in control. Our journey became a white-knuckle ride as the famous, wild wind of Provence pummelled the caravan with the subtlety of a steam hammer.

Caravans are relatively light, but have a large surface area, which makes driving in strong winds extremely hazardous. Without a deadline, we would never have continued. My stomach churned as visions plagued me. Caravan Kismet overturned. Our belongings strewn across the road then swept up in a tornado. At one point, the wagging nose of a blue SUP entered my field of vision at the top of the windscreen. We pulled over near a stand of thrashing trees to tie down the boards on Big Blue's roof more firmly. For the first time in two passionate decades of board sports, the power of the wind had loosened the cam-straps. Inches away, traffic roared and whizzed past. The shock waves from thundering lorries buffeted us as we fumbled to secure the knots.

After our delayed start, we had pushed on without lunch and were both starving. On the outskirts of Avignon, we passed a McDonald's drive-through.

"Shall I pull in here?" Mark said.

"Yes," I quipped, playing along with his obvious joke. Then, "What the hell are you doing?" as he swerved into an industrial estate.

The stress of the day caught up with us both, and there were tears before bedtime. Mark was upset by my reaction, but after an awful start to the day, followed by hairpins and high winds, I had undergone a full, eight-hour shift of absolutely terrified.

We have done some strange things with the caravan in tow, but I didn't think Mark was serious about taking a twelve-metre rig into a drive-through. Besides, I had lunch prepared in the caravan fridge. It was late afternoon and we had reached Avignon. I was under the misguided impression that we were only a few miles from our destination, and thought we could wait.

As we sat and starved in horrendous traffic and road-works through the industrial estates of Avignon, we settled our differences. I was heartbroken that we'd had cross words.

"We never argue," I lamented. As usual, Mark put it into perspective with his gentle wisdom,

"But when we worked, we used to be apart much more of the time. Now, we spend all our time together. We do well. We agree on all the big things. It's just an occasional misunderstanding about something small."

It's true – and our arguments usually follow the same pattern. Something shocks me into anger or silence, which Mark misinterprets as annoyance directed at him. Then, when all I really need is a hug, he gets angry with me for supposedly giving him the silent treatment.

As my blood sugar plummeted like a depressed lemming off a cliff, I wished wholeheartedly that I had agreed to the drive-through.

Our campsite was off the main road just beyond Avignon. A sinister stuffed red squirrel guarded the reception desk.

The site seemed slightly rough; several permanent-looking caravans and chalets mouldered away under the trees, and someone had stored their burger van opposite our pitch. Three vicious dogs, tied on long ropes outside one chalet, looked like their owners had abandoned them for the day and gone to work. They barked non-stop, adding to the cacophony of cicadas, who achieved a decibel level similar to that of a symphony orchestra composed of pneumatic drills. In case I put you off eating forever, I won't mention the toilets. We were glad of our own on-board facilities.

It was a blunt reminder of why we rarely book campsites and obligate ourselves to the unseen. This was a functional stop because of our appointments. As a sacrifice to certainty, we had made a reservation and paid a deposit. The site was in a convenient location and reasonably priced in an expensive area. We reassured ourselves that, on the upside, it was refreshingly shady in the mid-thirty-degree heat, but made sure that we locked everything securely when we took The Fab Four out for an evening leg stretch.

Unintentionally, we strayed through the vineyards towards a nearby castle, whose advertising promised, 'Eight Quality Activities for the Family'.

We happened upon part of their Quality Sculpture Walk and Quality Aviation Park.

Although our day had been a roller-coaster ride of the unexpected, with brake failures, multi-lingual cries for help, gales, and an escape attempt by a SUP from the roof rack, at no point had I expected to see a medieval turret juxtaposed with a Russian MIG fighter jet.

7

THE PENNY PINCHER'S GUIDE TO PONT DU GARD

The Stone Giant – one of the best things I have ever seen

Nous Sommes Citoyens de France – We Are Citizens of France!

Now, The Fab Four was officially *Le Quatre Fabuleux*.

I had been to the dentist and we had visited the vet. There, the pups got their outstanding vaccinations, a pipette for leishmaniasis – a sandfly-borne disease rife around the Med (Mediterranean) – and French passports. On American Independence Day, they gained the right to unlimited travel throughout Europe: a privilege Mark and I would lose forever in just a few months, at the end of the Brexit transition.

As a treat, we took *Le Quatre Fabuleux* to the river to cool off and chase sticks. It was so hot, I sought refuge by creeping under a bush. Then, we set out to scope out a back way into the Pont du Gard.

Official entry into the world's largest and best-preserved Roman aqueduct cost €9 per person – the equivalent of a night on a bare campsite. We might sound like penny pinchers, but it all adds up when you're on a budget and doing stuff every day.

"I've seen its picture on the internet," I crowed, so we nearly didn't bother to go to see it. That would have been a huge mistake.

The bridge has the decency to span the River Gardon, so we considered paddling up to it on the SUPs. Pont du Gard is also on the GR63 long-distance walking trail, and a *voie verte* cycle way. We assumed, correctly, that if we paddled or approached from a national route, there would be no entrance charge.

After parking on the roadside beneath an avenue of plane trees, we joined the GR63. The first 'Wow' came immediately, as the path turned to reveal a crumbling Roman aqueduct.

Pont du Gard is the masonry equivalent of Michael Jackson – the sibling whose individual fame eclipses its larger whole, i.e. The Jackson Five. The Pont is just one small part of a 50 km (31 mile) aqueduct, built to carry water from Fontaine d'Eure, near Uzès, to *Nemausus* – Nîmes, 'the Rome of France'. I was astonished to see how much of their creation remained.

The shady stroll was worthwhile in itself, although following an ancient aqueduct added an exhilarating frisson of excitement for me.

Then my jaw hit the deck.

Imagine yourself in an unspoilt pastoral area, filled with small scrubby trees and gnarly olive groves. You turn a corner and suddenly, a colossal structure appears like a mirage in front of you. Three tiers of monumental arches, stacked one on top of the other, to form a lacework of honey coloured rock. Roughly 50 m (160 ft) high and 270 m (895 ft) wide, it is two-thousand years old, and almost completely intact.

Even without the bridge, the setting was devastatingly picturesque. Ivory limestone bordered a sparkling river valley, which cut through a wilderness of verdant vegetation. I felt awestruck. Simultaneously dwarfed and elevated by the majesty of the scene.

Twelve arches which connected the bridge to the rest of the aqueduct were looted for stone in the middle-ages, but the state of preservation was extraordinary. When I reflected more deeply, the miracle of Pont du Gard blew me away.

First, a Roman engineer had to scout the best route for the aqueduct, and find the most suitable place to cross the Gardon. With no helicopters, drones, or Google Earth, this would have been on foot or horseback, through rough and untamed topography. Then somehow, vast quantities of materials had to be quarried, prepared, and transported to the appropriate site, through the same unfriendly terrain. For an idea of scale, the bridge alone contains about 55,000 tonnes of dressed limestone. The biggest blocks are two cubic metres in size and weigh up to six tonnes each.

Then, an army of craftsmen and labourers needed housing and provisions while they raised the immense structure by hand. I could still see some protruding stones, placed to support the wooden scaffolding used during construction.

As the crow flies, the distance between Uzès and Nîmes is only 20 km (12 miles), but to avoid the Garrigues de Nîmes hills, the architects used a more circuitous route. The mountains weren't the only obstacles. The aqueduct crosses approximately twenty bridges and passes through hundreds of metres of tunnels.

The bath houses and fountains of *Nemausus* consumed forty-four-thousand cubic metres (eight million gallons) of water per day. In an era before steam, oil, and electrical power, first-century hydraulic engineers made use of gravity. Over its fifty-kilometre length, the aqueduct descends just twelve metres (40 ft). How they achieved that so accurately, I don't know – and there is an additional layer of complexity. The gradient is not constant along the route.

Pont du Gard is the tallest Roman aqueduct bridge. Its height was right at the limit of the Empire's construction technology. If they had gone much higher, the bottom arches would have collapsed under the weight of the structure. However, varying the aqueduct's pitch enabled clever Roman engineers to build the bridge six metres (20 ft) lower. The precision of their measurements is staggering. The slope across the bridge itself is barely perceptible; 2.5 cm (1 inch) across the quarter of a kilometre span.

If I haven't yet impressed you with Roman engineering, they erected this immense structure without mortar. The *Gardonnades*, the Gardon's infamous, raging floods, have swept away many more modern bridges. In 1958, the surge engulfed the Pont's entire lower tier. But the Roman masons cut the stone blocks so exactly that gravity and friction has held them in place for two millennia, even in the face of such furious aquatic assaults.

Infrastructure rarely adds to the environment, but the

Pont du Gard is as much an aesthetic wonder as an engineering masterpiece.

We sat for hours on the riverbank. Our puddle-plunging pooches had a ball, exploring the pebble beaches and splashing in the warm shallow water. Now we had seen it for ourselves, Mark and I both agreed we would pay the entrance fee willingly. The spectacle was worth it, and we would not resent anything that went towards preserving this outstanding piece of heritage.

I've never seen Rome, but Mark told me,

"This is even better than the Colosseum."

As we approached the bridge, we felt diminished, like ants beneath its towering piers. I placed my hands against the stones. Warmed to blood heat by the late-afternoon sun, they seemed almost alive, and I felt an immediate connection with the energy and ingenuity of its creators. In the UK, we're not short of Roman ruins, but this structure made the grandeur and might of the Roman Empire real in a way I had never experienced before.

Pont du Gard was such an architectural inspiration that a thousand years later, it was still a must-see for journeyman stonemasons. You can see their emblems carved into the rock, alongside the inscriptions of its Roman builders. 'The Stone Giant' also became a blueprint for other bridges. The famous Pont d'Avignon, built in the 14th century, is one of many modelled on Pont du Gard, although less successfully, as we would find out.

A wrong turn up a flight of steps led to the highest point of the aqueduct, where we could peer along its water conduit. In the past, tourists could take a rather perilous and airy walk across the bridge's top tier, but perhaps rightly, 'Elf and Safety put an end to that.

We returned the way we had come, crossing the river on the adjacent road bridge that was added on the downstream side in 1743. Some accounts suggest the aqueduct was still in use for irrigation until the 6th century, but the channel was eventually blocked by debris and furred up with mineral deposits. Locals maintained the Pont du Gard because of its secondary usefulness as a toll route for pedestrians and traffic – and perhaps because it is difficult to loot dressed stone that is hovering fifty metres in the air.

The second highlight of our day came from watching fellow tourists enjoying our pups, particularly when I lined them up for a photo shoot. They were so well-behaved, one chap asked,

"*Agilité*?"

I told him we don't do agility with the dogs, but on the way home, as they bounced and leaped in the peachy-pastel light of sunset, it made me think I should appropriate the French national motto exclusively for *chiens*.

Liberté, Agilité, Fraternité – Liberty, Agility, Fraternity.

It seemed fitting, especially now they were citizens.

8

THE PENNY PINCHER'S GUIDE TO ORANGE AND AVIGNON

A Bridge Not Far Enough

What have the Romans ever done for us?

Well, they haven't passed on their gene for the unembarrassed use of public toilets to me.

Like the famous bathhouses, toilets in the Empire were a horrifyingly communal experience. Rows of Romans would align themselves side by side, exchanging small talk as they emptied their bowels. Afterwards, they would happily pass around the shared bucket and sponge-on-a-stick for their post-poop ablutions.

I could not be more different. Such are my sensibilities that, at work, I sometimes circled the entire office building two or three times to find a deserted convenience. Then, if someone entered the facility while I was in residence, so to speak, I cannot describe my mortification. Especially after a curry. The mere presence of another could strand me in a cubicle for hours.

French campsite toilets do nothing to aid my affliction. Their use requires a lot of front, because they lack certain items considered a necessity in the UK. Seats, for instance, would be nice, although that is not the worst omission. On most sites, the requirement to carry your own roll of loo paper marks out participants in the French walk of shame.

I go to great lengths to conceal my roll of Andrex. I try to keep one aside that is running low enough to slip surreptitiously into a pocket. If our tissue stocks can only furnish a plump new roll, burgeoning with the softness and strength of a Labrador puppy, I pop it into a large carrier bag. This dupes the casual observer into thinking I am going for a shower, until the very last moment, when I make my feint towards the can.

But a funny thing happened on the way to the forum. Before I even set foot in the Roman ruins of Orange, my day had hit a high, with unequivocal evidence of Caesar's heritage in action. With no qualms that onlookers might jeer, 'We know where you're going!' a chap strode proudly past the open windows of our caravan. Not only was his bog roll in clear view, but he had a *toilet seat* over his shoulder. I felt like giving him a round of applause.

As an impecunious nineteen-year-old, Mark toured France with two friends in a beaten-up Ford Transit van. From his unreliable memories of the region, Mark set out our objectives for the day. Théâtre Antique d'Orange – the Roman theatre in Orange, then Avignon, famous for its Pont.

"Orange is way better than Avignon," he said.

If you want to see one of only three Roman theatres in the world with their stage walls intact, you must go to Turkey, Syria – or Orange. In the days before amplifiers and microphones, the *scaenae frons* ('the big wall at the back') projected the sound perfectly, even as far as the cheap seats.

The incredible acoustics of the theatre helped propel its long career into the modern age. The *Chorégies,* an annual opera gala, started in the early 1900s. Then, in 1975, it hosted a rock festival billed as 'the French Woodstock', headlined by acts such as Bad Company, Procul Harum, and Wishbone Ash.

They allow dogs into the theatre, but I went in alone. Mark felt no need to refresh his forty-year-old memories, and since we're penny pinchers, we saved his €9 admission. As part of the coronavirus precautions, the reception staff aimed a laser gun at my forehead. They either took my temperature, or probed my brain...

Mark doesn't speak a word of French. As he waited patiently outside, a Frenchman came to see The Fab Four and struck up a conversation in English.

"He congratulated me on my excellent French," Mark boasted to me later. "He said, 'Most English say, 'Oringe', but you pronounce it correctly; 'Oronge'."

I mention this here, because soon, this minor incident would become a gargantuan source of irritation to me.

After we repurposed Mark's €9 entry fee into coffee and a fruit flan, we moved on to Avignon. Remember Mark told me that *Oronge* was much better than Avignon? His memory is notoriously flawed. I think he meant Avignon is much better than Avignon. My initial view invoked the same awe as my first glimpse of the New York skyline.

We found a free car park just over the river and walked to the town across the Édouard Daladier road bridge. Avignon must be a close contender with Oxford for the title 'City of Dreaming Spires'. Sandy-blonde castellated walls embrace a delightful jumble of towers, steeples, and campaniles, all jostling for attention above the formidable parapet of the ramparts. As we crossed the Rhône, we got a spectacular view of THE bridge, the Pont d'Avignon, made famous by the song, whose lyrics instantly sparked an argument,

"*Sur le pont, d'Avignon, L'on y dance,*" I ventured.

"No, it isn't. It's *'Ollie dances,'*" our fluent French expert assured me. His tone brooked no debate, so I didn't ask how Ollie landed the lead role in a fifteenth-century French ditty.

Perhaps he used his connections with the heroes of other French folk-songs, such as *Sunny Laymatina* and his chum *Jonty Alouette.* I always thought *Alouette* was a wholesome, blow-by-blow account of a sadist plucking a lark, written especially to traumatise children, but what do I know?

(*Alouette, gentille alouette. Alouette je te plumerai* means 'Nice lark. Lark, I will pluck you.' The song then continues with an explanation of how the *chanteur* will continue by plucking the nice lark's head, beak, nose, back, feet and neck. All a bit Hannibal Lecter to me.)

As we followed a marked walking tour through the labyrinth of tiny streets within Avignon's walls, we got lost. Very, very lost. The scale of our map was miniscule and showed hardly any street names. With fortifications obscuring the mighty Rhône, we had no visual reference. As we zig-zagged through alleys between tall, imposing facades, we lost our bearings completely. We felt like lab rats in a maze. The weird themed route we were following granted us views of strikingly unmemorable modern carbuncles, juxtaposed with sights of great historic importance.

Although we 'found' ourselves in Place St. Didier, we still departed 180-degrees in the wrong direction. I don't recall ever feeling so disorientated. The narrow streets were in perma-shadow, but the temperature was a sizzling 37°C (99°F). Even in the shade, the heat was debilitating. We had drinking water, but searched in vain for a fountain in which to cool off the pups. It was a sweltering few hours before our enquiries finally revealed an afterthought of a fountain; a few spouts which occasionally shot a jet of water out of the pavement.

Coincidentally, it was close to the *Palais des Papes* – The Popes' Palace, which was just the landmark we wanted. It is wonderfully grand, and surrounded by gardens, but you'll be missing out if I don't fill you in on a bit of history.

In the 14th century, Avignon, not Rome, was home to seven popes and two antipopes. I love the idea of antipopes – and the resulting Pope Wars. (As a highly advanced student of antiquity, 'Pope Wars' is a phrase I coined myself. The event is better known to history as 'The Great Western Schism'.)

I love to think of Pope Wars as pontiffs duelling with their pastoral staffs, much like the wizards Gandalf and Saruman in the second film in *The Lord of the Rings* trilogy. However, the real Pope Wars was a tale of two cities and three popes. The cast involved Clement VII, then Benedict XIII, who continued to rule as antipopes in Avignon, while the church moved back to Rome under Urban VI. Old Urbs VI became unpopular once he got

The Big Job and let power go to his head. Then, a third antipope, John XXIII popped up in Pisa.

Pisa's antipope eventually got everyone around the table, and he resigned. He persuaded Urban's replacement, Pope Gregory XII, to resign. Then he excommunicated antipope Benedict, who refused to resign.

In those days, Avignon claimed the title 'Babylon of the West' for being a hotbed of naughtiness. We can only speculate about Ben XIII's reluctance to step down. Like in the film *The Blues Brothers,* it might have been the certainty that he was on a mission from God. However, Petrarch, 'The Father of Humanism', had another theory. He was not alone in noticing Avignon's antipopes' bad boy behaviour. In his letters, Petrarch criticised them for being, "loaded with gold" and disapproved of their "licentious banquets...drinking bouts and what comes next on their scandalous couches." No one could accuse the antipopes of not taking a fully hands-on approach to shepherding their flocks, particularly the ladies.

Anyway, Rome elected Martin V as a new proper pope, and they all lived happily ever after. Well, almost. Six hundred years later, in the 20th century, the church was still passing religious laws to maintain Martin as the true papal line. There were also some alterations to the *Annuario Pontifico* – the papal *Who's Who*. For example, in the 1942 *Annuario*, they recorded antipope John XXIII as pope from 1410; then in 1958, they relegated him back to antipope when another Pope John claimed his number XXIII.

Pope Clement VI bought Avignon from Anjou in 1348 for 80,000 gold florins. It remained under papal control until 1791 and only became part of France when it was seized by force during the Revolution.

After soaking The Fab Four, we passed by a street café in a shady square. A lady leaned out of her chair to coo over our four dripping dogs. After an effusive fifteen minutes of lively conversation, we invited ourselves to join Ira and Tony at their table for coffee. We spent at least another hour chit-chatting and sharing stories. They had just moved to Avignon from the UK in circumstances that reminded me of us – they came, they saw, and they liked it. So, within months, they bought a flat and moved there.

We shared with them our impulse purchase; a 24.5 tonne 6x4 wheel-drive ex-army truck we bought blind off the internet from a dealer in Holland.

"It was when Boris Johnson became Prime Minister," Mark explained. "We wanted to escape the effects of Brexit and get as far away as possible, so we decided to go to Mongolia. We didn't think our hound cart (caravan) would make it across the Gobi Desert."

"Most people bought lockdown puppies. You bought a lockdown truck," Ira said.

"I suppose we did," Mark grinned. "We called her The Beast, because, well. She is!"

"And where is The Beast now?"

"I drove her back to the UK just before the first lockdown. She's in our mate's yard. He's converting her into our new home."

After coffee, Tony and Ira guided us to the Rhône. There, we parted company as they picked up the free boat shuttle to the Island of Barthelasse, which offers a splendid perspective of the Pont d'Avignon from the river.

Barthelasse also offered lots of pleasant walking paths, but we wanted to visit The Pont itself and were worried about our pooches in the heat. On our way back, we took a picture *Sous le Pont* – Under the Bridge.

As penny-pinchers, we weren't prepared to part with €5 each to go *sur*. However, I must inform you that, while it is not the accepted Avignon selfie, *sous le pont* is much more authentic. All this *sur le pont* nonsense is simply a demonstration of how fake news spread in the olden days, before Instagram set out to prove the camera always lies.

Like 'Ollie dances', *sur le pont* is a classic semantic change. All evidence suggests that if any dancing took place, it was definitely *sous le pont*. Let me explain.

The bridge is narrow, only 2.5 m (8 ft) wide, which leaves little room to strut your funky stuff, especially *tous en rond* – all in circles. If you attempted a mini hokey cokey, *sous le pont* was most likely where you'd end up, along with all the horses, wagons, and pedestrians, whose plummets over the parapets were reputedly all too common.

While you could forgive a bridge for its shortcomings as a dance floor, the Pont d'Avignon is a complete washout in viaduct terms. Besides being too narrow, it is a bridge not far enough – it doesn't even reach the isle of Barthelasse in the middle of the river. Its four arches are all that remain of twenty-two, which made up its 900 m (nearly 3,000 ft) span. Originally, it marched right across the island to connect Avignon with Villeneuve-lès-Avignon, and was the only fixed river crossing between Lyon and the Med.

The bridge's real name is the Pont Saint-Bénézet,

named after a shepherd boy from the Ardèche. Exactly like *The Blues Brothers*, he was on a mission from God, who had instructed him to bridge the Rhône at Avignon. Since no one believed him, he picked up an enormous boulder and lobbed it into the river to found the bridge. Then, he formed a cult, the Bridge Brotherhood, and oversaw its construction.

Despite its strategic significance, divine connections, and being modelled on the much older and long-lasting Pont du Gard, floods washed away the original bridge and every one of its subsequent wooden replacements. What you see today are the remains of the final stone iteration, which was abandoned in the mid-17th century. It collapsed so frequently in the Rhône's surges, it became too expensive to maintain.

You won't read this elsewhere, but Joe Strummer of punk band *The Clash* wrote his own Pont d'Avignon song,

"I fought the Rhône, and the Rhône won."

Yet, the disintegrated Pont is now world famous, and Bénézet is the patron saint of bridge builders. Industry has widely adopted this pioneering model of reward for abject failure. The Bénézet System ensures fat-cat bosses, who bankrupt their companies and raid the pension pot, are fast-tracked into multi-million-pound bonuses and a knighthood.

It will be some time before I forget our return journey to the car park. A trek through the magma chamber of a supervolcano could not have been hotter. Like a platoon of soldiers advancing under cover, we dodged from tree to tree along the Boulevard Rhône to stay in the shade. To cross Le Pont Édouard Daladier, we had no choice but to brave the merciless barrage; a few hundred yards under the full force of the blazing Provençale sun.

The scorching heat reflected from the pavement on to my shins, and I couldn't imagine how uncomfortable that would be on puppy paws and tums. They must have thought they were being spit roasted. In the short time it took to run to Big Blue, the strength of the afternoon sunshine had seared my cranium into the first stages of a headache – and I never get headaches.

As a treat on the way back to the caravan, we pulled over beneath some trees for one of The Fab Four's favourites; a refreshing swim in the river.

Back at base, a 37°C-day (99°F) seemed the perfect time to experiment with our new caravan air conditioning unit, bought especially for our trip to Spain. After forty minutes of operation on full fan and full cooling, it had raised the temperature inside the caravan from 34 to 35.5°C. We gave up, opened the windows and switched on our 12V twin-cyclone fan, which cost fifteen quid on Amazon and saw us through 40°C (104°F) in Romania.

Although the aircon is a fairly straightforward piece of kit, we wondered if we had missed something important, since the instructions provided were in Dutch, German, or French. My Dutch is non-existent and my German rusty and inadequate; so, we had arrived at Practical French, Random Challenge #26: Translate the Instruction Manual for a Caravan Air Conditioning System.

Thankfully, via the medium of Facebook Messenger, our delightful Dutch friend Casper sacrificed half an hour of his life to transcribe the instructions into English. We couldn't see any obvious omissions on our part; we bought it based on excellent reviews, and the caravan fell within the specification of a space small enough for the unit to cool. The supplier could offer no further tips to get the thing working. Somewhat after the fact, they emailed the manual in English, along with the assurance they would look it over if we returned it to the UK. Not helpful in our present parched predicament.

The following morning, when it was cooler outside, we tried the aircon unit again. In no time, it had warmed the caravan by two degrees. The weather forecast in Madrid was showing 39°C (102°F); a temperature even more torrid than the sultry feverishness of Avignon and her antipopes.

This was our third attempt to visit Spain. We recalled the legendary July heatwave that thwarted the first, with record highs of more than 50°C (122°F). Had we learned nothing? Even with an air conditioner that hadn't suddenly self-identified as a heater, the dog days of a Spanish summer would be too much for the pups and a transparent shade-dwelling creature like me.

It was third time unlucky. Once again, we decided to bail out of our trip to Spain and head north, in search of cooler climes.

Mark immediately got on to researching a re-route, with mixed success. At €7.90 per pooch per night, Bavaria soon provided a staggering record for extortionate campsite dog charges. Then, in his best faux-German accent, Mark read me this excerpt from the website of one site next to a windsurfing lake. It expressed what seemed to be an unnervingly widespread aversion to *Hunde* among the *Campingplätzen* of the Fatherland on our new northern route. It didn't fill us with hope,

"Dogs are prohibited throughout the season... The rejection of dogs requires no justification. For categories A and B, the dog ban applies without exception for the entire duration of the camping. In the event of violations of this, the campsite management reserves the right to issue an immediate referral."

In Monte Rosa, a lovely Polish couple had told us to go to Hel.

Not because we had offended them; Hel is a windsurfing destination on Poland's Baltic coast.

Before lockdown threw our plans askew, Poland had been one of our original destinations, and we had already worked out a route. Although the coronavirus delay meant we no longer had time to investigate the Baltic states, it looked like for once, we were in danger of sticking to at least part of a plan.

We would go to Hel in a Hound Cart.

PART II

JOURNEY TO THE CENTRE OF EUROPE

Map from Italy to Czechia

9

"I'M SORRY I HAVEN'T A CLUNY" – THE CITY OF THE HORSE, BOURGOGNE

We're sent on a fool's errand – twice!

Since the brakes hadn't failed and we had already used up the stress-inducing options of the Mistral and a head-on collision with a kamikaze lorry, Mark tried to add a different layer of excitement to our departure. As he loaded the bikes onto Big Blue, he attempted to amputate the end of his finger on my spokes.

Stemming the flow of husbandly blood is always a fine prelude to a road trip.

Our route north to Bourgogne (Burgundy) demonstrated how many delights there are on the doorstep of Provence, which had captured our hearts, but was just too hot to handle.

In quick succession, we passed signs for the Cévennes, Drôme, and Ardèche.

"We're not far from the Puy-de-Dôme and the Auvergne, either," Mark told me. More of our 'must-see-again' regions.

Our sudden change of plan would deny me the wild, white horses of the Camargue, another fantastic region on the fringes of Provence. However, it delighted me to discover that, while our destination, Cluny, was world famous for its medieval abbey, it was also an equestrian city.

Cluny is home to *Equivallée Haras* – The French National Stud, founded by Napoleon. For two-hundred years, Cluny has remained a horsey hub, with the stud, a club, and its own hippodrome to host various types of races.

Cluny's lovely municipal campsite was a short stroll from the town. The facilities were immaculate and the staff very friendly. As I checked in, Annette on reception asked whether I was English.

"It's really nice that you speak in French. Most English don't bother," she told me.

When I went back later to ask if there was a doggie walk nearby, Annette's partner, Chris, couldn't understand my French.

"Are you English?" he asked in a London accent.

"Yes..."

"I am too, but I've been in France for ages. Your accent put me off."

If you remember, a Frenchman complimented Mark on his grasp of the language simply because he pronounced 'Orange' correctly – and Mark doesn't speak a word of French.

Naturally, Mark chose to remind me of this.

ME! Who had been thrust into conversation with two Gallic mechanics about a caravan brake problem. Who presided over a visit to the vet for four pet passports, vaccinations, and a discussion about leishmaniasis. And who had my tooth filled (without anaesthetic, I'll grant you) – all in *Française*. I was livid.

We had no food. The previous evening, I had gone native and chucked everything together with some Herbs de Provence in a loose interpretation of ratatouille. After an already lengthy drive, we couldn't face further van time to go shopping, or, indeed, my cooking, so we wandered into Cluny.

The medieval high street was picture perfect and had a pleasing, relaxed buzz about it. The tourist office was closed, but we ambled into the vast precincts of the *Abbaye*. There, we found the weekly market in a cobbled square and a group doing something similar to T'ai Chi, but with swords, which really appealed to the repressed Ronin within me. (For many years, I was a student of martial arts.)

A pavement café boasted a daily special of *bavette* (skirt of beef) with *Béarnaise* sauce and *haricots verts,* so there was no argument about dinner. I always buy *bavette* if I see it; it's rare in the UK but a favourite for both of us. It is a well-flavoured cut which I usually stew, but which the French serve fried.

The service was wonderfully friendly and everyone cooed over the dogs. Kai, our little black and white boy, attracted loads of attention when he lay back in Mark's arms like a baby – that dude really knows how to do cute. Dinner was delicious and the aftermath of garlic from the *haricots verts* sufficient to repel vampires as far away as Transylvania.

The Fab Four behaved beautifully, even when other canines passed the restaurant. I was so proud of them.

As Mark paid the bill, I nipped off to buy some beers before the nearby mini market closed. The only cold ones contained an anaesthetic dose of 8% alcohol, so I opted for a chilled bottle of local white instead.

After so long in lockdown, Mark and I had shared our concerns that we'd lost the touring bug. While we enjoyed Provence, our previous campsite had been run-down, gloomy, and right next to a main road. It was no place to relax outdoors, although it had been cheap and convenient for the jobs we had to do.

Sipping a glass of chilled white Burgundy on a beautiful balmy evening, drinking in the splendour of Cluny Abbey and its medieval towers was the jolt we needed. It gave us the most obvious reminder of what our lifestyle was all about.

Although we had moved almost two-hundred miles directly north, the temperature was still 36°C (97°F) when we arrived. The following morning, we visited the tourist office to ask where we might find a cool river walk for the dogs. Madame informed me that the *voie verte* cycle path behind the campsite joined the river just off the map, which seemed far preferable to driving anywhere. Then, I asked if dogs could visit the National Stud. She looked at me as though I had enquired about the stud's breeding population of purple unicorns.

"*Pffft. Chevaux et chiens? Non.*"

I felt like saying "Horses and dogs? Well, it was fine in Lipica." *(Lipica is the famous stud in Slovenia, which breeds the noble Lipizzaner dressage horses for the Spanish Riding School in Vienna.)*

It didn't take long before I was furious with her. The only saving grace of her river walk was that it was mostly shady, which made it almost bearable for our pups. We walked for over an hour, but the path never came close to the river. When we ran out of drinking water, we asked two German cyclists whether we were likely to reach the river soon. They gave us a look not unlike the one delivered in the tourist office regarding dogs and the National Stud,

"We passed the river about 20 km back, but it is *schwartz* – black. Not even dogs would want to swim."

The following day, Madame achieved her 100% record. I visited the National Stud alone because of the dog ban. At the entrance, a sign revealed that dogs on leads were welcome.

"Are dogs allowed?" I clarified at reception.

"*Bien sûr* – of course," she confirmed. "*En laisse* – on leads."

Incroyable – Unbelievable!

On certain days, the stud offers guided tours and demonstrations, but I chose a €3, self-guided tour day. I saw the forge, the saddlery, a carriage museum, and a stable. I was disappointed that there were so few horses. Around half a dozen *Pur-sang* – Pure-bloods (a breed based on the English Thoroughbred, which has Arabian roots), and a couple of powerful Percheron and Comtois work horses languished in stalls behind full-length bars. Touching was forbidden.

There was no sign of the magnificent strawberry roan Belgian Ardennes they had splashed all over their literature. I have only ever seen one Ardennes in my life; in an Amish community in America.

The Comtois was a new brand for me – a draught horse originally from the *Franche-Compté* region, which incorporates the Jura. The Comtois was a popular all-round carriage-, war-, and farm horse. Comtois were originally bay (brown with black 'points' – mane, tail, and legs) although the predominant colour is now a striking dark chestnut with a flaxen mane. This is all down to a single stallion, *Questeur*. Bay is still acceptable within the breed standard, although a white blaze on the face which is more than half the width of the muzzle is not.

Apparently, the Comtois has a sweet temperament and is the most popular draught horse in France. En route to our next destination, we passed a restaurant called *The Convivial Comtois* – the perfect description.

I missed Mark and the pups, but they didn't miss much.

"How was it?" Mark asked,

"It's not Lipica," I replied; a response that was to become the start of a worrying trend of comparisons.

I had picked up an excellent booklet in the tourist office. Right at the beginning were four Discovery Driving Tours; they billed Tour No. 3 as *'Around Water – Rivers Guye and Gande'*.

Later, in the *'Ramblings'* section, it boasted of the *Balades Vertes* – "We can suggest over forty different walks in the area... leaflets are on sale at the tourist office." It recommended a further thirteen walks on the Massif Sud Bourgogne, along with three long-distance footpaths, including the Pilgrim's Way to Santiago de Compostela.

Why had Madame not recommended any of those?

During our two-day stay in Cluny, her mis-direction had nearly killed our pups from heat exhaustion on a non-existent river walk. Then, on Day 2, she had prevented Mark and I from enjoying the City of the Horse together.

I would thus like to invest a well-deserved title upon the tourist office.

'I'm Sorry I Haven't a Cluny'.

10

OF MICE AND MEN – EGUISHEIM, ALSACE

I'll be your dog – and REAL Pope wars!

"For breakfast, they have a massive dish of coffee, like a cereal bowl, and they dip slices of a huge, bell-shaped cake, called *Kugelhopf* in it."

This was wide-eyed culture shock, relayed to my parents, following my first ever trip abroad. Aged 14, I had been on a school exchange to Alsace to learn French.

As if cake for breakfast is not enough, Alsace is an enchanting place of wine and castles. It is tucked next to the River Rhine in north-east France, right on the German border.

Quite what the students from this beautiful region made of Blackburn, an ugly, industrial town in the north of England, where they ate Cornflakes and Sugar Puffs every morning, I don't know. Not only did this shimmering piece of paradise retain a special place in my heart, its language tuition was the solid foundation that had enabled me to solve the Practical French Challenges involving vets, dentists, and mechanics, which had characterised our road trip so far.

Two fortnight-long exchanges immersed me in Alsatian family life. They gained me an 'A' grade in my exams, and I returned to England with an inner monologue that conducted itself in French. While those forty-year-old linguistic skills have lain dormant, they somehow never abandoned me completely.

We have visited many wine areas, but Alsace's landscape is incredible and unique. Nestled beneath the Vosges mountains, it is a bright green undulating sea of vines. Unbroken and uninterrupted by any other crops, it stretches to the horizon in every direction.

"I've found a campsite in Roof-something," Mark said.

"Rouffach," I guessed correctly, to Mark's surprise.

"Big Bruv's first exchange was in Rouffach," I explained. "I stayed in Colmar, on the Route de Rouffach, although I've never actually been to Rouffach."

The satnav seemed even more unfamiliar with Rouffach than either Mark or me. It took us, seven-metre caravan and all, on a magical mystery tour of the village's winding, cobbled streets. To say we got some looks is an understatement – our passing saw more jaws drop than if we'd set up a table in the middle of the high street, with placards declaring our intention to indulge in the mortal sin of pairing red wine with fish.

The campsite looked closed, and that's how we ended up at Camping Les Trois Châteaux in Eguisheim – via a return route we chose ourselves. To avert a re-run through Rouffach's claustrophobic historic centre, we strategically ignored the satnav.

Even by Alsatian standards, which set a high bar, Eguisheim is something special. In 2013, the nation voted this enchanting, medieval village *Village préféré des Français* – Favourite Village of the French People. Obviously, it had made the cut for the list of 'Most Beautiful Villages in France' a long time before.

Eguisheim's streets are arranged in three concentric circles. These follow the lines of successive fortifications, although Eguisheim's importance was economic, not military. They built the walls to protect the sixteen *cours dîmières* – tithe courtyards, where aristocrats struck deals and collected taxes. Eguisheim also had five *colongères courts,* where the nobility applied a common code of law to groups of farmers ruled by the same lord. However, Eguisheim was not just an important centre for commerce and law. It claims its own pope. In June 1002, Pope Leon IX was born in Eguisheim's castle.

Although Leo pre-dated Avignon's Pope Wars by nearly four centuries, I am pleased to report he not only precipitated a schism of his very own, but had an actual war.

Leon's East-West Schism of 1054 split the Catholic and Eastern Orthodox Churches from each other. Unlike Avignon's Antipopes, Leon IX favoured celibacy and stamped out 'simony' – the religious variant of 'cash for honours'. Yet when the Normans threatened to attack Italy from the south, Leo rode out from Rome at the head of his army: I hope, wielding his pastoral staff like a wizard's wand. But even with God on his side, he got whipped at the Battle of Civitate.

It was an odd triumph for the Normans, who were devout Christians. Leon was their spiritual leader, so they celebrated victory by begging forgiveness and swearing fealty to the defeated pope.

Inside Eguisheim's walls lies a higgledy-piggledy mass of brightly coloured, half-timbered houses. Geraniums tumble from window sills, and storks nest atop the chimney pots. It's pure fairy-tale.

It fascinated me to learn that the houses' interlacing patterns of wooden studs, crossbeams, and braces have significance. The diamond represents fertility; the saltire (an X-shaped cross) protection; and the slanting posts represent the silhouette of a man. Inscriptions, such as tulips and five- or six-pointed stars, also protect against evil or lightning. The steeply sloping gables shed snow, and I discovered the long roof tiles with rounded ends were called *Biberschwantz,* because their shape resembles a beaver's tail.

The bright colours of the wattle and daub between the beams are a more contemporary innovation. Traditionally, the builders protected the timber by rubbing it with soot or red iron oxide, and coated the plaster with lime whitewash. Wealthier owners might have ventured boldly towards a pale, pastel hue, but with the advent of modern paints, the lure of *risqué* shades such as *'Mango Fandango', 'Dondarf',* and 'Elephant's Breath' proved irresistible. *(If you fancy Elephant's Breath in your lounge, it is a real colour by Farrow and Ball. I fabricated the others – but am expecting a call from a paint-naming team any day.)*

My younger brother exchanged with a family of winemakers in Eguisheim. Their cellar, Au Cheval Blanc, is on the main square, and is a great place to sample Eguisheim's *Grands Crus* – its most exceptional wines.

Another exchange student, Dominique, invited my

parents to his wedding in Alsace. A pair of English guests was a substantial coup for Dominique's household. They paraded Mum and Dad around the region, fêting them as aristocracy; possibly even minor royalty. Mum had a mischievous streak and would have played up to her rôle with more ham than Bayonne. Grudgingly squeezed into a suit, Dad would have borne the heat and formality with stoicism. I would lay odds that his ensemble involved sandals with socks, and that when Mum noticed, he earned a, "Bloody hell, Jim!"

I can certainly testify to "Bloody hell, Jim!" appearing at a friend's daughter's nuptials in Blackburn one hot July day. I'm afraid I was responsible for blowing Dad's cover. As we waited outside the church for photographs, I spotted his choice of footwear. I tried to withdraw to a safe distance, but completely failed to conceal my spluttering guffaw.

Later, he told me it was a protest.

"I had to go to a wedding, wear a suit – and it's my birthday. I should be able to do what I want."

While Mark set up camp, I walked The Fab Four through the vineyards. *Le Sentier Viticole des Grands Crus D'Eguisheim* is a marked route through the vines which started just outside the campsite, although I can't say it was well signposted. The trail takes in Eguisheim's two *Grands Crus*, Pfersigberg and Eichberg, which are the parts of the hillside that produce the most outstanding wines.

What have the Romans ever done for us? Well, they came, they saw, and they planted. It was they who spotted the potential of the gentle, sunny slopes of the *Schlossberg* (Castle Hill) – and created the first vineyard in Alsace.

It was a picturesque stroll beneath the *Trois Châteaux*. Named after the families who ruled them, the three ruined castles of Dabsbourg, Wahlenbourg, and Weckmund dominate the trio of wooded hills that sit above Eguisheim.

I enjoyed the walk, mostly. On the positive side, the castles gave me a reference point to sidestep a repetition of my trauma in the terroir – getting lost in the vineyards of Barolo the previous year. On the negative side, I caught Rosie crunching on something. When I told her to drop it, I was horrified to find it was the remains of a long-dead mouse. I kicked it into a bush, from where she retrieved it once again the following day.

Then, when I got back, I had to ask Mark,

"Is my sun dress too revealing?"

"It is low cut, like a bikini, but it's fine. Why?"

"A lascivious Frenchman in the car park leered at me and asked if he could be my fifth dog," I wailed.

I raced around Eguisheim's shops like a junkie, seeking to score my favourite Alsatian delicacies.

"I need *Kugelhopf*, Munster cheese, and *Choucroute,"* – the Alsatian version of *Sauerkraut*.

I was really looking forward to telling Dad where we were, since, suit aside, he has fond memories of Alsace and Eguisheim. Unfortunately, a poor telephone connection frustrated my attempt at surprise.

"*Bonsoir.* Guess where we are. We had *Kugelhopf* for breakfast."

"YOU'VE HAD TWO STOPS?" he bellowed down the phone, to compensate for the seven-hundred miles that our terrible line failed to bridge.

"WELL, YOU WERE IN AVIGNON, SO..."

"No," I tried to interrupt. "I said, 'We had *Kugelhopf...*'"

"TWO STOPS... LET ME THINK..." he yelled. "I KNOW. YOU'RE IN NICE!"

Later, Mark accused me of being a chip off the old block.

Mark mumbles, then accuses me of being deaf. Frequently, I am forced to point out that, within the preceding twelve months, an audiologist had proclaimed my hearing as 'that of an eighteen-year-old'.

When I try to fill in the gaps, he mocks me mercilessly. "It's the creativity of your answers that gets me," he said.

That very morning, I had popped my head out of the door of the *Traiteur* to offer Mark a choice,

"Do you want duck or rabbit pie for lunch?"

He made a suggestion based on Rosie's earlier misdemeanour.

"GET A MOUNTAIN BIKE FOR ROSIE?" I tried to clarify, completely thrown.

"No," he replied patiently. "I said, 'Get a mouse pie for Rosie.'"

Maybe he has a point.

11

ALTERNATIVE ALSACE: A WALK THROUGH HISTORY ON 'THE MOUNTAIN OF DEATH'

"Those who cannot remember the past are condemned to repeat it." – George Santayana

Alsace is best known for its wine route, castles, and fairy-tale villages. However, 956.5 m (3,136 ft) above the Alsace plain, at Hartmannswillerkopf, or HWK, you will find an extraordinary relic of World War I (WWI).

On a pyramid-shaped, rocky peak, there are around 60 km (37 miles) of trenches, tunnels, and shelters. They are incredibly well-preserved, due to both the location and the nature of the conflict that took place there.

Unlike many battlefields, once the fighting ceased, nobody claimed the mountainous land for other purposes, such as building or farming. In addition, a lengthy stalemate meant the troop positions remained static. The armies were well and truly dug in, so the trenches are well-defined and for much of the war, the layout hardly changed.

The reason this bluff became the epicentre of such

violent and merciless warfare was its key strategic importance. HWK has far-reaching views across the Alsace plain towards the Rhine and overlooks the Colmar-Mulhouse railway. For the French, HWK was also a matter of pride. When WWI started in 1914, Alsace had been in German hands since the Franco-Prussian war in 1871. Reclaiming this annexed French territory was a primary goal.

The combat on HWK was savage and relentless. While its strategic status diminished when the front moved north in the summer of 1916, a bloody stalemate endured until the conflict ended in 1918, with neither side giving ground.

HWK claimed the lives of 30,000 soldiers. Another 30,000 were injured or taken prisoner. The rows and rows of crosses in the cemetery hinted at what 1,200 vanished souls look like, but the genuine horror dawns when you realise the crypt contains the bodies of 12,000 unknown soldiers, and the ossuaries in the graveyard 384 more. In nearby Cernay, 7,000 German fighters are buried, but the whole HWK battlefield area is an open-air cemetery for those whose remains were never recovered. It was numbing.

The location took a bit of finding. Signposts for the 1914-18 graveyard, museum, and memorial actually said *Vieil Armand,* and it was neither in nor anywhere near Wattheim as advertised. HWK literally means 'head' (summit) of Hartmannswiller, which is the village at the foot of the mountain. L'illustration magazine christened it *Vieil Armand* in 1915.

The name *Armand* means 'army man'. My research

could not confirm it, but I suspect *Vieil Armand* means something akin to 'The Old Warrior'.

The soldiers who fought there were less euphemistic than the press. French troopers called HWK 'The Man Eater', while the Germans referred to it simply as 'The Mountain of Death'.

Just outside Wattheim, we drove up to the Col du Silberloch, where a stand of French, German, and European flags showed that by accident, we had found our destination.

The crypt, described as 'an underground cathedral', and the large, modern museum and café building, were closed due to coronavirus. Nevertheless, we went for a very fascinating and moving self-guided stroll through history.

Above the crypt, on the summit, sits 'The Altar of the Homeland', a glistening gilded stone sarcophagus, bearing the names and shields of various French towns who had supplied their menfolk as cannon fodder. From there, flowing down the green flanks of the hill, is a tide of plain, white crosses, each representing someone's husband, son, or brother.

From the Altar, we followed a marked track. The peaceful, sun-dappled woodland belied the horror that happened there. There was no sound but birdsong. Verdant green, natural forest had taken over from the barbed wire and trenches. Still, despite the resurgence of nature, it was easy to see shell craters, which pockmarked the whole area.

The walk started in the mostly earthen French trenches, then passed into no-man's-land before entering the German trenches. These were markedly different;

constructed from masonry, with shelters every few yards, where troops could seek refuge from bombardment.

Information boards along the way followed the timeline of the battle on HWK with incredible detail. There was an almost daily record of the skirmishes and lives lost in each area. Brief excerpts from soldiers' diaries gave an insight into their lives. Some are too upsetting to quote. André Maillet, a literature teacher in civilian life, described the result of a skirmish in December 1915.

"Dawn breaks. It is a horrible sight... Defeated, I am alone at the bottom of the abyss, where so many men cried out madly in their distress and pain. For a moment, the vision of my isolation on this bloody rock covered with bodies fills me with an endless despair."

As we walked through the regimented lines of crosses in the graveyard, I noticed the six stone-topped ossuaries. Each of these is a mass grave of sixty or more unknown soldiers. It was here that one quote really hit home. From the diary of Auguste Chapotte on 17th June, 1915,

"As soon as daylight allows, I get on the periscope... Imagine my surprise when I get a really clear view of several Huns about ten metres away from me, busy and very calmly digging a communication trench parallel to our trench...

"These Jerries are really young; they seem to be barely twenty years old."

As I investigated an underground bunker, Mark wandered off, and I experienced first-hand the disorientating character of the trenches. I shouted for him, but he didn't hear, and that was in the restful tranquillity of a summer's day, rather than the thunderous chaos and clamour of battle. Fortunately, Kai missed his mum and came bounding back through the labyrinth to find me.

Mark and I had set out in exactly opposite directions and were walking away from each other.

Our day was a very beautiful, interesting, and affecting walk through lush, shady woods.

By contrast, the information panels showed photographs of the devastation left behind by the campaign. What remained after the war was a lunar landscape of scorched earth and shattered skeletal trees, particularly in places where the Germans from the Dora fortress on the summit deployed two flame-throwers, called 'The Beasts Of The Apocalypse'.

The scale of the carnage in one minor theatre of The Great War was difficult to comprehend. So many lives destroyed in a fight over one small hill top. Multiply that by the rest of Europe and you can see why they dubbed WWI 'the war to end all wars'.

Yet, the site of such cataclysmic violence has become a place of hope. HWK stands as an enduring testament to the senselessness of arbitrary enmity and the pointlessness of warfare.

Because of its position on the border, Alsace has spent long periods as part of both France and Germany. WWI divided loyalties. Brothers fought brothers, and both armies suffered a high level of desertions as a result. Alsatian troops frequently elected to join the navy, rather than the army, to avoid the possibility of close combat with family and friends.

Another diary excerpt brought home that on both sides, these were just young men who had been instructed to be enemies, thrown together into a terrible situation that was not of their making.

March 4th, 1914: Artilleryman Henri Martin

reported, *"Yesterday, a mountain soldier was digging a shallow communication trench 50 m from them when he heard a voice, 'Hey! Hey!' And he saw one of the enemy who told him, 'Get down! Get down!'"*

With each attack and counter-attack, thousands of lives were squandered in the most inhuman circumstances, but neither party made any real gains. HWK was originally a place of remembrance for the French dead, but in 2014, on the 100th anniversary of the outbreak of WW1, it was rededicated as a testament to Franco-German reconciliation. They chose HWK because it is essentially 'neutral' ground, where neither side gained advantage.

No doubt the dead would rather have lived, but they can rest in some peace knowing the place they fell stands as a haunting memorial to all who made the ultimate sacrifice.

I also found it rather touching that nature has reclaimed the ground so completely that the diversity of the flora and fauna has earned HWK Natura 2000 status and protection. This place of brutal, unremitting death has developed into a vibrant place filled with life.

Paradise starts with the love we show each other here on earth.

Hartmannswillerkopf reminded me of that by opening up a brief glimpse into Hell.

12

HAUT KOENIGSBOURG CASTLE AND KAYSERSBERG, ALSACE

We discover the root of happiness

Being thoroughly modern, the visitor brochure featured a list of *Spots Instagrammables*. Alsace is a gorgeous region replete with plenty of competition, but Top of the Instagram Pops was Château de Haut Koenigsbourg.

This Disneyland collection of pinky-red sandstone turrets atop a green peak that dominates the flat surroundings is understandably a very popular attraction. To avoid the worst of the crowds, we parked at the side of the switchback road that led up to it. From there, we took one of many footpaths that zigzag through the cool shady woods.

The forest was enchanting. There is something magical about the light and character of a beech woodland. Our footsteps and the warm summer sun released the sweet, resinous scent of the pine trees, which were interspersed among the beeches and oaks. We followed a sign to the ruin of Petit Koenigsbourg, also known as *Château de l'Œdenbourg,* or 'Abandoned Castle'.

Œdenbourg dates back to the 12th century and was probably an annexe of the principal hilltop stronghold. Records show it was already deserted by the 1600s. In a quiet glade, sunlight played on tumbling but brutish walls, several feet thick, with massive boulders embedded in them. I found its dark and secretive aura more captivating and fantastical even than its grandiose neighbour.

Haut Koenigsbourg, which simply means 'High Royal Castle', has a mixed history. Records of the first fortress on the summit date to 1147. It was destroyed then rebuilt in 1462, but in 1633, it was burned to the ground during the Thirty Years' War.

What you see today is supposedly a historically correct reconstruction of how it looked before that fire. Kaiser Wilhelm II, who annexed Alsace after the Franco Prussian War, oversaw the early 20th century rebuild; however, he included a few inaccuracies – and flights of fancy. With Alsace under German rule, Kaiser Bill wanted to mark the boundary of his territory, show off his power, and fulfil his dreams of empire. Haut Koenigsbourg fitted the bill perfectly.

After several computer-related mishaps on our travels, Mark reminds me frequently of the importance of keeping back-up copies of everything. In an exterior courtyard, we found a small-scale model of Haut Koenigsbourg. Curiously, if you go to Kuala Lumpur, you can visit a full-size back up of Haut Koenigsbourg, along with the entire Alsatian city of Colmar, reproduced in the jungle by a Malaysian billionaire.

Even without the castles, the walk would have been amazing. The bonus ruin and the view from Haut Koenigsbourg were the rainbow sprinkles on the cup cake. With such a breathtaking panorama over the Alsace plain, the Vosges mountains, the Black Forest, and the Alps, the location of such a major fortress came as no surprise.

They didn't allow dogs inside the castle, which was not unexpected. It didn't worry us, since we're more impressed by a flying buttress than a Baroque interior. Instead, we retraced our steps through the woodland, then drove to the pretty half-timbered town of Kaysersberg.

We bypassed the attractions of Monkey Mountain, where Barbary macaques roam free, and The Eagle's Flight bird of prey centre, which are both close to Haut Koenigsbourg. Obviously, they don't welcome dogs either.

When we reached Kaysersberg, it was easy to kid ourselves we were in an Alsatian theme park, like the one in the Malaysian jungle. It was fairy-tale perfect, busy, and touristy. Look beyond the throng, though, and it is stunningly beautiful, with nooks and crannies that make it a genuine pleasure to explore.

We strolled through the cobbled streets to the centre, then ascended to the imposing remains of the 13th-Century Schlossberg castle, whose cylindrical tower stands sentinel above the town. The walking path continued beyond, but after our wander in the woods at Haut Koenigsbourg, we were happy simply to enjoy the vistas.

Kaysersberg is the birthplace of Albert Schweitzer, winner of the Nobel Peace Prize in 1952. Several placards on the route up to the castle bore inspiring quotes from the great man. In this epoch of instant gratification, where we have every material comfort but starve our souls, this one really struck a chord,

"A thousand times a day, advertising repeats this; not only do you need this new object, but you are eligible to have it. And right now! In an ideal world, where we live in nanoseconds, the sense of hardship and effort are absent... or reserved for those who work for you.

"This comfort taken for granted has impacted our representation of the real world. Is this doing us, or society, any good?

"However, contrary to what the 'spirit of our time' states, living in the physical, intellectual or moral comfort deprives us of our most essential food: the feeling of expanding our present limits."

After years of commuting into London at 4 a.m., I am so glad that Mark and I finally asked ourselves the question, "Is this doing us any good?"

In order to step off the treadmill and retire early, we had to choose a minimal life. We often say how grateful we are to have 'enough'. We are not rich, but so long as we are careful and stick to our budget, we have everything we need. Anything we buy is qualified with, "Is this a want or a need?" Sometimes, we permit ourselves a 'want' as a treat, but we think about it first. Not giving in instantly to every whim makes us appreciate what we have – and we wouldn't have it any other way.

While it is unlikely, we would never even aspire to the

obscene wealth that gives someone the means to replicate an Alsatian castle and town in Malaysia.

I feel so lucky to be in a position where there is nothing I could buy or own that would make me any happier than I am. It is a very contented state of existence.

At the bridge in the centre, we met a Romanian couple, Camille and Christian, who had moved to France with their beautiful young daughter, Sara. As born-again Romanians, following our road trip around their wonderful homeland, we chatted for ages. The pups entranced Sara, who cuddled our little black girl, Lani. She was so bright, and remembered all the dogs' names straight away.

Alsace has a very distinct identity. Although now part of France, after oscillating between French and German control throughout its history, it has its own Germanic language. As we drove around, we noticed graffiti demanding *Frei Elsàss* – Free Alsace in the local Alsatian dialect.

When I asked Camille whether Sara saw herself as French or Romanian, she told me,

"Sara considers herself not just French, but Alsatian."

Christian worked for a Romanian bank, now owned by the French. He explained one way that globalisation legally strips poorer countries of their wealth.

"They mark all the Romanian operations as a loss, so they pay tax only in France."

What a coup for Romania.

In my tourist pamphlet, I had highlighted a traditional Alsatian restaurant whose house speciality was one of my favourites; *Choucroute* – Alsatian Sauerkraut –

with four fishes; even better. It was only once we returned to the campsite I remembered that Au Lion d'Or was in Kaysersberg.

Unfortunately, in this case, Albert Schweitzer could not have been more wrong when he said,

"Happiness is nothing more than good health and a bad memory."

13

A WET WEDNESDAY IN WÜRZBURG – BAVARIA

Giga Blight and Cultural Comparisons

I was on my third language in three weeks.

Just as I'd got to grips with speaking French unsullied by a peppering of *Italiano*, we crossed the Rhine and entered Germany. On our radar were the historic cities of Würzburg and Bamberg; recommendations from our last German jaunt.

Exactly like our previous visit, as we departed France via Strasbourg, we joined the end of a traffic jam.

It was familiar territory. The same huge infrastructure projects were still in progress, which meant crawling through roadworks for much of our journey. Beyond the contraflows, we endured an inside lane filled with nose-to-tail lorries, while Porsches, BMWs, and one McLaren flashed past at an unexaggerated hundred miles an hour.

There is no speed limit on most of Germany's *Autobahn* – motorway. The fastest velocity recorded on the network under non-test conditions is 236 mph (381 kph). 'Non-test' means with other vehicles on the road – thankfully, not Big Blue and Caravan Kismet.

Our campsite was within walking distance of Sommerach, a pretty half-timbered village in the heart of the Frankish wine area. The campground was vast, made manageable by dividing it into three. My sketchy command of *Deutsch*, muffled by a face mask, saw me through check in. Even better, they awarded me a space right on the banks of the River Main.

We wanted to face Kismet's front picture windows towards the water. There wasn't enough room to drive onto our pitch, so we pushed her in by hand. It was flat, so we could manage, but as ever, our neighbours subjected us to the scourge of, "I will help you," but in German, which was more difficult to repel.

The chap opposite joined in unasked, which was kind, but unnecessary. It was also counterproductive. He pushed when we needed him to pull, then dragged Kismet sideways using the lever which engages the ALKO stabiliser. This is an important security device which stops the caravan snaking when towed. Thankfully, he didn't break it off.

Despite a swift en route reacquaintance with my old friend, *German in Three Months*, I could not vocalise, "Please don't manhandle a 1.5 tonne vehicle using a critical piece of safety equipment which is manifestly not designed for that purpose."

Unlike port, the family on our starboard side were very friendly. Jens and his daughter Mara soon arrived to say hello to the dogs, and Jens slipped in a polite enquiry,

"Do you have any Scotch?"

Throughout our travels, we have found that single malt is a perfect emollient to smooth international relations. We replied that sadly, we had polished off all our supplies during lockdown. He said it was his birthday, so we donated a bottle of *Weissbier* and told him,

"We're sorry we drank all your whisky!"

He accepted our apology graciously.

I had run out of my favourite hard-to-come-by sunscreen, the sort that binds to your skin and doesn't wash off when you're swimming or doing watersports. I had asked for it in a French pharmacy. The assistant gave me the purple unicorn look and followed up with something along the lines of,

"What new sorcery is this? Surely, such marvels cannot exist!"

I also wished to fulfil a long-standing desire for a new pair of exceedingly comfortable Reef 'Fanning' flip flops. My last pair disappeared mysteriously in the Auvergne. My sore and blistered feet missed them.

Surfing the wave of prior online ordering success in *Deutschland* (emergency replacement of Merrell walking sandals in Hohnstein three years ago), I placed an order and was assured of a two-day delivery.

Besides footwear and sunscreen, our third shortage was dog food. People often ask what we do about doggie dinners while travelling. During our first year of touring, we carted a 100 kg sack of kibble across France. Quickly, we realised that pet ownership has arrived in Europe, so most supermarkets stock the major brands. These days, as thrifty seasoned travellers, we beg campsite receptions to accept consignments of puppy provisions from an online supplier. That way, The Fab Four get their favourite brands of grub, and we pay less than supermarket prices.

Unfortunately, the German arm of our go-to supplier requires payment by bank transfer rather than a credit card. This wouldn't be a problem if we didn't have to factor in the likelihood of needing refunds for non-delivery. During our Italian lockdown, courier hide-and-seek was a primary source of entertainment. Our packages could be left anywhere in the village; from the adjacent hotel to some random corner of the three-storey underground car park. They never once arrived with Luisa, the 24-7 concierge at the reception of our apartment block.

Overnight, we heard a sound all too familiar from our previous German trip; rain battering the caravan.

As we awoke to a sodden morning and an equally dismal forecast, we resigned ourselves to a slack day and yet another critical shortage; we had run out of data. Just when circumstances demanded an afternoon of Netflix. When the deluge stopped around lunchtime, we made a sprint for Würzburg. On the drive, I glimpsed a sliver of blue sky and promised Mark,

"By the time we get there, it will be burning your eyeballs out!"

While it came highly recommended, we found Würzburg disappointing. It is a UNESCO World Heritage Site, and allegedly boasts Germany's oldest stone bridge, but it seemed like an ordinary town, with a smattering of nice buildings. However, our trip was not completely wasted.

For me, the highlight was the stop to purchase canine comestibles at Kölle Zoo, next to Ikea. It was a proper pet shop. You know, like the ones mums use for a free day out with the kids. It had an entire wall of fluorescing tropical fish, all manner of small furry creatures, and open crates of chewy treats. The Pawsome Foursome raced around on sensory overload.

Another question people ask about our lifestyle is, "How do you access the internet when you're touring?"

The answer is, we use our mobile phone as an internet hotspot, to which we tether our computers. For this trip, we had a 20 GB (Giga Byte) 'fair usage abroad' data allowance on our 'unlimited' UK contract. We could then bolster our allowance with a Pay-As-You-Go data SIM card in whichever country we were visiting. In Italy, we picked up 60 GB for €12.99 per month, while Romania held the record with 150 GB for €9 per month.

Sometimes, smug individuals say,

"Well. It's okay so long as it works."

Let me tell you, Romania is justifiably proud of her super-fast 4G network. It worked perfectly everywhere we went, no matter how remote. I can vouch that, even in major cities, this claim does not extend to the advanced industrialised powerhouse known as Germany – or, for that matter, the UK.

Our enquiries in various mobile phone shops revealed that buying a German data SIM was not a workable solution to our Giga Blight.

The best deal cost approximately €65 for a paltry 2.5GB per month. For our brief stay in Germany, it would be cheaper to pay the extortionate penalty for exceeding our UK limit, and hope that our upcoming destination, Poland, might offer similar deals to Romania.

We noted that coronavirus precautions varied widely in different countries. Italy had learned her lesson and was extremely fastidious about social distancing and mask-wearing. France was typically laissez-faire – wear a mask if you want, but it's not obligatory. In Germany, we encountered their legendary efficiency. We sat outside for coffee and cake at a pavement café, and they took our name, address, and telephone number.

"It's so we can contact you if there is an outbreak."

Masks were mandatory everywhere. Unlike in Italy and France, there was hand sanitising gel at the entrance to every premises – and not one dispenser was empty.

The café's choice of cakes was overwhelming. I studied the menu but had no idea what most of them were. They had ten different types of strudel! I panicked and stuck with the safe option; apple strudel and coffee. I made a bold attempt to order a flat white or latte, but received filter coffee with a plastic pot of milk; very 1970's.

A biblical downpour drenched us, even under the umbrellas. It matched our mood when we relinquished the meagre change from a €20 note as a tip. How could they charge so much for so little? In a miniature iteration of the Great Pacific Garbage patch, plastic milk pots and other pieces of café detritus floated by as the cobbled square flooded. I said to Mark,

"I told you it would be burning your eyeballs out once we got here!"

When the monsoon abated, we walked to the famous bridge. An inky black cloud loomed in the not-so-distant distance. We dashed back to Big Blue, parked somewhere on the street to the rear of the university. It was easier than we thought to navigate the labyrinth of alleyways back to her and miraculously, we didn't suffer a second soaking.

Even though it is the initial stopover on Germany's *Romantische Straße* – Romantic Road, personally, I wouldn't go out of my way to see Würzburg. Perhaps it was the weather, but it lacked the charm of some other places we have visited. Mark and I agreed,

"It's not Rothenburg ob der Tauber."

That pesky culture of comparison that we'd first noticed in Cluny had raised its head for the second time...

14

BITCH SLAPPED BY BAMBERG, BAVARIA

Fear and Loathing – plus a Fracas!

The monotonous, flat panorama buckled into a few low, forested hills as we crossed the Franconian wine country towards Bamberg. Another UNESCO World Heritage Site and once the epicentre of the Holy Roman Empire, the half-timbered medieval city came highly recommended.

There were even a few pretty villages en route. This contrasted with Düllstadt, a town near our campsite, which lived up to its name and epitomised the plainness of the immediate locale. The most exciting thing in Düllstadt was advertised on a brown sign. Its main visitor attraction was *Kartoffeln* – potatoes.

Despite showing early promise, our relationship with Bamberg got off to a shaky start. As we drove in, the tourist office with a surface car park nearby greeted us immediately. Bingo! Except somehow, we couldn't get near the car park. A plethora of underground parking was on offer, but we had second thoughts when we reached the entrance of a *Parkhaus*. We were plagued with roof rack anxiety. Not all *Parkhausen* make the two-metre-high cut, as we found out three years before, when we tried to park our van in Heidelberg.

With a parking disc, there was plenty of free on-street parking, but throughout Europe, we've never quite worked out where to purchase one. After several orbits in horrendous traffic, we eventually reached the surface car park. It was paid, but looked cheap: €2 for five hours seemed reasonable.

Bamberg dates back to the 9th century and is built on seven hills, which obviously invites the title 'The Franconian Rome'. A Kiwi can always annoy an Ozzie by referring to Australia as 'New Zealand's West Island'. With the same wry humour, local residents and tour guides label Rome 'The Italian Bamberg'.

I saw it more as 'The German Venice,' since water shapes the city. The River Regnitz, a tributary of the Main, splits around Bamberg to form several islands. Legend states the Church refused the citizens land to build their *Rathaus* – Town Hall, so in a show of defiance, they established it on a bridge above the river.

A wander over the bridges to the monumental *Rathaus* offered arresting views of the surrounding sea of timber-framed buildings. The tribulations of the morning demanded caffeine. €14 procured coffee with factory-made apple cake, and a waitress with no bedside manner. It was slightly cheaper than Würzburg, but we've had overnight stops that cost less.

Our mood did not improve as we wandered around the old town on the hill. Scaffolding over the cathedral and monastery was not alone in making them difficult to observe. The historic centre was not pedestrianised. The mêlée of traffic transformed admiration of the stunning medieval buildings into a game of Russian roulette. The chaos reminded me of Kathmandu, with psychotic electric scooters instead of tuk-tuks, although there were no kamikaze cows.

Despite the draw of its beer museum, we didn't visit the monastery, since scaffolding obscured the entire exterior. We took a guess that they wouldn't permit pups inside, anyway.

Instead, we opted for a river walk to the fishermen's village, unsurprisingly known as Little Venice. On the path, an old man abused us. I understood enough to grasp his accusations that we were not speaking *Deutsch*, the language of the Fatherland.

We have been told many times that *Bayern* – Bavaria – has its own distinct identity. Alsace displayed its uniqueness with welcoming pride, but Bayern's expression of 'distinct identity' was more 'massive chip on the shoulder'.

Other than our neighbour, Jens, the campsite was distinctly unfriendly. Most guests sported the joyous countenance of a person who had fallen out of the angry tree, hit every branch on the way down, then made landfall in a cowpat with a bear trap concealed within.

Along the riverbank, we chickened out of Little Venice amid showers of tuts and piercing stares directed at our Fur Babies. Scooters and bicycles gave pedestrians no quarter. The rule of thumb on shared pedestrian and cycle ways was, "Get the f*** out of my way!" It was a matter of time before someone collided with us or ran over our precious pups. The slow burn of stress bubbled over until I almost screamed,

"Mark, I hate it here. Let's get out!"

He felt the same and went one step further;

"Let's leave Germany and make headway towards Poland."

Bamberg was beautiful, its historic streets unsullied by modern monstrosities, but sometimes, when you travel, you just don't feel it. The reasons could be as arbitrary as the weather or simply your mood that day, but neither of us had warmed to the area. It seemed ugly and hostile, and we couldn't face the inevitable hordes of tourists at the other sights we had longed to see, such as the fantasy fortress of Neuschwanstein. Built by 'The Fairytale King', Ludwig II, it inspired Disneyland's Sleeping Beauty Castle.

In six hours, we could be in Hohnstein, which we had adored on our previous German tour. We could cross into the Czech Republic and the fabulous Bohemian Swiss National Park, which foul weather had forced us to bypass on that same trip. Our re-route would mean missing Berlin, but we were both city'd out.

The ultimate kick in the butt was that the parking cost €5, despite the price list not admitting to any time period in the sum of €5. If you remember, it advertised €2 for five hours. While the difference is not exactly a king's ransom, it was the principle. I felt robbed.

As for German efficiency, my sunscreen and sandals did not arrive. A text message said the courier could not find the vast campsite that dominated the outskirts of a tiny village because, 'the address information lacked vital information'.

Via an online chat, I explained that the address on the campsite's website had enabled literally thousands of campers, including two gormless foreigners like us, to find it. The operator assured me that she passed on some additional, magical piece of address information, even though there was nothing further to add. When the tracking didn't update, I braced myself for the inevitable. You don't need to be Nostradamus to predict whether or not my package ever arrived.

Even being in a country where I can say "*Gute Fahrt*" at will did not re-ignite my enthusiasm for Germany. (It means 'Have a good trip,' but sounds delightfully rude.)

Small, chilled, and with a pedestrianised centre, the capital of Slovenia is one of our favourite cities. We looked at each other and summed up Bamberg,

"It's not Ljubljana."

15

SOMMERACH TO KARLOVY VARY, CZECH REPUBLIC

We return to Living the Dream

Besides every plan going horribly awry, a further feature of our tour was a plenitude of Farmer Palmers. They seemed to lie in wait to lurch out of side roads with their heavy farm machinery the second they saw us approach with the caravan.

I laughed out loud as we left Sommerach, and got caught behind the slowest tractor ever. It crawled up the slope at a speed so leisurely it failed to register on our speedometer.

The tractor blankly refused to pull over, which forced us into a slight misjudgement that ended with white knuckles and a sharp intake of breath. We overtook him at the top of the hill, on a straight piece of road with a clear view ahead. Our misjudgement was failing to account for the velocity of German drivers. As we were parallel to the tractor, a black BMW hurtled out of the space-time continuum at twice the speed of sound. Mark and I released our breath when he deigned to decelerate sufficiently to avoid a head on. Chastened, we dropped hastily back on to our carriageway.

Otherwise, our break for the border was a charming drive through rolling hills of vineyards, barley, and maize, with the odd castle here and there. Sadly for me, our route missed Düllstadt, which denied me my final opportunity to capture a photographic record of its tourist-tantalising potatoes. I can only apologise for being so remiss and hope that one day, you might go to Düllstadt to experience its celebrated *Kartoffeln* for yourself.

As we crossed into the Czech Republic, the roads immediately became quieter and more relaxed. We remembered to buy a vignette (a road toll sticker) and even filled it out properly and stuck it on the correct section of the windscreen. That didn't spare me every anxiety, however. I worried they had sold us the wrong one, as it stated 'vehicles up to 3.5 tonnes'. While it is impolite to give away a lady's weight, Big Blue weighs about that, and Caravan Kismet adds another tonne and a half.

Being forced to buy it with a credit card was a sharp reminder that we had departed the Euro zone. We were in the land of the *koruna česká* – Czech koruna, and needed a currency exchange.

Our destination was a one-night stopover at Karlovy Vary, the Czech Republic's biggest spa city. As we drove through the outskirts, it looked awful; acres and acres of industrial estate. We considered going on, but since the campsite was out of town, we gave it a chance.

The campsite was next to a hotel, with no visible signs for campsite reception. We towed our twelve-metre length towards a building with Camp Vary emblazoned in huge letters across its gable, only to discover it was the toilet block. I left Mark there, contemplating how he might turn Kismet around while I roamed up hill and down dale looking for someone who could understand either English, French, Italian, or German. Someone told me to find the hotel reception, so I wandered lonely as a cloud through the terrace restaurant until a waiter finally directed me to the carefully concealed reception desk.

I laid out my linguistic possibilities for check in. The receptionist selected German, so I explained my limitations,

"*Mein Deutsch ist nicht gut.* – My German is not good."

Helpfully, she checked me in trilingually. She filled vocabulary vacuums by translating Czech into Italian on her computer, to which I replied in German,

"*Zwei Personen* – two persons" and "*Nein,*" for the use of the showers, which were extra. I was playing it safe, since I had no idea of the cost. I was in for a surprise.

Our stay came to 440 Kč – about £15, with no charge for pooches. That contrasted starkly with Germany. At €40 per night, our last site had hit our all-time record high for campsite prices.

In our experience, German campsites dominate the expense scale for Europe. Their pricing system often charges separately for absolutely everything. You pay a tariff for each person; your pitch; your caravan, your tow vehicle; electricity (which is sometimes metred); each dog; plus tax. Then, some demand extra for shower tokens.

Camp Vary was lovely and relaxed. It had only half a dozen pitches on top of a hill, with a scatter of wooden cabins on the steep slope between us and the facility block at the bottom.

I love it when our caravan loo has a view, and this was the first of our trip. Our bathroom window overlooked a pretty red sandstone folly on a mound, the Goethe Viewing Tower, and a zip line. That was a new and novel experience; be-helmeted zippers whizzing past during our ablutions.

We met Jan next door as soon as we arrived, because his elderly Vizsla was desperate to say hello to The Fab Four.

"You travel with four dogs!" he exclaimed.

Jan told us the industrial wasteland had grown up around the old town. He revealed a 4 km (2.5 mile) walk through the forest from the campsite into the pedestrianised centre of Karlovy Vary. Then, he pulled out his phone and demonstrated his app, Mapy.cz.

"It has all the tourist maps and walks on it, and you can use it offline. There are many footpaths through the trees. The spa visitors used to use them to take the air."

We decided immediately to stay another night and walk into Karlovy Vary the following morning. Jan pointed out a shorter route to a lake, so we chose that for a late afternoon puppy stretch.

The path led through a dark, pine-scented forest. By the lake, a group of youths encircling a campfire confronted us. Many bottles of vodka, a pall of pungent herbal smoke, and the white noise of Czech thrash metal surrounded them.

I was concerned they might decide to barbeque the dogs, but Mark and I recalled advice from a fun bodyguard training day we once did; 'Exude confidence'.

As we walked past in our shorts and sandals, with four fluffy, frou-frou pooches in tow, we oozed assurance. When we smiled and offered a friendly "Hi", they ignored us completely, which was excellent.

Half way round the lagoon, we encountered a chap with a Pit Bull, straining on a short leash. We clipped on The Fab Four's leads and gave him a wide berth. Exuding confidence provoked disinterest from the youngsters, but we were less certain of it working against a Pit Bull.

Once we had bypassed the hazards, The Pawsome Foursome got their swim. Aside from a fleeting sense of danger to life and limb in an unfamiliar country, it was a pleasant wander through the shady forest. It was hot in direct sun, but it wasn't Provence.

But I'm not making comparisons again. Cooler was a respite, and we enjoyed a beautiful sunset from our hilltop campsite. Peach and indigo streaks daubed themselves softly across the sky, while the lights of Karlovy Vary twinkled in the purple shadow of the valley below.

After a brief hiccup in Germany, we were back to Living the Dream.

16

CZECH PONT CHARLIE – KARLOVY VARY AND LOKET

"Today we were in Elbow, that about all description already loves and treats itself as a landscape work of art from all sides."
Goethe.

Founded in 1370 by Charles IV, King of Bohemia, Karlovy Vary is renowned for its thermal springs. 'Karl' is Czech for Charles and 'Vary' derives from the Czech word *vařit* – boil. Roughly translated, Karlovy Vary means, 'Charlie's Hot Tub'.

King Charlie also has a bridge. They named Charles Bridge in Prague after the same monarch. Following our acquaintance with the Ponts of Provence, I christened it Czech Pont Charlie.

I thank you.

From our campsite atop one of many hills overlooking Karlovy Vary, we walked into town through a mixed conifer and beech wood. The morning temperature edged towards 30°C (86°F), but it was bearably cool in the forest. Various glimpses through the trees afforded us some lovely previews of the eclectic mix of Karlovy Vary's tall, colourful buildings and surrounding hilltop folly towers.

The city had all the grace of a bygone era, but felt a little past its prime, like a heavily made-up aunt in a colourful but ill-fitting floral dress. An overpowering smell of drains assaulted our nostrils as we entered. We learned later it is a side-effect of the minerals in the water. However, a huge pipeline following the Teplá river contributed nothing to the view. A few individuals braved riverside cafés, but the foul odour would have put me off my food.

The stench subsided as we continued. The multi-storey facades on our riverbank formed an ornate and imposing wall, painted in a rainbow of pastel colours. Horse-drawn Cinderella carriages added charm as they clopped past on the cobbles. Facing us on the opposite bank were elaborate stone colonnades, housing mineral springs for all-weather enjoyment. In front of the largest, the Mill Colonnade, a violinist delivered an idiosyncratic repertoire. His rendering of *My Way* on a fiddle was more eclectic even than punk Sid Vicious' cover of the Frank Sinatra classic, especially when a howling hound contributed back-up vocals.

Since we were out of data, we searched for a phone shop to buy a SIM card. Our mission failed, so we crossed the water to compensate with coffee and a cake. In stark contrast to Germany, where such a treat rarely saw change from a €20 note, our delicious apple strudel and ultra-caffeinated latte for two cost the equivalent of about €3. Welcome to Czechia.

Our shady table had a view of what looked like a

white filigree metal bandstand, which was home to a small, undistinguished watery eruption. The steady stream of bodies stopping for selfies next to the barely perceptible burble perplexed me. They also seemed to be filling up small, squashed ceramic teapots, available to buy in a multitude of colours from the souvenir stands. This vision prompted me to say the first of two stupid things,

"Why are they posing and filling those tea pots and water bottles from THAT?" I demanded of Mark.

In his Einstein-explaining-the-simple-concept-of-subtraction-to-an-imbecile voice, he explained,

"It's a spa, Jackie. Like Bath. They are taking the waters."

Then I saw a Dachshund and wondered aloud,

"Is the German for Dachschund *Wurst Hund* – sausage dog?"

Mark launched straight into an unremitting barrage of ridicule.

"You're worse than George W. Bush. 'That's the trouble with the Germans, they have no word for Dachschund!'" he scoffed, paraphrasing George W's reputed castigation of our Gallic cousins, "That's the trouble with the French. They have no word for entrepreneur."

The signage was not hugely clear, but two police approached us politely to advise of dog restrictions in the colonnades,

"Dogs are not allowed on this side of the river."

"Sorry. We have seen lots of dogs there, so we thought it was okay."

"There are, because many people don't respect the rule."

We crossed back to where we could still enjoy the architecture, if not the bubbling curative springs.

Karlovy Vary's canine residents were all very smart; groomed to within an inch of their lives. We saw a Chinese Crested trotting along sporting a neat, pink jacket, although the majority of the poochy population did not deign to walk. Most were clutched beneath designer-clad arms, or languished in the expensive handbags of Beautiful People.

As budget-conscious early retirees, we groom The Fab Four ourselves. At the best of times, their hairstyles fall well within the realms of 'rustic'. By the time we reached Karlovy Vary, they had run four kilometres through a wood. Then, after lying in the shade beneath our table in the café, their chaotic coiffure was festooned with dead leaves.

I love to see little boys and girls with ruffled hair, scuffed knees, and their socks around their ankles (that was the younger me, by the way). Likewise, I am pleased The Pawsome Foursome are 'proper' dogs, who get to do doggie things. Nevertheless, it was no surprise that the Puppy Pawsers of Karlovy Vary looked down their noses at us, and dragged their pampered pooches away from our hirsute hoodlums.

Smart shops lined the streets. Some contained the most unbelievable *objets d'art*. If you were looking to kit out your Bohemian castle, Karlovy Vary is the perfect place to source enormous chandeliers or a gilded grandfather clock.

It was quite a climb back to the campsite, but the

ascent was gentle as the path wove and wound around the hillside. Karlovy Vary had been a most enjoyable diversion.

In the afternoon, we took a drive to Loket, a delightful medieval conurbation of grey stone, with a stunning hilltop castle. Loket is where James Bond and Vesper Lynd meet their MI6 contact in the remake of *Casino Royale.* I forgive you for thinking it is in Montenegro, as portrayed in the film.

On the way there, we stopped at a large Tesco, since the only help the phone shop in town could offer was advice that Czech supermarkets often sell SIM cards. It took about half an hour of sign language, but Mark returned triumphant with an £8, 3GB data SIM: somewhat more economical than the charges in Germany, and sufficient to keep us online for our week in Czechia. We also filled up with fuel for approximately 84p per litre. Coronavirus travel restrictions had pushed fuel prices down, but when we left the UK, a litre of diesel cost around £1.50. If only we had a bigger tank.

Loket was our kind of place. Its centre was small, pretty, and pedestrianised. Loket means 'elbow' in Czech, and is a reference to how the River Ohře cradles the town in the crook of its 'arm'. The current was very slack, so it would have been a great location to SUP, although we opted just to stroll. The Fab Four rounded off their day of shady forest walks with a swim. In doggie terms, a most satisfactory day.

Loket seemed to have been very popular with German writer Goethe. He was a frequent guest in one hotel, with his quote in Czech and German on the wall.

Mark and I stopped for an early beer opposite and I commented,

"It's like the Rosetta Stone. German translated into Czech. I wonder what it says."

Our resident language expert, Mark, didn't skip a beat,

"Up your ass with a gallon of gas!" he elucidated.

We sniggered like naughty schoolchildren as we offered the bastardised words of Goethe to toast our newfound fluency in Czech.

On our trip around town, we had seen a shop selling *Suvenyry* – Souvenirs. In Tesco's we had bought *Krakersy* – crackers, and according to our neighbour, Jan, *Mapy* is Map. We quickly worked out that *Pivo* was beer – a similar word in most Slavic languages.

We were sorted.

That night, my sleep was troubled by a dream that Mark was being executed. Throughout our life together, Mark has conjured silver linings from the darkest of clouds. When I suffered the body-blow of redundancy, he said,

"Well, we were thinking of giving up work, so this gives us a chance to learn to manage with less cash coming in, rather than losing two well-paid jobs at once."

In my dream, in his irrepressibly positive way, he held my hand and told me gently,

"Not many couples get to be together at the end."

Thankfully, Mark's shackles in the dream were a puzzle, so he deployed his excellent lateral-thinking skills and escaped.

Nevertheless, I was relieved the rain woke me before living in my dreams got any further out of hand.

17

KOKOŘÍN CASTLE AND KOKOŘÍNSKO NATIONAL PARK

Czech-erboard landscapes, Czech Points, and Strange Questions at Czech-in

"Prague, of course," is most people's answer to, "Where did you go in the Czech Republic?"

But not ours...

As Adventure Caravanners, our aim is to reach the parts that other road trippers don't. Kokořínsko National Park was in our sights, with its beautiful landscapes, historic villages and, naturally, castles.

The first part of our journey from spa town, Karlovy Vary, to Kokořín was enchanted. We followed a sparkling river as it slithered through a verdant forest.

Then, it was flat, flat, flat, boring, boring, boring, culminating in a huge open cast mine at Spořice. With no exaggeration, the desecrated apocalyptic wasteland extended to every horizon.

Things improved as we approached some domed, volcano-shaped hills. One was topped with imposing twin turrets, surrounded by a chequer board landscape of apple green, brown, and golden fields.

Things returned to enchanted as we drove into the protected area surrounding Kokořín; pronounced Cock au Gin.

Sandstone cliffs, softened and eroded by time, bordered our route through dark, shadowy forests. Small caves and grottoes pockmarked the walls. Some housed statues of the Madonna. It was like fairyland.

Our campsite was a quirky little place, tucked at the head of a slightly damp and gloomy cleft between the sandstone crags. Enveloped by dense forest, we loved it immediately. The lady proprietor and her delightful teenage family welcomed us like one of their own, and footpaths galore led straight from the door.

At first glance, it looked like there was no room for us, but the owner squeezed us into a quiet corner. The squeezing required a perilous reverse through an obstacle course of campers, caravans, tents, awnings, and an electricity bollard. To make it easier, we persuaded a misadventure of kids to move their detritus of tricycles, an inflatable whale, mini tables and chairs, plus a paddling pool to the side.

Once again at check in, our only shared language was German,

"*VIER Hunde?* – FOUR dogs?" she exclaimed. My heart sank as visions of dog bans flashed into my mind. Then she said, "I will make a charge for two..."

What an endearing phrase.

Since we had run out of clothes, we were grateful to be next to the facilities. Our portable, twin-tub washing machine had to be filled with hot water, so having a supply on tap was a bonus. Caravan Kismet's boiler supplied seven litres – barely sufficient to cover the bottom of the tub. Wash day usually involved lots of buckets carried from the shower block, plus a steaming array of pans and kettles on the hob.

Of course, the second we had finished all our laundry, it rained, but we put our home-made 'awning' over it. Thankfully, it dried in the following morning's sun.

Besides a lack of attire, we had no food. On our way to the campsite, we had seen no shops or supermarkets. Fortunately, the site had its own small restaurant. Ribs, two beers each, and a local walking map cost less than €20 – or coffee and a cake in Germany.

The new day arrived with no grub to break our fast either. Even though breakfast finished officially at 10 a.m., the owner's son, Frankie, offered to cook us ham and eggs at 10:30. I don't want you to think we had overslept. We had just been bewitched by our morning walk through such entrancing surroundings. The Fab Four absolutely adored it. They bounded through the trees and chased each other, although The Terrible Two, Lani and Rosie, kept disappearing, hot on the scent of some elusive woodland creature.

After breakfast, we set off into the wood, following the *Rundweg*, a circular walk to *Hrad Kokořín* – Kokořín Castle. We loaded our backpack with gingerbread. Not to lay a trail to get back. It was a forgotten delicacy we had imported from Alsace – and the only thing we had to eat.

At check in, Frankie's mum had posed a rather strange query,

"How heavy are your dogs?"

I wondered if they determined dog charges by weight,

but in German, she explained the *Rundweg* had ladders and steps, so it was more a question of whether our pooches were petite enough to be portable.

The walk was gorgeous, weaving between sandstone cliffs in the mottled light of beech woods, and we had it all to ourselves.

Close to the castle car park, we found an ice cream trailer and two outdoor restaurants. Plunged into the heat beyond the forested shade, ice cream seemed a sterling idea. Mark went with the easy option of *Karamel*, while I pointed at *Meruňka*. I had no clue what it was until I tasted it. To my relief, it was not garlic and kipper flavour, but a very delicious apricot. There was no sign of the castle, but we had no problem finding it. From the food stop, we simply followed the crowds up a narrow, shaded lane that cut through the woodland.

Kokořín is an impressive mini castle of exactly the sort that I would love to live in. With white walls and an orange terracotta tiled roof, its charming turrets give it a fairy-tale quality. It seems to float above the treetops on its sandstone outcrop. *Hrad Kokořín* started life around 1320 as a fortified palace with a tower, built by a Bohemian knight, Hynek Berka of Dubé.

In the 1400s, the religious 'Hussite' (or 'Bohemian') wars badly damaged Kokořín. Later, it got a Gothic facelift, but had fallen into disuse and disrepair by the 17th century.

Even in ruins, Kokořín inspired the imagination of notable poets and painters, which attracted tourists. In the late 19th century, aristocrat Václav Špaček bought it and between 1911 and 1918, reconstructed it in its current Romantic style.

Entry to the courtyard and turrets was free, and dogs were welcomed on leads. There was a small charge to see the restored interior, plus an additional 10Kč to photograph it. I didn't go inside, but climbed a spiral staircase to the top of the main tower. There, I experienced stupendous views across the treetops, along with that uneasy feeling of vertigo in the pit of my stomach.

By the time we got back to Caravan Kismet, I had a different feeling in the pit of my stomach. Even after a sunlit relaxation session, we couldn't summon the energy to drive out and find a shop. We plumped for a second indulgent dinner on site. Despite adding gingerbread and ice cream for variety, the Czech diet of meat, with meat, plus a garnish of meat, left us hankering for something fresh.

We settled at what was now 'our' table on the outside terrace. The menu was in Czech, but Frankie spoke good English. We requested a dish that came with vegetables.

He brought a delicious grilled pork loin with chips. Mark and I peered at it and asked,

"Frankie, where are the vegetables?"

"There!" he said, as his trademark smile lit up the whole place.

Proudly, he pointed at an extra-large dollop of horseradish sauce.

18

POKLIČKY AND THE SCARY SECRETS OF HOUSKA CASTLE

We discover the gateway to Hell!

We're often asked "Where's the absolute best place to go?"

Our answer is always:

"It depends what you like."

Our day was a classic illustration of that.

Over another ham and egg breakfast on the terrace, young Frankie shared his recommendations in the Kokořínsko Protected Landscape,

"Houska Castle and the Pokličky rocks. 'Pokličky' means 'pot lids' – they are the symbol of the area."

Local advice is invaluable, so we embarked on a scenic circular drive to incorporate both. It took us past Bezděz, a striking hilltop fortress, and through traditional Czech villages, replete with distinctive timber houses with their thin, horizontal black and white stripes. Kruh was especially attractive. Residents used the topography as sheds, with doors fitted over the mouths of caves in the sandstone cliffs.

Dating to the 13th century, *Hrad Houska* – Houska Castle raises many questions in the mind of the casual onlooker.

Why was it built in a marshy, forested wilderness, unsuitable for hunting, distant from any trading routes, and with no strategic value?

Why are there no stairways from the upper floors into the courtyard, and why are so many of its windows fake?

Why is there no kitchen, well, or water source?

And why is it named after a bun? (In Czech, *houska* means a braided bread roll, as illustrated by the sculpture of a plaited loaf on a banister.)

Even more puzzling, why are all its defensive fortifications on the *inside*?

If you asked, "Who lives in a house like that?", the answer for most of the castle's history is – nobody.

Houska was not built as a home. The folklore surrounding its location reveals its true purpose.

In the Middle Ages, a split in the rock on which Houska now stands became known as 'The Gateway to Hell'. It was a bottomless pit, impossible to fill, from which demonic, winged beasts reportedly emerged. Part animal, part human, these fiendish creatures attacked people and dragged them into the void.

The locals promised a young prisoner on death row a pardon if he agreed to be lowered into the chasm and report what he had seen. According to legend, within seconds, the convict was screaming uncontrollably. When they pulled him out, he had gone insane. His face had aged thirty years and his hair turned white. Within two days, he died of unknown causes.

The purpose of *Hrad Houska* was not to keep enemies out, but to keep them in. They deliberately constructed the chapel directly over the abyss to seal the portal to the underworld.

The castle is still renowned as one of the most haunted locations in the world. Visitors report hearing scratching and screams; supposedly demonic creatures trying to claw their way to the surface. There are reports of cars failing to start and dogs going mad.

Houska appears in many annals of the paranormal – and some even claim it is a time portal.

It boasts a plethora of ghosts; from a full cast of human characters, including the classics such as a white lady and faceless monk, to a headless horse gushing blood and an intriguing human/bullfrog/dog hybrid.

The Nazis occupied the castle, reputedly to conduct experiments into the occult. Of course, when they retreated, they destroyed all records.

Despite its status among the best-preserved castles of the early Gothic era and all its apparent fame, Houska hadn't come up in our research. Once we arrived, we realised why.

What confronted us truly was the gateway to Hell.

A courtyard overflowing with tourists, stalls, and an entrance to a tacky ghost train ride held zero appeal for Mark and I.

I am normally rather sensitive to the atmosphere of buildings. As a scientist, I have a healthy scepticism regarding paranormal phenomena. However, I have occasionally sensed something strange, only to discover later that disturbing events had taken place there. At Houska, I felt nothing.

Our decision was instant. We did an about turn and went for a short walk in the woods. The dogs did go mad, but that was perfectly normal behaviour for them in a woodland. The views across the sunlit, rolling countryside were lovely, but we decided to flee the crowds and find somewhere nice for a coffee.

We left Houska to complete our loop on a spectacular raised causeway that led through the canopy of the forest. As we passed cyclists, I tried not to look at the drops that fell away on both sides of the hairpins.

The town of Kokořín drew a blank on the caffeine and lunch front, so we continued on towards the eateries that we knew surrounded Kokořín Castle. A long, low, wooden cafeteria offered pizza for €3, but we opted for the posher restaurant across the road. All in Czech, the menu was impenetrable, but after a diet of nothing but meat for nearly a week, we once again requested a dish with veggies. We hoped for a tad more vitamins and fibre than Frankie's well-meant dollop of horseradish sauce.

Our waitress spoke some English and recommended two typical Czech pork dishes, which came with cabbage and dumplings. The tablespoon of cabbage was an afterthought, but after half a kilo of dumplings, we were definitely not hungry when we waddled off in search of the Pokličky.

I'm not sure *Hrad Houska* is a portal to the past, but the Pokličky certainly are. The origin of the curious, mushroom-shaped sandstone pedestals starts during the Cretaceous period, 145 million years ago. Their 'lids' contain more iron, which weathers less easily than the soft sandstone and clay pillars beneath. They stand an impressive twelve metres (40 ft) high.

The Pokličky were only a few steps from the car park. We climbed a steep wooden ladder to view them from above, then set off on a circular course. First, we took a forest track, which was pleasant, but ordinary.

"It's not the Saxon Swiss National Park," we grinned at each other. We are so spoiled...

Things improved when our route entered a sunken lane with twisted tree roots winding through its banks. This led to an area of golden sandstone pillars and stacks, which we clambered over in the variegated sunlight filtering through beech leaves. The crunch of leaf litter and dancing light in a woodland never fails to delight me.

One of the side canyons was alive with grottoes and caves. We followed it and explored a narrow pothole in its walls. Our little black girl, Lani, was not too keen. She whimpered and started shaking, so we abandoned our underground explorations.

The path was quite messy with fallen logs, which the pups trotted along daintily like expert tightrope walkers. As soon as we were near the car park, Princess Ruby found some lovely sludge-filled puddles to paddle in. It would be bath time once we got back.

Luckily, our hearty lunch meant we did not need dinner. So far from a supermarket, our choices at the caravan were the last piece of gingerbread, half a rotting melon, and some bread purloined from the breakfast buffet.

While our agreement to bail out on Spain was based on the soaring summer temperatures, we noted a huge

COVID spike in Catalonia. Perhaps we'd made a good decision to avoid Iberia, although as I said to Mark,

"I haven't seen a mask, other than my own, since we entered the Czech Republic."

"I think we'll be okay," he reassured me. "We eat outdoors and only use the facilities in our caravan."

It came as no surprise when, soon after, Czechia declared a national COVID emergency.

19

KOKOŘÍN TO ČESKÝ RÁJ – 'BOHEMIAN PARADISE'

Paradise is in the eye of the beholder...

Squeak, squeak, squeak, squeak...

"Can't you see the funny side?" I asked a rather grumpy Mark.

Children playing nicely often adds to the ambience of a campsite. As we tucked into Frankie's breakfast special on the terrace that morning, the background of three toddlers enjoying the sandpit had been a genuine pleasure. Kokořín had exceeded all expectations, although moving to a place called Český ráj – Bohemian Paradise – launched our hopes into the exosphere.

But we made a terrible mistake.

We pitched near a trampoline.

The new campground sloped, and a large swathe was cordoned off to accommodate a group. Our task was to identify a level area within reach of an electricity bollard. There was a small trampoline that looked privately owned. No one was using it when we arrived, so we didn't give it much thought.

By 7:30 p.m., however, it had been going like the bedsprings of a nineteenth-century brothel for five hours. The elastic excruciation started shortly after we reached the critical point of setting up: i.e. when we couldn't be bothered to pack everything up again and move.

As if to compensate for the bedsprings, the gentle strumming of a guitar drifted through the fading sunlight. Then, we heard a sound that should never sully any campsite, anywhere.

A tone-deaf musician warmed up for a recital. Desperately in search of a tune, he blared out discordant scales and arpeggios on a trumpet. Then, he skirled a flat rendition of *When the Saints Go Marching In* across the campground. Having truly hit his stride, he continued his quest to purge any trace of melody from a series of musical notes. What followed was the musical interpretation of migraine; a cacophonic zigzag; a racket sufficient to make even modern jazz sound like the heavenly trill of angels.

Who brings a trumpet to a campsite?

My advice is don't, unless you're a genuine expert.

And even then, still don't.

Unless you wish to risk a sharp bonk on the bonce with your bugle.

The day's challenges didn't start with the trampoline. The 60-mile hop from Kokořín to Český ráj took hours. Mark contradicted my claim we had no food,

"You've forgotten that half a salami in the bottom of the fridge. It's been there since France."

Mmmmm. Appetising.

It was a bonus to find a huge, out-of-town supermarket en route, although our stop there was not without incident.

Dipped headlights are compulsory while driving in many European countries. Due to language difficulties, I took so long to trawl the aisles that Mark played *Marilyn Manson's Greatest Hits* in its entirety before he remembered to switch off Big Blue's headlamps. He'd left the ignition switched on to power the iPod, so perhaps having Caravan Kismet connected had also affected the battery. When we'd put away the provisions and he turned the key, nothing happened.

It is difficult to convey the desolation you feel when stranded with a caravan in the car park of an isolated Czech supermarket.

What to do?

In desperation, I approached a man in a high-visibility jacket as he patrolled the car park. I think he was collecting trolleys, but he was in possession of a peaked cap and a walkie-talkie, so he looked official. Our only shared language was a smattering of German, so, my prior knowledge of *les pinces* was useless to me. To explain our issue with *das Auto*, I resorted to sign language.

Travelling has cultivated my ability to deal with mechanical difficulties in foreign languages. Jump leads – '*les pinces*' had entered my French vocabulary the previous October. In order to make an early morning getaway, we had left Kismet hitched overnight, not realising it would flatten Big Blue's battery. Sadly, this incident led to a misplaced confidence that we wouldn't be stupid enough to drain the battery again.

So, my advice is, don't get complacent. And learn to say *Starthilfekabel* in a variety of languages.

Luckily, our Hi-Vis Hero was just the man to administer a hefty heave. After we unhitched Big Blue, he and Mark propelled her across the tarmac in a supercharged trolley dash. The pressure of responsibility to execute the jump start was all mine. I could have sobbed with relief when I dropped the clutch into second gear and Big Blue lurched and spluttered back into life.

We had narrowly averted *The Car Park* – a tedious adaptation of the Tom Hanks film, *The Terminal*, featuring a couple trapped for eternity in a Bohemian supermarket.

Our next challenge was to reach our destination without stalling, like the film *Speed*.

At least I had picked up some consolation. Although the cellar section in the supermarket was filled with Bordeaux and little Italian numbers, I decided when in Česky...

So, here's my Connoisseur's Guide to Czech Wine. I deployed my full oenological expertise – and bought something with a stupid name. Considering our situation, it turned out that 'Palava' was irritatingly appropriate.

We rarely book campsites in case we don't warm to our destination. Our first choice endorsed our strategy. Ruby, our water-loving pup, was ecstatic when she spotted the private lake. On paper, the camp was central to all the notable sights in Český ráj and a short walk from a castle, but it was huge, noisy, and commercial. The young man guarding the gate said it was full, which avoided the embarrassment of saying we didn't want to stick around, anyway. He handed over a list of local campsites, but particularly recommended one,

"It's in a forest. I would stay there if I came here on holiday," he assured us.

Mark's research had already highlighted it as a possibility. After a tight U-turn, we re-traced our route past the lake. We were relieved to retreat from the commotion of sun-singed pot-bellies and inflatable watercraft that troubled its surface.

But the nearby autocamp would not relinquish its secret easily – we couldn't find it. I nipped into a post office near where we thought it was. All I found was a corridor lined with blank doors, which looked like apartments. Some had signs pinned to them, written in Czech, which was no help at all.

I asked a man parked outside. When I pointed at the name of the campground on the list, he stuck up two fingers. I was quite shocked until he said,

"Two kilometres."

It was two kilometres to the turning, but the campsite was *waaaay* beyond that, down a long, winding forestry road. For once, check-in happened in English, which had pros and cons. It meant I understood only too well that payment was cash only, and they wanted it immediately, preferably sooner. We didn't have enough currency, so Mark had to drive to the closest ATM – almost all the way back whence we came.

By mid-afternoon, soon after we'd settled up for two nights, the brothel opened for business. The trampoline continued with no rest or respite until 10.30 p.m.

"I know we've paid, but what do you think about moving on tomorrow?" Mark said.

That was when I mocked his lack of humour over the trampoline,

"It's more commercial and less natural here, but the dogs and I had a lovely walk while you set up. There are sandstone formations in the woods here, like Kokořín. I know there's not a castle in walking distance, but we're spoiled. This is 'It's not Ljubljana!' all over again."

"I s'pose there are a few castles and a palace to see," Mark conceded, although the description of one highlight, Valdštejn Castle, did not reassure him.

"It says it's a 'restored hilltop castle with a pub'."

The US special forces used heavy metal music to wear down Panama's General Noriega and force him out of sanctuary. Delta Force threw everything at him, including Van Halen, Guns N' Roses, and The Clash. It was musical torture – or an epic line up at Glastonbury Festival. It's all in the ear of the beholder. The opera-loving General held out for ten days.

I said to Mark, "I reckon trial by trumpet and trampoline could have saved the Americans a week."

The trampoline sealed our surrender. The tuneless trumpet was an unnecessary flourish.

By 8:24 a.m. the following morning, I had joined Mark in a catastrophic sense of humour failure. Our bordello had already been in action for an hour.

Despite the language barrier, it was easy to recognise that the bouncing babes were playing a counting game. It went something like;

Squeak, squeak, squeak... "Five million, seven-hundred-thousand, four-hundred-and-twenty-seven," ... squeak, squeak, squeak... "Oh no! I've lost count. One, two..."

Squeak, squeak, squeak through breakfast. Squeak, squeak, squeak as we drank our coffee. Squeak, squeak, squeak as we packed, and then realised that the critical hour of 10 a.m. had passed and reception was closed.

To prevent theft by those who had not paid the power premium, The Management had locked our electricity supply cable into the bollard. Our desperate attempt to pick the lock failed.

What to do?

Mark found a notice in Czech with a phone number affixed to reception's locked door. A couple of teenage lads were hanging around nearby, so he asked them,

"Do you speak English?"

"I do a little," one of them volunteered.

"Can you tell me what this note says?"

Mark was almost paralysed with laughter when he returned. Without the slightest hint of humour or irony, the boy had read the note aloud in Czech.

Our Czech SIM card from Tesco's, with its free calls and data, saved the day. With our already meagre hope waning rapidly, we called the telephone number. Shockingly, we got through to someone sensible. They divulged, in English, the location of the keys for the electric bollard, hidden under some tourist leaflets outside the office.

At last. We were free! But we couldn't leave because the caravan brakes were locked again.

Squeak, squeak, squeak, CLANG.

The trampoline provided all the motivation he needed. Like a meerkat fleeing a hawk, Mark shot beneath Caravan Kismet. His trusty torque wrench delivered the restorative whack to the *freins de caravane.*

Within seconds, we had pulled away. I don't think I have ever been more delighted to hightail it from a campsite.

Maybe it is unfair to rename Český ráj 'Bohemian Crapsody'. Evidently, it appeals to the masses, but it really wasn't for us.

What to do?

Finally, we hit the Road to Hel.

Next stop – Poland.

20

JOURNEY TO THE CENTRE OF EUROPE, BOLKÓW, POLAND

We discover the geographic centre of Europe – depending on how and when you calculate it

A Polish man is having an eye test.

"Can you read the chart?" the optician asked.

"Read it?" he said, "I know him!"

My home town of Blackburn, Lancashire, has a large Polish community, so unlike Czech, I can claim some form with Polish pronunciation.

My Dad once asked how I might pronounce the surnames of two Polish colleagues, Hyrcaj and Dzrombak, which he spelled out for clarity.

"'Ritzy' and 'Chumbug'," he told me. I didn't even get close.

As Confucius says, "Real knowledge is to know the extent of one's ignorance."

It was a warning of things to come. Never think it will be simple to ask for directions in Poland.

But I'm getting ahead of myself.

When we departed the Czech Republic a few years ago, we blew our remaining Czech currency on chocolate marzipans in a supermarket. Confused by the exchange rate and unsure how much cash we required to settle our campsite bill the previous day, Mark had panicked and withdrew about €200 in koruna. Since we paid only €24 for two nights, we now needed to rid ourselves of €176 before we reached Poland that evening.

Even for us, that was too much chocolate marzipan.

We filled up with fuel at a petrol station beneath the impressive ruin of Trosky Castle. With two towers seated atop two basalt pillars, the eroded remains of lava tubes, the fortress was never conquered.

As I admired Český ráj's most visited sight, Mark exchanged every koruna for diesel, LPG, wine, plus a coffee each. He emerged without firearms, despite a sign advertising guns for sale above the door. In Eastern Europe, there is nothing extraordinary about purchasing an entire arsenal of offensive weapons with your fuel and morning coffee.

Mark's carefully calculated supermarket sweep came to 4,977 Kč, but he only had 4,976 Kč. The kind man in the garage waived the 1 Kč – about 4 cents.

The area around Trosky continued the theme of tourist hell. Several huge rafting outfits defiled the far bank of the river, but as we drew away, the scenery became more natural and unspoiled. Near the border, we went through the ski resort of Kořenov, then crossed into Poland, which was the original geographic centre of Europe – before the EU, German reunification, and Brexit. It was a new country for everyone – and our fifth in four weeks.

As we passed a forestry site, I said to Mark,

"We'd never get a job there."

"Why's that?" he asked.

In my best Dublin accent, I replied, "Because they want tree fellers and there's only two of us."

Silence.

"I said they need tree fellers and there's only two of us. And one of us is a girl."

"I got it the first time," Mark replied witheringly. "There's no need to embellish it."

"You'd miss it if I didn't make terrible jokes. These long journeys would be boring..."

Our route was anything but boring as we ventured through further tourist hellishness. A troll-themed rope park stood out as particularly memorable. Thankfully, as we continued, things once again became quieter and more picturesque.

I was jubilant as I noted a snack stop approximately every ten yards. This instilled hope that Poland wouldn't be another Romania, where I endured most lunchtimes with a rumbly tum and low blood sugar, as we searched in vain for somewhere that sold food.

The journey was only 60 miles, but it took hours. Many roads were brand new, so for much of the way, the satnav insisted we were in the middle of a field. After a bit of nip and tuck, an overshoot, and yet another U-turn, we finally arrived in Bolków from an unexpected direction. We stopped outside our planned destination, but the campsite looked deserted. I tried the gate, which was firmly locked. It was definitely closed. Possibly even abandoned.

According to the satnav, the next nearest site was

about 23 miles away. Parked on the side of a narrow road with traffic flashing past, we grabbed the laptop. Mark was sure there was a campsite nearby, so he investigated hastily while I took the pups on the verge for a nature stop. He found Camping Pod Lasem, which was considerably closer than 23 miles. It was just around the corner.

We pulled in to find a derelict field containing nothing but a pair of mouldering caravans and a man working on the roof trusses of a half-built building. Our hearts sank. Was every site in the area closed? Perhaps it was because of the pandemic. We berated ourselves for not checking.

I circled reception – it was empty and locked. Then the chap in the distance on the roof truss waved his mobile phone, which seemed to indicate he had made a call. I wandered to the back of the campground and found several beautifully kept grassy terraces, with tents and motorhomes in residence.

By the time I returned from my investigations, Mark was already checking in with Richard, the friendly owner. Richard was Polish, but had lived in the Netherlands for twenty years. Naturally, his English was impeccable, and his approach differed greatly from some of the abrupt receptions we'd received elsewhere. He gave us each a cold beer as a welcome gift and, by coincidence, allocated us pitch number 2, which was the pleasant, shady space upon which I had already set my heart.

Pod Lasem means 'near the forest'. It was serene, the pitches spacious, and completely devoid of trumpets and trampolines. The Fab Four could run free around our terrace and play with Bo, a bouncy, black Cocker Spaniel. Bo belonged to Marianne and Carola, a chilled-out

Dutch couple who were our only neighbours. Woodland surrounded us and we had two castles, Bolków and Świny, in our sight.

As we contemplated the sunset with our cold beers in hand, we figured we might stay awhile.

21

BOLKÓW AND ZŁOTORYJA

Medieval Castles and The Oldest Town in Poland

"They will be *fine*!"

Mark's report of the man's claim embodied my worst fears. Vans and caravans have specialist tyres. My primary worry about getting them changed abroad was that we would end up with the wrong ones – and this chap's offering could not have been more wrong.

Tyres had been a concern since Provence. It's best practice to change caravan tyres every five years anyway, although in her last half decade spent schlepping around Europe, Kismet had burned more rubber than most. We had also noticed some unnerving hairline cracks developing in the walls of Big Blue's summer tyres.

From our base in Bolków, Mark visited a tyre fitter in nearby Jawor. Despite Jawor having a castle, a 17th-Century UNESCO-listed Church of Peace, and being on our list of places to see, Mark described it as,

"Somewhere you want to keep your windows up."

As for the tyre shop, he said,

"It seemed legitimate – it had a large sign and a lorry on the forecourt. They didn't have the correct tyres for Big Blue, so they offered me some others. I told them they were no good, but they insisted they would be okay. They only stopped trying to sell them to me when they wouldn't fit under the wheel arch."

Mark told them we'd be around for a week and asked if they could order tyres of the right size. Dismayed, they shook their heads and replied,

"In a week? Not a chance!"

Tyre-less, we walked to Świny, the most local of our two castles. Now a ruin, *Zamek Świny* started life on its hilltop as a fortified wooden settlement, established as early as the 5th century. Its role was to protect the Czech side of Lower Silesia, but it fell into disuse when they built neighbouring Bolków castle in the 13th century. Many castles can claim destruction by fire and sword, but this was my first encounter with one ravaged by hurricanes.

Our route passed a bug-infested lake, before rising via a stony footpath through a scrubby forest. Shards of broken glass strewn along the path made us worry about puppy paws. The aroma of burning plastic suffused the air. A group of sultry teenagers occupied a viewpoint on a crag, with drum and bass music thrashing out of their boom box. Tentatively, we approached to admire the view over Bolków, then continued on to the castle. In deep, mossy and mosquito-ridden shade outside the gate, a spherical chap in a check shirt with spectacles like the base of bottles waited on a wooden chair to collect admission. We had no money with us, but the ruin looked less than inviting. We feared that once inside, its soaring but cracked and ramshackle walls might collapse on us.

The following morning, we drove into Bolków. The town itself was not the prettiest, but I genuinely enjoyed the castle, which is one of the most important medieval monuments in Lower Silesia. Like Świny, it is a ruin, not a palace, but unlike its neighbour, it overflowed with atmosphere. I felt an immediate connection with the past as I wandered through the various ruined rooms and outside spaces, enclosed by forbidding, fortified walls. My favourite part of the visit was my own unique adventure when I climbed the tower.

I ascended part way on some wooden steps, then entered a gloomy stone chamber. Inside was a hole in the floor; probably a dungeon or prison. I had spotted people on top of the tower, but couldn't see how to climb any further. There was no one else around. Mark had stayed in the courtyard with the hounds. It took me a few minutes of groping around the walls to discover a narrow aperture in a shadowy corner, barely big enough to squeeze through.

The opening led into a claustrophobic passage with a spiral staircase. In a complete blackout, I fumbled my way up the uneven stone slabs that formed the steps. My hair brushed the rough stonework of the roof, and the damp musty smell of age-old mortar enveloped me. Near the top, two shiny and deathly pale disembodied faces with dark slashes for mouths suddenly floated into view. Like vampires, they came at me out of the darkness.

It was a pair of heavily made-up lady tourists wearing headscarves, but they gave me a start.

The views from the ramparts took in agricultural land and the town. They were both commanding and vertigo-inducing. Unfortunately, the lights were back on for my descent through the tunnel. If you ever wish to shatter ambience and ruin the mystery, a row of fluorescent tubes works a treat.

Sadly, *Zamek Bolków's* July Festival of Darkness was yet another casualty of coronavirus. Having experienced the castle's aura, I loved the idea of a gothic get together in such a moody setting.

That afternoon, we drove to Złotoryja.

"We won't go through Jawor, it's a dump," Mark said.

Fewer than five miles short of Złotoryja, the road was closed. The diversion sent us all the way back via Jawor and Bolków.

"It's nice to see a bit of Poland," I chuckled as we retraced our steps around three sides of a thirty-mile square.

The countryside reminded me of Merrie England, with half-timbered barns dotted in a rolling agricultural landscape. It was not unlike Hampshire, but with hills in the background, storks nesting on chimneys, and a red squirrel who ran across the road to shoot up a tree.

En route, we screeched to a stop on the roadside when we spotted a footpath to a rock outcrop called Czartowski Skały. It looked like a great place to give the pups a run. From an information board in Polish, I surmised that Czartowski Skały was geologically different from the surrounding area, but beyond that, I hadn't a clue. Despite my developing understanding of

Russian, cultivated during lockdown, and command of several Latin languages, I couldn't even take a punt at Polish. Other than obvious words such as *restauracja,* which means banana.

I'm kidding.

It does mean restaurant.

Later, after looking at the website, I can tell you that the *skały* are basalt; solidified lava from the inside of a volcanic cone, which eroded away.

With lockdown delays, it was some time since Mark had planned our trip, so he'd forgotten why we needed to visit Złotoryja. When we arrived, the central square was buzzing, packed with families enjoying their Sunday afternoon at pavement cafés.

We joined in the fun, so our abiding memory of Złotoryja is of a sun kissed festival of pizza and beer at an outdoor café. I took a photo of the fountain opposite our *restauracja* because it was so hideous. It appeared to be a stack of grotesque, writhing fish with swollen Mick Jagger lips, moulded from donkey-coloured concrete.

After our visit, curiosity got the better of me. Why was Złotoryja on our sightseeing list? I discovered that, besides being among 'the ten most beautiful villages in Poland', it's the oldest town in Poland and has a long history of gold mining. While we had been making the most of its pizza and beer, we missed out on two hundred historic monuments, the opportunity to pan for gold, and its very own extinct volcano in a nearby quarry. The website exposed the fountain as a renowned 17th-Century work of art.

Back at the campsite, Mark and I discussed our intentions. Toothache had kept me awake most of the night, along with a gnawing sense of dread. The protracted series of small niggles, disasters, and disappointments was getting to me, but the icing on the cake was the previous night's dream in which Mark and the dogs all died.

"I feel like we're blighted," I said to Mark. "So many things have gone wrong. That truck nearly killed us all on day one. We've had problems with the caravan brakes, our tyres are dangerous and we can't get them changed..."

But like beauty and fish fountains, bad luck is in the eye of the beholder.

Mark replied, "But everything worked out superbly well in the end. We got out of the lorry situation really quickly – we could have been stuck there for hours. In fact, it couldn't have turned out better. There's nothing seriously wrong with the caravan brakes, and now we know how to fix them. And I promise you we will get tyres tomorrow in Wrocław.

"We have options," he continued. "We could run for home or go windsurfing in Brittany. Mind, both will be tourist hell in August. A few things have gone awry and we've had to change our plans, but most of our trip has been wonderful. We've just had a few bad experiences recently."

We were both a little disappointed with Poland so far, but rationalised that we might feel the same about Britain if we judged the entire country on a weekend in Slough. *(Former Poet Laureate, Sir John Betjeman, wrote a poem about Slough. He invited friendly bombs to fall upon it.)*

By the end of the day, my tooth was hurting less. The ache was the same with or without painkillers, which was an improvement. My heart filled with a new optimism that I may not be forced into sourcing antibiotics or organising a root canal in Polish.

"It would be a shame to miss Wrocław," I said. "It's the capital of Silesia. And we do need tyres..."

We had arrived at a consensus; we would persevere with Poland.

22

GRAVESTONES, GNOMES, AND ZŁOTY PIES, WROCŁAW

We discover Poland's Ljubljana

In our sights was a cosmopolitan municipality whose university produced nine Nobel laureates and a quirky anti-communist resistance movement. A centre for locomotive manufacture, it's the last place in the world where you can stand on the footplate of a scheduled steam passenger service.

It has had many names, including Breslau and Vratislav. Like a prism, these separate out the individual threads of Poland's history. Vratislav derives from Old Czech, while Breslau is German.

Wrocław is not only the largest city in Western Poland and the capital of Silesia, but one of the oldest and most beautiful.

'Poland's Venice' straddles twelve islands on the Oder River, connected by more than a hundred bridges. Cathedral Island – *Ostrów Tumski* is the most ancient department, dating to the 10th century.

At a crossroads in Central Europe, Wrocław has been part of the kingdoms of Poland (1000-1335), Bohemia (1335-1526), the Austrian Habsburgs (1526-1741), Prussia (1741-1871) and Germany (1871-1945). The Allies restored it to Poland following the Second World War.

Our trip there from Bolków was a pleasant hour-long drive across rolling country. Mostly, it resembled the Hampshire downs, except for one very flat section which looked like the edge of the earth, where the horizon fell away into the clouds. En route, we passed a quarry – and many more than the average number of establishments involved in the manufacture and sale of gravestones.

"It's probably a granitey, stony sort of area," I ventured.

"That's the technical term, is it?" Mark mocked.

Yet it wasn't just local geology that made the DK5 a hub for headstones. The highway was a fast, straight, single carriageway with deep ditches on either side. It definitely generated its fair share of demand. Horrible memorials lined the verges; crucifixes and flowers, each crowned with a motorcycle helmet.

My own experiences on two wheels led me to christen motorcyclists 'Temporary Englishmen' – and persuaded me to curtail my riding career. Initially, to stay safe on my bike, I rode with the assumption that I was completely invisible to all other traffic. It is no coincidence that, *Sorry Mate: I Didn't See You!* was the title of my motorcycling safety handbook.

Even so, being forced off the road and having my handlebars clipped more times than I care to mention by cars overtaking me rashly brought home a few truths about motorbiking;

1. It was not a matter of if, but when I had an accident;
2. It would most likely not be my fault;
3. I would come off worst.

Following nasty accidents, several of my fit and active biker friends had been told they'd never walk again. Thankfully, they were a tough lot who defied their prognoses, but physical activity is everything to me. Although I loved the exhilaration of a motorbike, the risk:reward ratio convinced me to hang up my leathers for good.

We planned to meet a friend, Zuzanna, in Wrocław, but our first job was tyres. After navigating around an unexpected road closure, we eventually rocked up to an industrial area that resembled a post-apocalyptic version of Fort Apache, The Bronx. Magda, the receptionist, spoke a little English and was much more helpful than the tyre fitters in Jawor. At least she didn't try to fit something akin to tractor tyres to Big Blue.

"These are not a common size" she said. We will have to order them in. They should be here this afternoon."

We showed her the caravan tyre and left with some uncertainty whether we had also ordered a pair of those.

How to find Zuzanna was the other uncertainty. Prior communication had been sporadic and rather non-committal, but we put it down to cultural differences. We had a date (today), a time (in the morning) and a place (Wrocław – Poland's fourth largest city) but beyond that, no other detail.

As uptight Brits, we would have synchronised watches and selected somewhere central, obvious, and easy to find, even if it was totally inconvenient for us. We would have deployed our Five-Point Plan for meeting up:

1. Send printable maps, directions, and grid references.
2. Recommend parking nearby.
3. Confirm and re-confirm the details by call, text, and email at suitable time intervals both leading up to the appointment, and on the day.
4. Submit a selection of potential itineraries, or at least a short questionnaire, to identify which sights and attractions might be of most interest to our guests.
5. Then, arrive two hours early to ensure we were on time.

Seemingly, that was not the Polish way.

In the centre of Wrocław, we parked in a multi-storey. While I quizzed random strangers to help me decipher the signage and identify whether Big Blue was in a tow-away zone, Zuzanna called us.

"Where are you? I'm in a restaurant called *Mleczarnia.*"

Trust me, that's not how it's pronounced.

"We don't know," and "Can you spell that?" we answered.

Zuzanna sent a text which we showed to many individuals as we tried to discover first, where we were, then how to locate her.

I photographed a few landmarks and street names so we could find our way back to the car park. This was a navigational *aide-mémoire* pressed home by an Amsterdam taxi driver late one Friday night. During the initial stages of a hen weekend, he was the lucky man selected to drive home a gaggle of giggling girls to somewhere they could neither spell nor pronounce, even before they had imbibed a vat of distilled and fermented beverages.

"What's your hotel called?"

"Er, we can't remember," we cackled.

"What road is it on?"

"We haven't a clue!" Hilarious.

Luckily, someone recalled that our accommodation was near the station, so he returned us to base amid a barrage of abuse along the lines of "Bloody tourists who come here, get plastered, and don't know their arses from their elbows."

In Polish, a man delivered directions to the main square, which we mistakenly assumed was an excellent bet. It was not the location of the restaurant, but the tourist information office. Further quizzing of a second guy directed us away from the square. Then Lani wagged her way over to a little dog, which got me in conversation with a lady who spoke English.

"Don't you have Google Maps?" she said.

"Um, no. We're too old-fashioned," I confessed.

She delivered a lesson in technology, but was as perplexed as us when our phone would not admit to being closer than a socially distant 290 km from Wrocław. She pointed out the restaurant on her own phone, then reminded us of the most important thing about Google Maps,

"Don't forget to turn off your mobile data."

Within minutes, we were lost again.

"Don't you have Google Maps?" another young guy asked. Two themes were developing. No one knew *Mleczarnia*, and we needed to bolster our tech knowledge.

Eventually, I spotted a plumber's van, sign written in English. The plumbers came good. We surprised Zuzanna and her friend Athena not only by taking so long to locate them, but also by turning up from an entirely unexpected direction. Zuzanna saw nothing wrong with her choice of meeting place. Rather than selecting somewhere in the easy-to-find centre, she had opted for an obscure back street in the Jewish quarter,

"It's nice here. They do excellent food – and Athena lives nearby."

There was more.

"The restaurant is confusing," she admitted. "It doesn't have a name above it on a sign – it's on the glass doors and they are folded away."

Well, there's nothing like setting your guests a challenge on their first visit to a strange city with an unfamiliar language. She probably assumed we had Google Maps.

We originally met Zuzanna and her husband, Piotr, while skiing in Monte Rosa. Her daughter Kalina befriended the dogs and visited them every day. We got along well, although they did tell us to go to Hel – to windsurf, you understand. After coffee, Athena, who had lived in the UK's St. Albans, departed to go shopping and Zuzanna took us for a wander around the *Rynek*, Wrocław's medieval market square.

"It's one of Europe's largest," Zuzanna said. "Kraków's *Rynek Główny* is the biggest."

An elegant, multi-coloured jumble of tall Renaissance town houses embrace the square, which was alive with bars and restaurants. In the basement of the magnificent, gothic town hall, *Piwnica Świdnicka* is reputedly the oldest restaurant in Europe. Founded in 1273, its name refers to a favourite tipple from the middle-ages, brewed in nearby Świdnicka.

"It's so quiet," Zuzanna exclaimed. "At this time of year, the square is usually full of people, shoulder to shoulder."

If you hate crowds, as we do, there are some advantages to touring in a pandemic.

In front of the town hall, an entertainer released flurries of oversized bubbles with a special rope contraption. Rosie, who is always full of fun, ran, leaped, and twisted in the air to catch them, and attracted her own crowd of onlookers. If only we'd brought a hat to collect donations.

We passed another famous pub and microbrewery called *Złoty Pies.* I was disappointed that the pronunciation is less amusing than the written form. Zuzanna explained,

"The L with a line through (Ł) is a W in Polish and *Pies* is pronounced P.S. Zwoty P.S. means 'Golden Dog'."

Kalina was desperate to visit McDonald's, but we stopped at the PRL Communist Bar to meet another friend from St. Albans, who had returned to live in Wrocław, "for the climate and the vibe."

Like Athena, Dan was instantly likeable. A mild-mannered student of philosophy, he was the most chilled and laid-back person I've ever met. A wonderful air of serenity surrounded him – perhaps philosophy does that to you. Dan didn't seem to commit to anything and responded to most enquiries with another question. I heard a possible urban myth of someone gaining a top degree in philosophy with their response to,

"Is this a good question?"

Their first-class-honour-worthy reply was,

"Is this a good answer?"

How cool is that? Perhaps the road to peace and enlightenment is to sit on the fence and avoid strong opinions. Mark and I took note.

Zuzanna and Dan asked what we intended to see in Poland. We told them our plans, and they tried to guess where we meant.

They both claimed zero knowledge of Białowieża, Słowiński, and Woliński; all famous national parks.

"You must have heard of Białowieża. It's where the bison are."

"Ah. Biawoviedjza!" they chorused.

Zuzanna betrayed us to Dan.

"They are staying in Bolków and they pronounce it Boll-Cow," she sniggered.

She also corrected our BBC pronunciation of Wrocław,

"It's 'Vrotswaff', not 'Rock-law'."

"Well, you told us to go to Hel," we reminded her. "At least we know how to pronounce that."

We sat outside, but I checked out the historic interior of the bar, filled with communist era artefacts and propaganda. PRL stands for *Polska Rzeczpospolita Ludowa* – The Polish People's Republic, which existed from 1952 to the collapse of the Soviet Union in1989.

We asked Zuzanna if she remembered life under communist rule.

"I'm 75," she replied, as if that clarified everything.

"You don't look a day over 30." Mark and I laughed at her odd answer.

Zuzanna explained that in Poland, you don't give your age, but the year you were born.

"I'm younger than you then," I claimed. "I'm only 64."

"I remember communist times," she said, "but mostly as not being able to get anything or go anywhere. My mum once told me to queue for oranges, but I refused. I just said, 'I can do without oranges.'"

The coronavirus pandemic, with its panic buying and lockdown travel bans, has given everyone a taste of what life is like with shortages and restrictions on liberty. In the West, pampered by privilege, we can assume that these hardships will end. For many communities across the globe, that may never happen.

But while we're on the subject of communism and oranges, I'll tell you about the miniature bronze dwarfs or gnomes we'd been tripping over on pavements all over the city (locals refer to them as both). They originated with the surreal anti-authoritarian resistance movement, *Pomarańczowa Alternatywa* – Orange Alternative, formed in 1981 by art student Waldemar 'The Major' Fydrych. Orange Alternative combatted Poland's oppressive martial law with humour and peaceful defiance.

Wrocław's gnomes started as graffiti. On walls where police painted over anti-government slogans, Orange Alternative drew a gnome with an orange hat, holding a flower. Thousands of these appeared all over Wrocław, and the movement spread to other cities.

Orange Alternative also arranged 'happenings', such as the Revolution of Dwarfs, where a ten-thousand-strong crowd marched through Wrocław wearing orange gnome hats. They carried banners which stated, 'There is No Freedom Without Dwarfs!' The 'happenings' posed a conundrum for the communist militia; how do you arrest thousands of illegal gnomes – or seventy-seven Santa Clauses (true!) – and maintain your dignity?

Communism controlled people's lives and repressed free expression. The Orange Alternative's insolent actions and cheeky gnomes cheered folk up, while poking fun at the absurdities of the regime. Along with *Solidarność* – the Solidarity movement, Orange Alternative played its part in the fall of Soviet rule in Poland. It possibly also inspired other political protest movements around the world, such as the Church of the Flying Spaghetti Monster in Kansas, USA, and the Ukrainian Orange Revolution.

I wondered if it had anything to do with the birth of the UK's Official Monster Raving Loony Party (OMRLP) set up in 1983 by the late musician, Screaming Lord Sutch. The OMRLP mocks UK politics and provides a choice for protest voters in 'safe' seats, where the mainstream candidate is unlikely to be toppled.

When the communist regime fell, Wrocław commemorated its history of resistance by immortalising the gnomes as tiny bronze sculptures. When we visited, there were nearly four hundred. Each has its own character and backstory, and they add more every year. If you want to discover them, there are dwarf maps and free gnome walking tours – and you can even commission a gnome of your own, so long as you get permission from the landowner.

Finally, as a reward for her patience, Zuzanna agreed to take Kalina to McDonald's. Dan floated off on his ethereal wave of serenity, while Mark and I left to find the shopping mall to purchase a Polish data SIM card. In an English-speaking pharmacy, I asked about topping up our dwindling supplies of prescription medication and getting amoxycillin for my toothache. They told me that my challenge, should I choose to accept it, was to make an appointment with a Polish doctor. At least the SIM was straightforward. 25GB of data cost 25 Zł – about €5 – which was approximately two thousand per cent cheaper than Germany.

Back at the tyre shop, we were on the receiving end of what Brits do abroad. Magda wasn't there, so a tyre fitter yelled the same thing at us with ever increasing volume to assist our understanding of his mother tongue. Eventually, he gave up on the English idiots and called Magda on his mobile. She said the tyres wouldn't arrive until the next day.

As we left Wrocław, we happened upon a bizarre seventy-foot sculpture by Andrzej Jarodzki plonked in the middle of a roundabout.

'The Train to Heaven' is an original full-size ninety-tonne PKP class Ty2 steam locomotive. Upended on its track, it heads for the sky at a rakish, seventy-degree angle. Known as *Kriegslokomotiven* – War Locomotives, the Nazis built these simple, reliable engines to aid their expansion into conquered territories.

Ironically, the Nazis forced Poland to build them.

When World War II ended, the Ty2s went into civilian use with *Polskie Koleje Państwowe* – the Polish State Railway. With plentiful coal, the world's last steam passenger train service remained active in this area. Sadly, it was due to be decommissioned, although Wrocław remains a manufacturing centre. Bombardier makes London Underground trains in Wrocław.

The Train to Heaven sculpture reminded me of how Caravan Kismet looked the time we used a levelling app.

Our return journey to Bolków was terrifying. The motorway section, which led to the border with both Germany and the Czech Republic, was one long queue of lorries. Driving skills, such as anticipation and lane discipline, were not a feature of Polish roads.

"Poland is second only to Romania for lunatic driving, with the Czech Republic a close third," Mark said. "They make the Italians look like *Driving Miss Daisy*."

We've had close shaves in all these countries. The previous weekend, on our trip to Złotoryja, I dug my nails into Mark's shoulder so hard that I nearly drew blood. My panic originated with a set of headlights overtaking a line of oncoming traffic, which missed us by a whisper.

"I knew he'd pull in," Mark assured me, although at that point, we were in the ditch.

Nevertheless, we decided we were back in love with Poland.

Charmed once again by a small, relaxed city, we both agreed,

"Wrocław IS Ljubljana!"

Albeit a delightfully Polish version.

23

THE UNPRONOUNCEABLES – BOLKÓW TO OJCÓW

If you think seeking directions in Polish is difficult, try setting up a mobile phone!

"Watch that lorry," I screamed. "He's all over the road." I hid my face in my hands.

"He's just avoiding the bumps," Mark replied.

Our replaced van and caravan tyres had excellent grip, and we were grateful. The two-lane autoroute had a few surprises up its sleeve. The surface looked new, but despite the speed limit of 110 kph (70 mph), the carriageway occasionally morphed into sections of deep hollows and humps the size of sleeping policemen. The errant HGV was simply dodging potholes, albeit at motorway velocity.

When you're retired, every day is a weekend. It's a pitfall we try to avoid, but midweek alcohol became a certainty when, besides the wildly weaving wagon, the air horn of a tanker nearly shot me out of my seat.

To impress upon us that sticking to the speed limit

was unacceptably slow, the thundering behemoth held its position an inch from Caravan Kismet's rear bumper. As he pulled out to overtake, he blocked the second lane. At 80 mph, a car impatient to pass us both zipped up our inside on the hard shoulder, then sliced inches from our nose to screech around the outside of the vehicle in front of us.

Romania, Costa Rica, and the Philippines were all filled with crazy drivers, but Poland was different. It combined craziness with aggression – a toxic fusion.

"This is the most stressful country to drive in, EVER," Mark said.

As we recalled the broad, empty roads, we both agreed, "It's not France."

I came late to the innovation of satellite navigation. After a quarter of a century in field sales, I became adept at finding my way around most of the UK. Like 'The Knowledge' for a London cabbie, my apprenticeship taught me every major road, all the back routes, and many shortcuts. For years, Mark and I toured Europe in the same manner; using nothing more than maps and memory.

Foreshadowed by its fabled aptitude for stranding the unwary in fields, this new-fangled electronic invention held no appeal. In addition, I was cautious of overreliance on technology. A hysterical phone call I received from a trainee representative, Anna, was a perfect illustration of why.

"I don't know where I am. My satnav stopped working," she howled.

From the other end of the country, I was able to pinpoint her whereabouts with three simple questions:

1. "Where were you last?" "Newcastle."
2. "What was the last road sign you saw?" "Scotch Corner."
3. "Are you on a big dual carriageway?" "Yes."

"BOOM! You're on the A1 southbound."

Her navigational ineptitude was most surprising, since she was still within the bounds of her home county. But Anna was part of the iPhone generation, and had never needed to use a map.

Despite this, Mark and I still slipped inexorably into the technology trap. He bought me a satnav for my birthday. It stayed boxed and shrink-wrapped for months – until we tested it on a weekend trip to Cornwall. We were impressed when it led directly to the tiny concealed entrance of our cottage, in the middle of nowhere. So impressed, we started to rely on it.

We didn't learn the time we spent sixty minutes and twenty euros lost in toll tunnels beneath Paris. We didn't learn when the signal disappeared in a series of French underpasses, forcing a full caravan U-turn in city traffic. We didn't learn when the device we later christened Naffsat denied the existence of the DN4 in Romania and led us, rig and all, across two cornfields and along a footpath...

Naffsat's replacement obviously felt much the same disdain for Polish motorways. Since we entered the country, it had mostly identified our position as in the midst of some mythological meadow. On this journey, we lost faith when we noticed that as we progressed through its fantasy field, our distance from destination was actually increasing.

After tackling the outskirts of Wrocław and 120 flat miles of wheat on winding roads, it was disheartening to join the A4 and see a sign for Wrocław. If only we had checked a map, the main road could have saved hours. The satnav had clearly not completed 'The Knowledge' regarding some of Poland's newest motorway infrastructure.

Our target was Ojców, Poland's smallest national park. Electronics would not get us there, so Mark pulled over, and we went retro. Stupidly, we hadn't acquired a road atlas – who needs one when you have a satnav? So, by scrolling through the route, he made a list of towns we needed to pass through. These were Dąbrowa Górnicza, Sławków, Bolesław, and Olkusz. Jerzmanowice was the village that hosted Camp Nasza Dolina, which we hoped to find from its address, since the campsite itself was not listed in 'points of interest'.

Asking for directions was out, because we couldn't pronounce any of them. If you think I'm making too much of this Polish pronunciation business, let me advise you that to enunciate Ojców like a native is Oytzov.

I'll bet you didn't see that coming.

Eventually, we hit something familiar: the A1, although we were following signs to Łódź, not Scotch Corner. That would have confused Anna.

We stopped for lunch and supplies at an immense out-of-town Carrefour supermarket. Foiled by a touch screen upon which there was nothing familiar, I bailed out of ordering Kentucky Fried Chicken when a long and angry-looking queue formed behind me. A sandwich stall was more straightforward; I simply pointed at what I wanted. They overcharged me for a brace of butties and two *lattes*. I felt utterly impotent, lacking the speech and sign language skills to argue.

Like a superhero, Mark swooped in to save me from further linguistic stress and humiliation. After we ate our sandwiches, he did the shopping. For its size, he reported the supermarket had very little stock, but he did return with a few treasures. A new mobile handset to replace our ancient, overheating Blackberry (do you remember those?), plus a bottle of... wait for it... Fairy washing-up liquid.

We travel light, but carry a few indispensable British home comforts, which are mostly unknown in foreign lands. I'm talking tea – specifically PG Tips – and Fairy Liquid.

I was still packing PG Tips, but my Fairy ran out in Italy. My joy at being re-united with longer-lasting bubbles was ample compensation for the adverse impact of my procurement problems.

In fact, my entire mood was lifting.

Following an out-of-kilter month on the road, I was getting back into my stride with travelling.

As a teenager, I worked on various farms and once saw a battery chicken escape from captivity. Given her first taste of freedom, you might think she would spread her wings and soar joyfully into a bright new existence of liberty. Instead, she stood transfixed; overwhelmed by the enormity of the farmyard and paralysed by the vastness beyond. To catch her, the farmer simply walked over and picked her up. She didn't move. She was probably relieved to be returned to the tranquilising safety of her small, familiar, and soothingly predictable enclave.

I suppose her reaction was unsurprising, when you consider the space allocated to each intensively farmed bird is slightly smaller than an A4 sheet of paper. A lifetime spent crammed in a cage with eight to ten companions, too cramped to extend her wings, had eradicated every trace of instinct. She probably clucked to her mates that the world outside, free of boundaries, had been a very scary place indeed.

We had been confined in an isolated mountain village in Italy for eight months. In the previous five years, aside from our ski seasons and a summer of family nursing duties, we'd barely spent a full week in one location. Yet, emerging from lockdown, I thought of the hen. My world had shrunk. Freedom felt unfamiliar. Then, the secure but comfortingly claustrophobic boundaries of my existence in a tiny mountain village had suddenly exploded, and my brain didn't know how to handle it.

After miles of flat wheat fields and industry, the scenery transformed to limestone ravines and stacks. Bartek, our host at Camp Naszna Dolina, gave us a warm welcome without cracking a smile. He was the coolest dude I've ever met. With a tanned face and short black hair, his greeting from behind mirrored sunglasses was laconic and deadpan. The site was an open field and his attitude to our pups was as phlegmatic as his shades.

"Park down the end. There is electricity there and you can let the dogs run free."

It was music to our ears after a long day. Our poor puppies had been so patient. We had driven only two hundred miles, but between the supermarket stop and navigation issues, we had been in the van for nine sweltering hours.

We celebrated our arrival with an excellent bottle of wine, selected by Mark.

As sommeliers, Mark and I employ very different wine selection procedures. I give weight to absurd or entertaining names, but I'm not fooled by anything contrived, such as Goats do Roam, Ein Zwei *Dry*, or Planet of the Grapes.

I admit to being conflicted by Bastardo; a legitimate grape variety, hijacked by marketeers to hoodwink hipsters, who, like me, use it to pretend they have a sense of humour.

Mark operates on the simple principle of 'you get what you pay for', and allocates an appropriate budget.

Without doubt, Mark's strategy is superior, although his selection of Springer wine, with its doggie double-entendre, almost spanned the budget and silly-scale divide. Almost.

At the very least, Springer helped us through an interesting evening.

Impassive in shades, and staring straight ahead, Bartek passed by a few times aboard his sit-on mower. Each time, an avalanche of needle-sharp grass cuttings rained in through Caravan Kismet's front picture windows. In between cloudbursts of clippings, we attempted to set up the replacement mobile phone.

The things you have to do while Living the Dream.

We've fallen into the 'purchasing electronic gadgetry

abroad' trap before. Mark purchased a bargain laptop online in Monte Rosa. It took him ages to work out the Italian keyboard and I still find it almost impossible to use. Of course, the firmware on the new mobile was in Polish, and the instruction manual translated into a comprehensive suite of Eastern European languages.

Fortunately, just prior to the tipping point, Mark did something which somehow switched the handset to English.

So, he didn't launch it at the wall.

24

PIESKOWA SKAŁA CASTLE AND THE HERCULES CLUB, OJCÓW NATIONAL PARK

"We don't know where we are, but we're not lost!"

"There's nothing to see here!" I told Mark as I scanned the tourist brochure.

"Only castles, over four hundred caves, seventeen of Poland's twenty-one species of bat, and The Hercules Club."

Silently, I wondered about the facilities and membership requirements of The Hercules Club.

"Other exciting attractions include 'Buildings in Ojców' and Energylandia, which is not like the inimitable Museum of Electricity at the back of the Waitrose in Christchurch, Dorset, but Poland's biggest theme park."

We had set up home on the doorstep of Ojców, Poland's smallest national park. Just sixteen kilometres (10 miles) from Kraków, Ojców is a bijou 21.5 sq km (8.3 sq mile) garden of Eden, stuffed with verdant meadows ensnared by outcrops of jagged Jurassic limestone.

Its spectacular canyons and sculpted white rocks are

the eroded remains of a 140-million-year-old ocean. Many of the formations have fanciful names, 'The Fossilised Wanderer', 'The Prelates' and 'The Kraków Gate.' Quiet relief flooded through me when I spotted 'The Beach Clubs'. They alerted me to the possibility that *Maczuga Herkulesa* – The Hercules Club – might be more stone than social.

I was so glad I'd kept my thoughts to myself. It meant that unwittingly, I had slipped beneath Mark's sarcasm radar. I imagined his likely diatribe about a gentleman's club filled with the testosterone-fuelled male offspring of Zeus, bragging at the bar about their twelve labours,

"I slew the Hydra and a bulletproof lion of Nemea."

"Call yourself a man? I pilfered Diomedes' man-eating Mares and the Amazon Queen's girdle-of-virtue."

"Last one to scrump the Nymphs of the West's apples buys the beers!"

But before we could go out to explore this lush and leafy gem, we had some typical traveller's tasks to complete. This included purchasing solar panels and leisure batteries for The Beast, our new expedition truck, arranging an MOT test for Big Blue, a pandemic-backlog-beating three months hence, and putting our house on the market to fund the conversion of The Beast into our new home.

Mark also booked his visit to Auschwitz; 'a three-hour guided trip in your chosen language'. I had mixed feelings that, being so close, perhaps I should go. However, I rationalised that since I have yet to recover from watching *Schindler's List* at the cinema in 1994, I would spare myself the trauma and babysit the dogs.

Our Ojców explorations started 400 m from the

campsite at Pieskowa Skała, a spectacular hilltop castle which dates to the 14th century. Its white and ivy-clad walls, red roof, and onion-domed clock tower are the result of an elegant Renaissance restoration in the 1580s.

We bought a walking map in the shed-like shop near the car park and climbed through darkly wooded shade to the castle. Although *Pieskowa Skała* means 'little dog's rock', our little dogs didn't rock enough to be allowed inside, so we briefly enjoyed its classy exterior then continued on our way.

Our circular walk would have gone more smoothly had I not spotted a board detailing Nordic Walking Trails. One was marked in green and led to The Hercules Club, which I had now confirmed beyond doubt to be a giant limestone pillar.

Unfortunately, the shop window forced some unwelcome thoughts about The Hercules Club and its male members straight back into my mind. Plastic replicas of this famous landmark resembled a battery-powered device ladies might buy from an emporium supplying erotica. As a souvenir, it would be a phallic asset to any sideboard.

The woodland walk was beautiful, but it wasn't Kokořín (I'm joking!) Navigation went really well until the point where we were due to join the green Nordic trail. Three quarters of the way round, we ran out of coloured trail markers and found ourselves off piste among fields and a tiny hamlet of pretty country homes.

An elderly man with dinner all around his face shot out of his cottage to greet the dogs. We showed him our map. His stabbing finger and a spray of comestibles confirmed our location, but we couldn't work out whether his effusive guidance in Polish was confirming or contradicting our onward directional hunch.

We were reasonably certain we were on the right track. It seemed odd that there were no trail markers to match the bold green line we were following on the map, but the worst-case scenario was a network of unmarked footpaths that would lead us back to Pieskowa Skała. As we waded through desiccated fields of golden crops, which crackled and swayed in the sunshine, Mark gave a classic appraisal of our situation,

"We don't know where we are, but we're not lost!"

It was sunny, but we were not too worried about the pups. Even in the open, it was cooler than the mid-thirty-degree temperatures of recent days, although most of the walk had been in delicious woodland shade. A few tinklingly clear chalk streams crossed our path, which provided The Fab Four with opportunities for a refreshing splash and a good drink.

It got interesting once we re-entered the woods. Almost immediately, the footpath petered out completely. We could see the edge of the forest and decided that if we kept close to that, we'd not go far wrong. It was rough underfoot and at one point, we took a compass bearing just to be sure.

Eventually, we intersected with the yellow-marked path we wanted and, after a quick descent, popped out of the trees right next to *Maczuga Herkulesa*. The self-congratulation at our navigational prowess was as vast and tumescent as The Hercules Club itself, or any mighty masculine members thereof.

Back at the shop, we sat under a sun shade and treated ourselves to an ice cream and a debrief. Only then did we realise that the green line we had followed so faithfully on the map was not a Nordic walking trail. It marked the boundary of the National Park.

We made a pact and, like my secret thoughts about The Hercules Club, vowed never to speak of it again.

25

CRACKING KRAKÓW

A Story of Dragons, Cheesecake, and Sibling Rivalry

We made a mistake with Kraków.

Our drive into Poland's former royal capital took us on a journey back through time. Like the growth rings of a tree, modern outskirts encircle the old town, while in the centre, thousand-year-old buildings lie atop the site of a 50,000-year-old Palaeolithic settlement. Kraków's many layers also mirror the history and changing fortunes of Poland.

Towering communist architecture loomed above us as we delved towards Kraków's ancient heart. Dark and brutal, like the regime, their grey concrete and stone exuded an obstinate, stark, but powerful beauty. As we approached the Vistula River, the views opened up to reveal a limestone outcrop topped by the vast battlements and towers of the red brick Wawel Royal Castle. Along with Kraków's Old Town, this was the planet's very first UNESCO World Heritage Site.

As we looked for somewhere to leave our van, the signage for the surface parking confused us. A square blue 'P' sign is pretty universal, but here, they displayed the confusing addendum: *Płatny Koniec*. Worried about what terms and conditions this might imply, we found the Wawel underground parking and abandoned Big Blue there. (I can now report that *Płatny* means 'chargeable' while *Koniec* means 'end' – so we passed up on free parking.) Fully aware of our navigational shortcomings, even Mark and I were confident that we could find our way back to our vehicle. Wawel is one of Poland's largest castles and is visible from most parts of the city.

Dragon Street – *ulica Smocza* skirted the Wawel's walls and followed a shimmering bend of the Vistula. Kraków was founded on dragons and the 12th-Century *Polish Chronicle* tells of Smok Wawelski, a dragon who inhabited a limestone cave beneath the Wawel hill. Smok made a nuisance of himself by devouring sheep and local virgins, but here's a question for you. How do you deal with a delinquent dragon?

To save you time, I have abridged Paul Simon's famous song, *Fifty Ways to Slay a Dragon.*

'Spear it with a lance, Vance' and 'Pierce it with a sword, Claude' pretty well cover numbers one through forty-seven. Dragon-dispatching aces Lancelot, Beowulf, and St. George were all disciples of Simon's 'Stab it in the back, Jack' system.

At forty-eight comes 'Hit it with a dart, Bart'. Arrows are the leading cause of death among dragons in *Game of Thrones* and *The Hobbit*.

However, a few mavericks made bold departures from mainstream methods of wasting a wayward wyvern.

'Turn it to Stone, Tone' was the method favoured by Perseus, who swooped in aboard Pegasus, brandishing the severed head of the Medusa. Once he was stony-faced and petrified, sea dragon Cetus could no longer harass Andromeda, tied naked to a rock as a sacrifice. In a fabulous display of toxic masculinity, Perseus then claimed Andi as his bride. To get around the inconvenience that Andromeda was already engaged, he re-used the Gorgon's head to turn her fiancé to stone. He threw in a bonus petrification of some bloke who was annoying Andi's mum, then niftily disposed of his murdered murder weapon by presenting it to the goddess Athena as a lovely gift.

However, King Krakus and his sons, Princes Lech and Krakus II, top the podium for theatricality when it comes to dragon-slaying.

'More Bang for your Buck, Chuck' charts at fifty – and our princes certainly fought fire with fire. They fed Smok a sheep stuffed with smouldering sulphur. To dampen his dyspepsia, Smok drank heartily from the river.

Then he blew up.

But the story didn't end there. Lech killed Krakus and blamed it on the dragon. Once he became king, however, someone rumbled him. So, the city founded on the detonated dragon's lair took the name of his brother. Or dad.

An alternative legend concerns cordwainer, Skuba, although shoemakers killing dragons might be cobblers.

You can visit the Dragon's Cave beneath the castle. As we walked past, a metal sculpture of Smok delighted the crowd by breathing fire every few minutes. Bones of prehistoric creatures, allegedly a dragon, adorn the exterior of the Wawel Cathedral. If they ever fall, the world will end.

Dogs could not go inside the Wawel precinct, so with four in tow, we admired the immense structure from the outside and continued on our quest to find the Old Town. Mark had diligently researched our tour and marked all the sights on a map. His hard work is invaluable when we explore a new city, but only when he remembers to bring along the map.

As we hit the road junction beyond the Wawel, I took a guess,

"I reckon it's left for the city centre."

"I think it's right," he insisted.

Since our second date, I have known that Mark has a superpower. I noticed it when he took a shortcut to avoid a traffic jam in his home town, where he'd lived man and boy. Quietly, I questioned myself. It seemed we'd followed three sides of a square, but I bowed to his superior local knowledge. I kept a straight face when we emerged half a mile further back in the same traffic queue, having discovered that although two wrongs don't make a right, three lefts definitely do. Mark, it seems, is even more directionally challenged than I.

Since Mark had been staring at maps of Kraków for weeks, I stupidly overlooked his superpower. He did not disappoint. Few visitors to Kraków will see the unique and unforgettable sights we took in; a busy, four-lane road junction, a three-wheeled van advertising the *Kraków Pinball Museum,* and a café which claimed to offer at least two items on a menu advertising 'Coffee: Tea: Cocaine'.

Enquiries with passers-by revealed we were en route to *Kazimierz* – Kraków's Jewish quarter; exactly one-hundred-and-eighty degrees off course.

Twenty years after our second date, I still maintained a tactful silence as we retraced our steps towards the ancient centre and the map-restoring opportunities offered by the tourist information office. I could claim it was solidarity following the incident that slightly preceded the aforementioned traffic jam and superpower revelations. Mark had also maintained a poker face when I rushed to the bathroom, hacking like a cat with fur balls. I was trying to hide that I was choking on a fish-bone from the sea bass that he had lovingly poached in white wine as an impressive pre-theatre supper. As I sashayed back to our tryst, I slipped on the top stair and slid down the full flight on my backside.

He asked what the noise was when I returned to the dining room.

"Nothing!" I said, as I deployed my most coquettish smile and hair flick combo.

"It sounded like someone falling down the stairs."

"Did it? Ha ha ha hack hack hack." Ever the gentleman, he did not pursue the subject.

He left me with my dignity intact; a lesson I've not forgotten.

The lesson being that silence and a smug grin convey so much more than words.

Although truthfully, rather than preserving Mark's dignity with silence and a smirk, I was busy staring open-mouthed at the stunning ancient architecture that bordered our route towards Rynek Główny, the largest market square in Europe. With each side measuring two-hundred metres (656 ft), the square encloses an area of nearly 9.4 acres.

Most of Poland's major cities were rebuilt following absolute destruction in WWII, but Kraków survived the war relatively unscathed. Previously, the accepted wisdom was that, led by Marshall Ivan Konev, the Soviet Red Army took the Nazis by surprise when they attacked and liberated Kraków. However, recently discovered documents suggest that because of the risk of being surrounded, the Germans never intended to defend Kraków. Instead, they left and simply mined the bridges. This preserved their line of retreat while hindering the Red Army's advance towards Poland's industrial heart-lands, which were critical to the Nazi war effort.

As we wandered up Grodzka, our first notably historic encounter was the 15th-Century Baroque church of St. Peter and Paul. Its domed roofline dwarfed the octagonal twin towers of its older Romanesque neighbour, St. Andrew's church and monastery, which pre-dates St. P. P. by five centuries. One of Kraków's most ancient buildings, St. Andrew's is a rare example of a fortified church, which provided refuge when the city was under attack. It was the only church to survive the devastating Mongol invasion of 1241.

After a quick dive into the tourist information, we repaired to the shady pavement umbrellas of a café in the main square to study our newly acquired map. There, we re-planned our city tour and enjoyed the best coffee of our trip so far, with a sliver of Cracow Cheesecake on the side. (Cracow is the Anglicised version of the city's name.)

Although it didn't make the cut for the song in *The Sound of Music*, baked cheesecake could account for a few of my favourite things.

I love it so much, my signature speciality for dinner parties is baked lemon cheesecake on an *amaretti* biscuit base.

"It tastes like Prussic acid," was Uncle Norman's appraisal of my *pièce de resistance*.

After a long afternoon in the kitchen, I can't say, "Hydrogen cyanide," was the reaction I expected to my culinary masterpiece.

Thankfully, *Sernik Babci,* the famous and delicious Polish curd-cheese classic, does not share that tang of bitter almonds with cyanide-based poisons, plastic explosives, or gangrene. If only the dragon slayers had known about my cheesecake. They could have stuffed it full of cyanide and Nobel's Explosive No. 808 and Smok would have been none the wiser.

As we savoured our slices, we drank in the quintessential vista of the square, which took in the Clock Tower and Cloth Hall. I knew it was the quintessential vista, since it matched the panorama emblazoned on the sides of electric council vehicles, which were buzzing around emptying the bins.

Like so many Polish cities, colourful, four-storey Renaissance and Baroque town houses encircle the market square, which was rebuilt in 1257, following the aforementioned Mongol invasion and sacking. Today, many of the medieval cellars are subterranean bars and bistros.

The layout of the buildings within the square has

changed over the centuries. We found evidence of this immediately as we stepped away from our coffee and cheesecake. The seventy-metre gothic clock tower, constructed from red brick and white stone, is all that survives of the old town hall. Dating from the 14th century, it was one of Poland's oldest seats of government, but was demolished in 1820 to open up the square. If you have a head for heights, you can enjoy a bird's-eye view over Kraków from the top.

Talking of heads, you will find one of Kraków's weirdest landmarks next to the tower. A popular meeting place, The Head is a massive bronze sculpture of a hollow bodiless bonce, bound with bandages and laid on its side. Created by Igor Mitoraj, this rather eerie artwork is *Eros Bendato* – Eros Bound. It is the neck and noddle of the Greek god of love, depicted as though it were a toppled fragment from an ancient monument.

In case you think, "What's that all about?" interpretations vary.

As a highly erudite art critic, I can reveal that the figure represents someone who was accidentally beheaded in a game of Blind Man's Buff. It was placed there by the *Health and Safety Executive* as a warning to us all.

However, pseudo-philosophers have come up with all kinds of ludicrous explanations. Some say the blindfold symbolises that love is blind. Others say that the hollow eyes are a window to the darkness within, or that the bindings show the imprisonment of ideas and desires. Another theory is that it explores the paradox of whether civilisation is broken beyond repair, or held together despite destructive powers. Or perhaps that it represents the suffering of the artist's home country, Poland, throughout its troubled history.

Whatever it is, if you want to see where else Eros was bound, you can come face to face with copies of the same corpse-less cranium in St. Louis (home of Lambert International Airport), Vancouver, and Lugano, Switzerland.

The Cloth Hall – Sukiennice, has been a centre of commerce for over seven centuries. It has undergone several rebuilds, with its characteristic stone arcades added towards the end of the 19th century. On the ground floor, you will find market stalls selling souvenirs, with an underground museum beneath, and an art gallery and café above. Whether you're Usain Bolt or just need a hundred-metre dash to work off all that cheesecake and culture, the length of this iconic building is conveniently pre-calibrated.

The sight of magnificent horse-drawn carriages drew me towards their taxi rank between the Cloth Hall and the twin towers of *Kościół Mariacki* – St. Mary's Church. Consecrated in 1320, St. Mary's gothic towers are noticeably asymmetric. Legend has it that another pair of *Kraków's* belligerent brothers built them, but in a classic, "Mine's bigger than yours!" argument, one allegedly stabbed the other before turning the knife on himself. Don't believe it? The knife is on display in the *Sukiennice*–although, as with any good legend, the knife might be there as a reminder to Kraków's population that crime was punishable by death. I think Paul Simon missed a trick here; the follow-up sonnet *Fifty Ways to Cleave Your Brother* has commercial success written all over it.

Every hour, the five-note *Hejnał mariacki* – St. Mary's Trumpet Call toots four times from the top of the taller tower. The call goes out to each point of the compass, although they cut it short to commemorate the trumpeter shot in the throat as he called the alarm to warn of the fabled Mongol attack. This legend inspired the book, *The Trumpeter of Kraków,* by Eric P. Kelly.

The *Hejnał* is to Poles what the chiming of Big Ben is to Brits. They broadcast the noon trumpet call live on Polish national radio. Noon is also the time when they unveil St. Mary's Gothic altarpiece. Among the largest in Europe, renowned German sculptor and Kraków resident, Veit Stoss, carved it in the late 1400s.

Past the obligatory Irish Pub, we found ourselves at the Barbican, one of the few remaining parts of the old defensive walls. This circular, moated brick building with seven watch towers also dates to the late 1400s and has walls three metres thick. It saw active service through many sieges, and was once connected to the Florianska Gate, the principal of the seven entrances into the city. The Florianska gate is the start of Kraków's Royal Route, which we had unknowingly trekked in reverse from the Wawel.

In need of respite from the brilliance of the sun and the city's history, we looped back to the Wawel via the Platny gardens. These surround the ancient centre and follow the path of the city's former defensive walls and moat. They planted the trees in the 1800s, when the walls were demolished and the moat filled in. It was less relaxing than it might have been due to the hipster scourge of electric scooters whizzing past. Like the

Mongol invaders, they were relentless and showed no mercy.

Although we had barely scraped the surface of the Old Town and hadn't even made the Jewish Quarter to see the Oskar Schindler factory and remains of the ghetto, we called it a day. It was then that we realised our mistake. It wasn't misinterpreting parking signs, getting lost, or forgetting our map. The simple truth is – you need more than a day to see Kraków.

Koniec - End (Of the chapter, not the book.)

I have provided the recipe for my Prussic Acid cheesecake in Appendix 1.

NOTES: In case you ever visit, this was Mark's list of things to see:

- **Out of Town**

- Kosciuszko Mound

- **Centre**

- Wawel Castle, Cathedral and Dragon's Den
- Market square, Sukiennice, St. Mary's Basilica
- Eat Zapiekanki at Plac Notwy

- **North**

- Florianska Gate – start of the Royal Route
- Barbican

- **Jewish Quarter**

- Schindler's factory

- Heroes square
- Bohateron Getta – fragment of the Ghetto, Lwowska street

- **Zakrzowek Lake for doggie walking**
- **Salt Mines**

26

A WALK IN THE WOODS, OJCÓW CASTLE AND NATIONAL PARK

The Curious Incident of the Dog in the Light Grime

Our early start to miss the crowds paid off in every way, other than making us fugitives from the law.

'Buildings in Ojców' featured on the campsite's list of 'must sees'. This rather underwhelming description prompted us to drive there one evening to check their credentials. The quaint wooden houses and lush, pastoral scenery suggested at least 'worth a gander', although the heaving mass of humanity crammed on to every footpath was off-putting enough to take us way off piste.

We set an alarm for 6 a.m.

For Mark and I, a working life filled with 4 a.m. commutes to London had removed the sheen from early starts. Now, with the daily option of an afternoon nap, I don't know why we don't do it more often. Just the pale honey-coloured stillness and warm fragrance of a summer morning is well worth rolling out of bed for.

Since Big Blue was the sole occupant of the deserted car park beneath the ruins of Ojców Castle, we had a luxurious choice of shady spaces. Big Blue's aircon had packed up weeks ago, so it was a relief to know that driving back to the campsite would not leave us all gasping like goldfish trapped in a hydrothermal vent.

The paths were devoid of jostling crowds, allowing us to linger and admire the curling filigree carvings that adorned the gables of the dark wooden houses. We climbed a deserted promontory above the village and felt like planting a flag to claim the vista along the Prądnik valley for ourselves. Shimmering limestone cliffs and the ivory-white cylindrical turret of the castle shone in the transluscent saffron light, framed to perfection by opulent tousles of greenery.

As we dropped from our knoll, we passed a series of tranquil pools. Unknown to us, Ojców trout is a well-known delicacy. The valley's microclimate and the gin clear waters of the Młynówka stream, oxygenated by a waterfall, provide the perfect habitat for brown trout. We noted a scatter of shaded wooden tables and a rustic barbeque on the lawn surrounding one pond and shared a thought; "That's lunch sorted."

At the end of the footpath, beyond the trout hatchery, we came face-to-face with two towering boulders. Each around fifteen-metres (50 ft) high, they form *Brama Krakowska* – the Kraków Gate, a narrow, foreboding yet entirely natural portal into the forested gloom of the gorge. The gateway formed part of the principal trading route between Kraków and Silesia, now replaced by the metalled road that follows the Prądnik valley floor.

A few yards from the gate is *Jaskinia Krowia* – the Cow

Cave. The cavern was formerly used as a shelter for sheep or cattle, and latterly made into an ice house and Polish film set.

Źródło Miłości – The Spring of Love used to bubble up from the left pillar of the Kraków Gate. Legend has it that a sip from this spring would bind couples eternally; ancient wisdom you can trace all the way back through the mists of time to Ojców's first tour guides.

The Spring of Love moved when a mineral water company gave it a romantic re-route through a ditch under the road to a now demolished bottling plant. These days, the water bubbles out over a tender and passionate slab of concrete opposite the Gate. According to the explanatory placard, *Źródło Miłości* has adopted a new and much dreamier name; 'The Secondary Love Source'. With the Cow Cave in mind, we surmised that taking the waters was more likely to perpetuate E. Coli than everlasting adoration.

Following a figure of eight route, we planned to return triumphant through the Kraków Gate later, so after a brief exploration of the Cow Cave, we continued up the valley. The cobbled road was a delight. As it wove its way through rustling meadows, it played a meandering duet with the Prądnik river. Limestone cliffs festooned with vegetation stood guard on either side, while an occasional timber house shimmered like a mirage, nestled into its idyll, surrounded by lawns the colour of vibrant green tree frogs. A golden peace surrounded us: silence, with a muted background of birdsong, insects, and the river.

The pups added an explosion of exuberance to the day with an abandoned splash in the fresh waters, just before we reached a little coffee shop. Kawiarnia Niezapominajka is allegedly renowned for cakes and special Polish pancakes filled with cream cheese and sugar. It was too early to sample its wares, but as an almost messianic convert to bacon, banana, and cheese jacket potatoes in Zimbabwe, I'd urge you not to knock any weird combinations of foodstuffs and flavours until you've tried them.

Before you could say Kawiarnia Niezapominajka, we found a conveniently staired pathway and struck upwards into the fresh green forest. It led to the Okopy plateau, an extensive area protected by sheer drops on most sides. Woodland now conceals the remains of the 13th-Century Wisegrod hill fort, but for millennia before that, Okopy provided a perfect refuge for people and livestock. Evidence of habitation on the plateau dates to the Neolithic era.

A dusty pathway at the top of the ridge seemed too much for Rosie. She rolled enthusiastically until our smartly contrasting white and black dog acquired the indistinct, ashen hue of a laundry accident. *(My brother achieved the zenith of washday woe when, to save time, he placed all his clothes into the machine at once. Undaunted, his characteristically optimistic spin on the sombre, washed-out result was; "I've always wanted a matching wardrobe!")*

We put Rosie's rolling down to high jinks. However, The Curious Incident of the Dog in the Light Grime was a mystery we would not solve until we reached our next destination.

Gaps through the trees offered tantalising glimpses of the picturesque vale and its ragged, chalky walls. At one point, we found the viewpoint that overlooked *Skała*

Rękawica – The Glove Rock. This five-fingered formation looks for all the world like a giant Jurassic hand, eighty-five metres up, waving travellers on their way through the Kraków Gate.

On the subject of gloves, the time had come. It forced us to run the gauntlet through the morning's first stampede of tourists as they swarmed up to tick The Glove Rock off their bucket lists. As we descended the steep steps through the throng, we passed the entrance to *Jaskinia Ciemna* – The Dark Cave; also known as The Ojców Cave. 120,000 years ago, it was home to humans and is one of the most important archaeological sites in Poland. Excavations discovered more than a thousand stone tools, which are now on display in the museum.

To sate any pressing desire for visitors to know what a family of naked Neanderthals might look like, the park authorities had thoughtfully provided a realistic 3D installation in plastic. Unfortunately, we missed this Stone Age selfie stop because social distancing is tricky in a 230-metre tunnel. Understandably, the cave was closed because of COVID restrictions.

I was a little disappointed, since a clue to one particular charm of The Dark Cave is in its title. As you might expect from a 150-million-year-old cavern, it has no mod-cons like electricity. They conduct guided tours by candlelight, which sounds rather enticing.

The cave gave me a sudden urge to examine Mark's subterranean scholarship,

"How do you tell the difference between stalactites and stalagmites?"

He noted my grin and offered me a resigned, "Go on..."

I was educated at a Catholic convent school, where my geography mistress, Miss Taylor, tutored,

"Stalac*tites* grow on the roof, so they hang on *tight*."

However, a backpacker in Oz taught me a strikingly different denotation for dripstone differentiation:

"Toights come down!" I mimicked him gleefully, in my best Australian accent.

Tights coming down was definitely not on the Convent's curriculum. Indeed, that was exactly the sort of thing my saintly sex education aimed to prevent. The nuns offered a single, straightforward solution to avoid sins of the flesh, which was,

"Don't do 'it'."

'It' being a euphemism for... well. You know. That messy 'business' you learn about in biology.

In a vague nod to the real world, they did equip us with additional practical advice,

"If you *must* sit on a young man's knee, place a thick book beneath your bottom," and "don't wear patent leather shoes, as they show off your knickers." The knickers in question being a pair of brushed cotton pants the size of Berkshire, in regulation bottle green. Doubtless, a glimpse of those reflected in a patent leather shoe would whip up even the most chaste young man into a frenzy of desire.

Mark and I emerged from the forest, squinting into serious sunlight. As we strode through the Kraków Gate for the second loop of our figure of eight, the scene was very different. High-heeled horses and traps disgorged cartloads of tourists before reloading to trot back to Ojców. The horses had wedges on the rear of their shoes to aid traction on the cobbles.

Once again, we dodged into the forest's coolness. A pleasant ramble away from the crowds led gently uphill to *Grota Lokietek,* also called the Royal Cave. Ironically, they named Ojców's largest cave after Poland's smallest monarch.

A diminutive Duke, Władysław Łokietek, or 'Władysław the Short', allegedly used the cave as a hideout while at war with Bohemian ruler Wacław II. As Kingly cognomens go, his other name, 'Władysław the Elbow High', is not the worst. I know of one Shit (James the Shit of England, Ireland and Scotland), a Cabbage (Ivailo the Cabbage of Bulgaria), and at least three Bastards, the best known of whom is William I of England, although he preferred the handle, 'Conquerer'.

The tall tales surrounding this pint-sized Polish prince say he escaped death when an obliging arachnid spun a web to cover the entrance to his secret passage. What else can I tell you about cave-dwelling Władysław Łokietek?

'Though he be but little, he is fierce.'

I know. I misquoted.

Shakespeare's sisters were the feisty ones, but just like the girls in *A Midsummer Night's Dream*, Łokietek got his happy ending. He defeated his enemies, got crowned King of Poland in 1320, and ruled happily ever after.

Until 1333, at least, when the 'ominous and fearful owl of death' swooped in for a visit.

The finest fish I have ever tasted was a fillet of Arctic Char I ate in Sweden's Ice Hotel on the occasion of Mark's fortieth birthday. Our lunch at *Pstrag Ojcowski* came the closest to toppling this spectacular *Salmonidae* from a near two-decade reign atop our piscatorial podium. The lightly smoked trout was tender, sweet, and juicy. Caught in the pond next door and cured on the premises by a mother and daughter team, it was almost fresh enough to claim negative food miles.

I'm sure location enhances the pleasure of a meal. In Sweden, ice plates, ice glasses, and a glistening sculpture of melting ice, all hewn from the frozen River Torne, complemented our flavoursome Arctic Char. In contrast, a tinkling stream, balmy sunshine, and the scent of summer accompanied the earthy flavours of our trout. Washed down with lavender-flavoured lemonade, that fish remains a feature of my foodie fantasies.

After our delightful lunch, it was a short skip back to explore the ruins of Ojców Castle. King Kazimierz III Wielki – Kazimierz the Great, son of The Elbow High, built the castle. He was the ruler who welcomed the Jewish community into Kraków; which is why they named their Jewish quarter 'Kazimierz' in his honour.

Along with Pieskowa Skała just up the road, Ojców Castle forms part of a chain of twenty-five medieval castles and watchtowers which comprise The Trail of the Eagles' Nests. In the 14th century, Kazimierz the Great established many of these strongholds to form a defensive line between his Poland and the Bohemian Kingdom of Silesia to the south. The Trail runs approximately 163 km (100 miles) from Kraków to Częstochowa. Until the 17th century, Kraków was Poland's capital city. Obviously, the trail derives its name from the lofty locations of the fortifications, many of which cling to the steep limestone rocks and bluffs of the Polish Jura.

As you do when you're following tourist routes, we kept running into the same faces.

"You're dressed as the Polish flag," Mark said to one chap, who stopped with his family to fuss over the dogs while we were in the forest. At first, he looked confused,

"You're wearing a white T-shirt with red shorts."

"It's not deliberate," he laughed when Mark clarified.

Yet it was quite appropriate on the anniversary of the Warsaw Uprising; about which we would discover more later.

We met Mr. Flag Man again at the castle. I was still struggling with pronunciation, so I asked him to remind me how to say Ojców,

"Oyt-Zov."

I scrawled it on my hand in biro and, to Mark's delight, repeated it like a mantra all day.

"Ojców comes from the Polish word for 'father'," Mr. Flag explained. "Kazimierz named the castle for his father," – that Elbow High guy again.

Though he be but little, he was unquestionably held in high regard.

Like many of the Eagles' Nests, Ojców Castle is mostly in ruins. The restored tower was closed for COVID reasons, but the site's elevated position still gave us a splendid view up the valley.

Back at the car park, we got a nasty shock. With every space rammed full, a car conga dribbled out on to the road. Mark lifted a piece of paper from our windscreen. Covered in undecipherable hieroglyphics, the only part we understood was a number, followed by the symbol for Polish złoty.

It was a clear case of the early bird getting the parking ticket.

We scanned the area, but as when we had arrived at first light, there was no sign of a parking attendant to collect our money. What could we do?

Mark and I are upright and law-abiding citizens, although I am ashamed to admit that insurgency is not new to me, albeit my crimes were inadvertent.

Warsaw's famous son, Fryderyk Chopin, visited Ojców in 1829. Once, at a party, I performed Beethoven on a piano reputedly played by Chopin while I was Brahms and Liszt. At the time, I didn't realise how seditious my drunken recital was. Luckily, it happened in Scotland a decade after Soviet rule in Poland ended. In another time and place, my actions could have been insurrection by association.

It may not surprise you that in 1977, the BBC banned punk band The Sex Pistols' controversial song *God Save The Queen*. However, would you believe that classical champion Chopin was so synonymous with Polish nationalism that Tsarist Russia deemed his music subversive and forbade celebrations of his birth?

The Nazis took it even further and prohibited him completely. Under German occupation, a soiree with Chopin was punishable by death.

In 1830, following the brutal suppression of the November Uprising, after which Poland lost its sovereignty and was absorbed by the Russian Empire, Chopin fled Poland. 'The Poet of the Piano' carried a jar of Polish soil with him into voluntary exile in Paris. He never returned to his homeland, but like his jar of earth, his loss and yearning never left him. Although Poland no longer existed, it lived on in his soul, and he poured all this pain, displacement, and love of his country into music.

His fifty-nine Mazurkas are based on traditional Polish folk songs, which embody his countrymen's proud spirit and desire for freedom. Chopin showed that, besides being heartrendingly beautiful and stirringly emotional, music can wield political power. This was not lost on German composer Schumann, who described Chopin's melodies as "cannons buried in flowers" – aimed at Russia.

Chopin's body is buried at Père Lachaise Cemetery in Paris. Mourners sprinkled his coffin with Polish earth from his jar. At his own request, his sister, Ludwika, sneaked his heart back to Poland, pickled in cognac. Reclaiming his nation in death, Chopin's heart is buried beneath a pillar in Warsaw's Church of the Holy Cross.

We're not revolutionaries like Chopin. If we'd had the slightest clue how to do so, we would have paid the fine. Instead, like Bonnie and Clyde, Mark and I made a furtive withdrawal from the car park and went on the run. As mentioned previously, I was brought up Catholic, a liturgy that centres around guilt. As we drove past the grotto of Our Lady with the electric halo, her eyes bored into me, although religious people can be anarchists too. Nearby, we passed the wooden Chapel of St. Joseph the Craftsman, also known as 'the Chapel on the Water' because it's built on a bridge. Tsar Nicholas II forbade construction of sacred buildings on land in Ojców, so like the good people of Bamberg, they built it over water.

We hoped that for the rest of our stay in Ojców, a large blue van with British plates might slip beneath the radar – and that the long arm of the law in Poland might be modelled on someone the size of Łokietek.

When they are open, dogs are not allowed in the caves. Year round, the temperature inside the caves is around 7°C (44°F), so take suitable clothes. The caves are popular, so at peak times, booking a tour is advisable – and don't forget to pay for parking.

27

OGRODZIENIEC CASTLE: ON THE TRAIL OF THE EAGLES' NESTS

A lesson in life...

A few miles from Podzamcze, population 1,011, a magical castle appeared, afloat in the sky. As we drew closer, we saw how it seemed to meld organically with the landscape.

Some of its shapely white towers were man made, others were natural pillars of limestone, all integrated into the structure by pale curtain walls. The spectacular ruins had an other-worldly look. Mark and I agreed; on all our travels, it was one of the most impressive castles we'd ever seen.

Ogrodzieniec Castle sits 515 m (nearly 1,700 ft) above sea level on the highest outcrop of the Polish Jura. It is close to the centre of the trail of the 'Eagles' Nests'. We love a castle. Recommendations had directed us towards Ogrodzieniec, along with a plethora of signs jostling on roadsides around the area, which proclaimed it was 'The Best Tourist Attraction of 2020'.

Really, we should have known.

Ogrodzieniec hides a secret far darker than the ghost of the black dog dragging a length of golden chain, which allegedly patrols its battlements on moonlit nights.

Traffic in the tiny village of Podzamcze was as crazy as rush hour in London. Even at 4 p.m. on a Saturday, the vast castle car park overflowed. Conscious of our outlaw status, caused by our inability to decipher, never mind pay the parking ticket we'd received that morning, we didn't want to add further misdemeanours to our unintended criminal record.

A spiralling black hole of unparked cars seeking spaces sucked us over its event horizon and imprisoned us. The circulating melee then propelled us along a street where a line of identical ladies in identical headscarves sat on identical chairs outside every garden gate. We took a guess at this peculiar aspect of the local economy and escaped the fray when one beckoned us into her yard. As the dogs sprang out of the van, she greeted them with an enormous smile and told us we could park for as long as we wanted for the equivalent of €3.

Our walk up to the castle was beyond strange. For at least half a mile, stalls packed both sides of the walkway, peddling everything from plastic swords to candy floss. More sinister was the array of authentic weaponry for sale. Since picking up guns, knives, and pepper spray with your takeaway coffee at gas stations was perfectly normal in these parts, perhaps we shouldn't have been surprised.

As we approached the splendid 14th-Century castle, I felt a disconnect with the ambient soundtrack. It called to mind an anecdote regarding a radio programme scheduled to start with a clarion of trumpets. It actually opened to the clamour of fairground carousels, because the sound unit mistakenly supplied 'a funfair' instead of 'a fanfare'.

Ogrodzieniec was surrounded by an army – of giant trampolines, dodgem cars, and bouncy castles. As if the real thing were not enough.

What do you need to complement a breathtaking medieval monument? A monstrous theme park. How it won the vote as Number One Tourist Attraction was instantly clear; it was huge, grotesque – and a testament to the triumph of money-grabbing capitalism.

The socially distanced queue at the entrance was long and slow-moving, so we opted to walk around the outside. Rock Jocks scaled the magnificent pillars with ropes. The area is popular with sport climbers; a few miles from Ogrodzieniec, also in the Eagles' Nest Landscape Park, is another picturesque limestone climbing area known as Kroczyce Rocks.

Our Rosie knows she is gorgeous and loved by everyone, so she did what she does best and bounded over to introduce herself to a lovely young Polish couple relaxing on the grass. Of course, Nosy Rosie never takes her eye off the ball regarding investigations; she is well aware that anyone sitting outdoors on a sunny day could be packing a picnic... The couple both spoke perfect English, so we joined them at a safe distance while they played with the dogs.

As we chatted, the sudden, plaintive blare of an air-raid siren ruptured the warmth of the afternoon. It was 5 p.m. The hubbub of fairground fun and laughter died away instantly.

The couple explained what was going on,

"Today is the 75th anniversary of the Warsaw Uprising."

Not one person, adult or child, broke the minute's silence.

Poland has had such a tragic past. For 123 years leading up to WWI, it was annexed by Prussia and didn't even exist as a country. The same thing happened after WWII, when the Allies hung the Poles out to dry.

Since he is a scholar of history, I will hand you over to Mark:

At the mention of the Warsaw Uprising, my heart skipped a beat, and a lump came into my throat. I despair of the depths that human behaviour can reach when circumstance removes societal boundaries, and neighbour turns on neighbour with vitriol and violence.

The Warsaw Uprising was an organised attempt by the citizens of this brave city to expel the Nazis. The Allies actively encouraged them to do this to support their own advance. Initial efforts were successful, but for post-war political advantage, the Soviet Red Army deliberately held back from relieving Warsaw, which enabled the Nazis to reinforce. For fear of Soviet wrath, the Western powers dithered and took no decisive action – until it was far too late.

During two months of fighting, estimates suggest that Nazi reprisals and mass executions caused the deaths of 200,000 civilians and 20,000 Polish resistance fighters. The Nazis levelled a further third of the city (on top of what they had already destroyed) and sent residents of those areas to Auschwitz, where they almost certainly perished too.

After the war, the Allies handed Poland over to the Soviets. Polish war heroes, a squadron of whom were the most successful in The Battle of Britain, were denied the right to take part in the UK Victory parade, for fear of aggravating Russia. Polish servicemen who returned home risked imprisonment, torture, and execution as enemies of the state. Post war, Poland did not regain her independence; instead, she was given over for occupation by the USSR.

Six-million Poles – around 20% of the population – died during WWII. 90% of these lives were not lost in combat, but in prisons and death camps, or through over-work and starvation.

No one should forget that even after the war, the freedom and privilege we enjoy in the West was built on the foundation of bravery and suffering that for some did not end with the conflict, but continued for decades under a brutal and oppressive regime.

We shared the couple's grief and happiness – they told us they were getting married in three weeks. They seemed pleased that a pair of foreigners understood and empathised with the plight of their countrymen during those terrible times.

On our walk back, there were plenty of reminders that sadly, terrible cruelty is hardly a 20th century invention. We could peer through loopholes into various rooms and courtyards within the ruins, which oozed history and atmosphere. On the north side, one was possibly *Meczarnia Warszyckiego*, the torture chamber built by 17th-Century scoundrel Stanislaw Warszycki.

According to legend, Warszycki tortured his peasants, imprisoned his wife (in mitigation, some stories say she did try to poison him!), and made a pact with the Devil. Demons transported him to Hell before his death, where Old Nick ripped out his soul, transformed it into a giant black dog, and condemned him to haunt the castle and repent his sins forever.

Folklore suggests that Warszycki's bargain with Beelzebub is the reason that his stronghold at Danków was not destroyed in the wars known as the Swedish Deluge. Apparently, Warszycki also haunts Danków Castle, although there, he appears as a headless horseman.

At this late hour, we didn't have time to investigate the other sights around Ogrodzieniec. A reconstructed 13th-Century wooden hill fortress, Biröw Stronghold, was a short walk away on the adjacent hill. A chapel in Podzamcze was rebuilt from stonework and statuary taken from the castle, and contains a cannonball from the Swedish Deluge. One of the most famous attractions nearby is the Wieliczka Salt Mine, which has a connection with Ogrodzieniec. Of course, I remained extremely mature about a gentleman banker; one of the richest men in Europe, who managed the mine and took over the castle at Ogrodzieniec.

His name was Jan and he came from a long line of Boners.

As we left, we reflected that perhaps the castle at Ogrodzieniec is a metaphor for life.

If you can just strip away all the superfluous crap, what remains is arrestingly beautiful.

28

AUSCHWITZ-BIRKENAU – THE INDUSTRIALISATION OF GENOCIDE

"Think occasionally of the suffering of which you spare yourself the sight." – Albert Schweitzer

I stepped, blinking, into the bright afternoon sunlight on Ealing Broadway. The buzz of a busy Saturday filled the space; the rumble of West London traffic; chattering shoppers; pigeons flapping and cooing as they sent flurries of litter and dust into the air from the warm, white paving slabs. The scene was entirely normal, yet I was completely unable to speak.

It was 1994, and I had just seen Steven Spielberg's film *Schindler's List*, which follows the story of ordinary people. Ordinary Jewish people in Kraków, going about their everyday business in the same way as the bustling crowds in Ealing. Until the day the regime declared them undesirable. Then, they were rounded up, confined in a ghetto, stripped of their possessions and wealth, then shipped in cattle trucks to one of the most notorious death camps of the Nazi era.

What if the authorities suddenly deemed Ealing residents with knobbly knees outcasts? Declared those who worship at the temple of the wrong TV soap opera enemies of the state? Pronounced a death sentence upon all those wearing shell suits; a perfectly acceptable sartorial choice in the 1990s?

I know I'm being flippant, but such criteria are as arbitrary as any made over race or religion, and as trivial as those that lie behind genocide and ethnic cleansing.

I don't like you.

I don't agree with you.

You don't deserve to exist.

It takes courage to pass through the gates of Auschwitz and stare into the dark heart of humanity. Courage I do not possess, so once again, I must hand you over to Mark.

I was nervous the day before my planned visit to Auschwitz.

We had been on the loveliest four-hour walk in Narodowy Ojców that morning, then spent the afternoon at Ogrodzieniec Castle. Although I'd already purchased a ticket online, I was still deciding whether to go, because of the emotions it stirred.

I don't want to dwell on the rise in populism, or liken the current situation across the world (including Poland and the UK) to Nazi Germany, since nothing can compare to a period in history so repulsive it should never be allowed to happen again.

As a society, we must not blame other ethnicities for our woes, and it is critical to recognise that many of those in power dispense this sort of hateful narrative to control our thinking and manipulate our behaviour. The 99% of us need to guard against the 1% who try to use us like sheep.

I don't hate the German people for the atrocities of WWII, but I hold them to account for letting themselves be duped into giving power to a despot. Before Hitler, Germany was a liberal democracy. Humiliated after WWI, Hitler promised jobs and prosperity; to make Germany great again. Does that sound familiar?

The Nazi party was not elected with a majority, but Hitler was given emergency powers the day after the burning of the Reichstag, an act which some believe he ordered. Four weeks after being sworn in as Chancellor, he used this free rein to appoint his own people into key positions, then, in The Night of the Long Knives, simply murdered all who opposed him. The rest, as they say, is history.

It seems surprising that Auschwitz is utterly synonymous with the Holocaust, yet Auschwitz Kommandant Rudolf Höss, the man who industrialised genocide, (not to be confused with Deputy Führer Rudolf Hess), is so little known.

The arch above the gates at Auschwitz bears the words Arbeit Macht Frei – Work Sets You Free. The B is upside down; perhaps a gesture of rebellion from the prisoners forced to make it. The slogan appears at other Nazi camps, and was appropriated by Höss from Dachau.

Auschwitz has two killing sites. Auschwitz 1 was an old Polish army base, handed over to Höss with the instruction to massacre the Polish elite at the start of the war. Höss was reportedly a quiet family man, born in Baden-Baden to devout

Catholic parents. He believed in following orders. Arbeit Macht Frei could apply to him without irony. Given a task, he applied himself to it with ruthless efficiency. At Auschwitz, he excelled. He created the largest single site of mass murder known to history.

By 1941, the derelict old army camp that had been Auschwitz 1 held 10,000 prisoners and was the largest in the Reich. However, it had only a small furnace and couldn't perform mass killings on the scale necessary to implement Hitler's 'final solution of the Jewish question', which began in earnest in 1942. The Führer ordered, "Every Jew we can lay our hands on is to be destroyed now, without exception."

To achieve this ghastly aim, Höss employed forced labour from Auschwitz 1 to build a second camp nearby. Birkenau (Auschwitz 2) had four massive furnaces. That solved the problem around disposing of the aftermath of mass murder, but to increase the efficiency of extermination, Höss experimented with different gases. His deputy, Karl Fritzsch, discovered that the pesticide Zyklon-B, used to de-louse inmates' clothing, produced cyanide gas when exposed to air. A grisly trial on Russian prisoners showed it was far more efficient than the exhaust fumes from truck or car engines employed previously.

When he was tried for war crimes at Nuremberg, Höss testified that it took between 3 and 15 minutes for the victims to die using Zyklon-B, and that they knew when the people were dead because the screaming stopped.

Thus began the ruthless, industrialised process of extermination. Daily, the Nazis shipped trainloads of Jews, Roma gypsies, the handicapped, and other 'undesirables' to Auschwitz. As each train arrived, the SS and doctors, including the infamous 'Angel of Death', Josef Mengele, carried out an immediate callous selection on the platform. Most Jews went straight to gas chambers, along with any deemed unfit for work. This included children under 15, pregnant women, the elderly and infirm. They sent the young and fit to Auschwitz-Birkenau to be worked to death under starvation conditions. Many captives died en route to the camp; for example, 65% of Greek Jews perished on the 11-day journey. Each rail cart was the size of our four-berth caravan, crammed with 100 people.

To maintain a calm order on the march to the gas chambers, guards chatted to prisoners and told them they were going for a shower. They ordered detainees to strip and place their belongings in numbered cases. Guards instructed them to remember the numbers to reclaim their things after 'Disinfektion', and told children to tie their shoelaces together, as this would be their only footwear in the camp. This was, of course, a false hope. The Nazis took everything of value, including gold fillings, and shipped the murder victims' clothes and shoes to Germany to help with the war effort.

Up close, the mechanics of Hitler's golden ideology were profoundly disturbing.

Noting the effect on the psychological health of his own men, Höss appointed Jewish prisoners the gruesome task of removing the 900 or so bodies from each chamber after gassing, ready for cremation. To maintain secrecy around the activities of Auschwitz, he had these Sonderkommandos – Special Commandos murdered and replaced every few months.

Life was brutal for those interred in the camp. Prisoners were forced to work hard on minimum rations and lived in cramped and unhygienic conditions. Mengele conducted his twisted experiments on inmates. Summary execution by public hanging awaited any who stepped out of line; including recaptured escapees, anyone who assisted prisoners, or the families of those who escaped. If there was no family, they killed a random selection of people who shared the same work detail or barracks. A rail around the perimeter to facilitate hangings served as a warning and deterrent. Every day there was a roll call; the longest required prisoners to stand in scorching temperatures in the courtyard for nine hours.

As the war was drawing to a close, the Nazis added a railway line directly into Auschwitz-Birkenau to speed up their plans as they focussed attention on eradicating the last remaining Jewish enclave: half-a-million Hungarian Jews. By now, 'improvements' meant Auschwitz could kill and cremate 12,000 people per day.

To conceal the atrocities from the German citizens and the world, Heinrich Himmler forbade record-keeping and at the end of the war, the Germans destroyed most of the gas chambers. At Nuremburg, Höss refuted the accusation that he murdered 3.5 million people at Auschwitz. In his testimony, he stated, "No. Only two and one-half million – the rest died from disease and starvation."

Census figures pre- and post-war show that Poland's Jewish population fell from 2,700,000 to 100,000; there was a similar fall in her non-Jewish population. In total, the Nazis annihilated over five-million Polish people.

These are some of the facts and figures. I can't possibly describe Auschwitz, and if you want to know about it, then visit. For me, it was too commercial and had lost much of the horror. The guide tried to dramatise what happened there; it didn't need that. The facts are stark and grotesque enough on their own. There are all kinds of fables about Auschwitz; they say no birds sing there. That is true, but there were few trees. Like you wouldn't hear birds at a scrap yard. My visit didn't upset me in the way I thought.

I shed tears just the once when I saw what the Soviets found when they liberated the camp. Seven tonnes of human hair, bagged up ready to ship to German textile factories. To put this into context, the average weight of hair from one person is twelve grammes.

When Mark got back, the guys in the caravan next door asked him how he got on at Auschwitz. They seemed disappointed when he replied honestly.

"I didn't find it as upsetting as I'd anticipated."

Later, he asked me,

"Do you think I shouldn't admit that to people?"

"I think you should tell the truth," I said. "It's a very personal thing, and your feelings about your visit are just as valid as anyone else's."

In the Instagram age, there seems almost a pressure to outdo everybody else's horrified reactions with emotional one-upmanship. "You didn't cry? I wept buckets!" "That's nothing, I wept buckets, then vomited at the repugnance of it all."

The following day, Mark rationalised his feelings.

What happened at Auschwitz was awful, but it's now a tourist attraction. It's a story that absolutely should be told, and you hope that, as a memorial to the millions who suffered and died there, it stands as a warning to history. However, for me, having it as an attraction lessens it.

What I find THE most upsetting is that nothing has changed. With the right people in charge, the same would happen again in a whisper. It's happening around the world now, but we stand by and don't lift a finger.

Next time you look at your boss, your colleagues, your friends, or your neighbours, think about whether they would act against such behaviour. Would they collaborate for personal gain? Would they be the ones holding the knife to your throat? And what about you? If the price was your life or the life of your loved ones, would you resist?

Decency lies in unexpected places. Contrast Rudolf Höss, who at one time considered entering the Catholic priesthood, with Oskar Schindler, the Nazi chancer who came to Kraków to make his fortune from the war. While Höss murdered millions without question, Schindler risked his life and bankrupted himself to rescue 1,200 Jews from certain death in Auschwitz.

Back in Ealing on that sunny afternoon, the reason I couldn't speak after seeing *Schindler's List* was not just because I was choked from seeing the horrors of Auschwitz recreated so vividly on the big screen. I was overwhelmed with a feeling that it should never, ever be allowed to happen again, although the second the thought came into my mind, I knew it already was.

In 1994, the genocide was taking place in Rwanda and the Balkan war was in full swing, with appalling atrocities committed on all sides.

George Santayana said,

"Those who cannot remember the past are condemned to repeat it."

By the 75th anniversary of the Holocaust, over fifty-five-million civilians had perished in eighty-nine major genocides around the globe. *(Source – A Journey into the Holocaust).*

29

ŁAŃCUT

Poland's Hampton Court, A Dance with the Devil, and The Revenge of the Ghost Mouse of Eguisheim

It was at Łańcut where we finally solved The Curious Incident of the Dog in the Light Grime.

We had intended to go to Kazimierz Dolny, 'The Most Beautiful Town in Poland', set amid a landscape of spectacular gorges and lakes. However, as we checked out of his campsite in Ojców, our host, Bartek, told us,

"Kazimierz Dolny is infested with mosquitos at this time of year. There's a really lovely campsite at Łańcut, with lots of things to see close by."

Recommendations rank highly in our route planning hierarchy, but Mosquito Avoidance trumps everything, so we set a course for Łańcut, whose claim to fame is Poland's largest palace. With three-hundred rooms, Łańcut Castle is one of Poland's National Historic Monuments.

Once again, the drive there was plain.

"You know that photo of a sea of barley that I took on our first leg between Bolków and Wrocław? I could use it for every journey we've done across central Poland," I said to Mark, although as we pushed east, the scene did change from bread basket to scrubby forest and poor agricultural land.

I still found items of interest to point out to Mark. "Look. There's a field full of Przewalski horses. They're really rare."

Przewalskis are the horses you see depicted in cave paintings. They are the equine equivalent of wolves or wildcats – the closest you can get to the original, prehistoric, non-domesticated animal. They are notable for their chestnut-dun colour, stocky build, and erect mane. They have donkey-like features, such as a pale mealy muzzle and belly, and black stripes down their backs and on the tops of their legs.

As we passed road signs to Belarus, Slovakia, and Ukraine, Mark said, "We could clock up ten countries on this trip." For once, I urged caution,

"With the coronavirus situation, I'm not sure we should go outside the EU. What if the borders close? They might not let us back in."

Within a few days, another reason not to stray too far came to light.

So often, 'The Lamberts are coming' is the match to the blue touch paper of public unrest. It happened in Romania, Nepal, and Zimbabwe. Less than a week after Mark and I had this conversation, Belarus confirmed President Lukashenko, 'Europe's Last Dictator', for a sixth term. Anti-government protests started amid claims of widespread electoral fraud. Despite brutal suppression, the unrest escalated and continued. While President L. is unpopular at home and abroad, he has powerful friends; notably one named Putin in the Kremlin.

The campsite was as lovely as Bartek had promised. Eddie, the owner, and his wife had lived in Chicago for twenty years, but set up the site when they returned home to Poland. As a trucker, Eddie had roved all over the United States and Canada. We met his late-teenage daughter, Anielka, who was a sweetie. She had moved back to Poland aged eight and spoke English fluently, with a strong hint of stars and stripes.

I had a long conversation with Anielka, but first things first. I asked her,

"How do you say Łańcut?"

"Wine-Suit," she said.

Well. If you can have a Smoking Jacket, why not a Wine Suit?

When Anielka revealed that even she struggled to pronounce some Polish words, I felt vindicated. In return, I introduced Anielka to Welsh, one of Europe's oldest languages. I still think Welsh is easier to articulate than Polish, despite all those Ls. All you have to remember is:

- F = V
- Dd = Th
- W = Oo and
- Ll = a kind of Cl or Hl made with a hiss from both sides of the tongue to replicate the sound of a moderately outraged rattlesnake.

Anielka was suitably awed by my party trick, a recital of the second longest place name in the world: Llanfairpwllgwyngyllgogerychwyrndrobwllllantysiliogogogoch. Fifty-eight letters whose translation makes it sound way more fascinating than it is; '*St. Mary's Church in the Hollow of the White Hazel Near to the Rapid Whirlpool of St. Tysilio of the Red Cave*'. The reality is a mini-village, barely more than a train station, on the Isle of Anglesey, reputedly named by an enterprising local tailor to attract tourists, which worked a treat.

My careful research suggests the length of place names is inversely proportional to their significance. Capital cities rarely stray beyond three syllables. However, the longest place name in the world belongs to a small hill near Hawke's Bay in New Zealand. This eighty-five-character classic is Taumatawhakatangi-hangakoauauotamateaturipukakapikimaunga-horonukupokaiwhenuakitanatahu, named to commemorate an auspicious occasion; '*The hilltop, where Tamatea with big knees, conqueror of mountains, eater of land, traveller over land and sea, played his koauau to his beloved.*'

I can tell you two interesting things about Taumata, as it's known for short. You can hear it spoken on the intro of *The Lone Ranger* by Quantum Jump, since the band cunningly appropriated the hill's Māori name as Tonto's Native American chant.

The second interesting fact is that the name is actually an anagram of Whakatangihangakoauauotamatea-turipukakapikimaungahoronukupok-aiwhenuakitanatahutaumata. (I made that up!)

Anielka told me she wanted to attend University in England or Scotland, although the Brexit spanner had clogged those undergraduate works.

"I'm sure the government will sort out some kind of study visa," I said. "Overseas students are so important – they need someone to fill up and pay for all those University places."

Anielka sent me away with a few Post-It notes listing Polish culinary specialities to try and the best restaurants in Łańcut to try them. Mark and I took an evening stroll into town along the road and through some waste ground. Clearly, we had deviated from the 1 km route through the park that Eddie had suggested.

After some further navigational detective work (we still hadn't mastered Google Maps) we found a pavement café that was both open and welcomed dogs. There, we sampled our first *pierogi*, the famous Polish dumplings filled with variations on the theme of meat, cabbage, and cheese. We lingered over this very hearty plateful, which cost less than €20 for two, including a two-litre jug of beer. Our leisurely approach to dinner made our stroll back along the road and through the waste ground in the dark considerably less enjoyable.

The following day didn't start well.

Back in Ojców, I had confused our neighbours when I told them,

"I like Polish rain."

I had to explain,

"Today's forecast was for rain, but it's forty-degrees and full sun."

Yet the grey liquid version of Polish sunshine that blessed our morning was the least of our problems. When Mark returned from taking the dogs for their pee poo run, he announced,

"Rosie's got worms!"

At last, an explanation for The Curious Incident of the Dog in the Light Grime. We noticed Rosie had taken to rolling abundantly in all kinds of dust and dirt. It must have been because her poor little tum was so uncomfortable. Her worming treatment wasn't due for a couple of weeks, so these were nuclear worms.

A quick internet search revealed the likely culprit. Way back in Alsace, we recalled Rosie treating herself to a crunchy snack as we walked through the vineyards – a long-dead mouse. A conversation with our vet at home confirmed our strong suspicion that the Ghost Mouse of Eguisheim was the most probable cause of Rosie's vermicular infestation.

Thankfully, a single dose of Milbemax exorcised the ghost.

My own medical problems were less straightforward. I had no further need for amoxycillin, since my toothache had calmed down of its own accord. However, I was rationing my prescription medications because even pleas of lockdown hadn't got me past the ferocious gatekeeping of my doctor's receptionist. Issuing an international prescription was out of the question, she told me. Now, I had almost run out.

Kraków's tourist office had supplied details of the private company in Poland through whom I could see a doctor. Since I suffer from phone-o-phobia, Mark rang the purportedly English-language help line. Communication was such a stressful experience that within an hour, Mark and I, the couple who don't argue, were barely on speaking terms. At one point, a very frustrated Mark snapped out an order,

"Go and find Eddie or Anielka."

They could have acted as interpreters, but were nowhere to be found. The result was that Mark may or may not have made a doctor's appointment at some building located somewhere within the Lublin city limits.

After an entire morning Living our Dreams via the medium of worming dogs, mis-communicating, and being put eternally on hold in a rain-lashed caravan, we planned our afternoon. While places of interest looked nearby on the map, almost everything of note, other than Łańcut itself, was an hour-and-a-half's drive away.

Thankfully, our mood brightened with the day as the liquid sunshine made way for another scorchingly blue sky. We drove into Łańcut to avoid the roads and waste-land, parked at the castle gates and bought an enormous compensatory ice cream.

Since we travel with four dogs, our expectations had never encompassed going inside the castle. In the grounds, a man taking photographs lamented,

"I can't go inside. Entry slots are limited because of COVID. You have to buy a ticket, and they're all sold out."

We had noted wildly varying responses to the coron-avirus pandemic. Now, in Britain, the Eat Out To Help Out scheme was launching to boost business. Taxpayers would subsidise half-price meals – up to £10 per person – between Mondays and Wednesdays throughout August. Mark and I felt no gratification when our entirely predictable prediction about the rise in UK case numbers came in September.

Back in Łańcut, we finished our ice creams and wandered around the outside of the grand red-brick palace. Our friend, Kazimierz the Great, son of The Elbow High, founded the town in the mid-1300s on an important trade route linking Western Europe with Ukraine, Hungary, and Poland. The palace dates to 1642, although it was reconstructed and modernised over many years. By the 1800s, its rambling Baroque elegance made it one of the finest residences in Europe, fit to host exalted guests, including Louis XIII of France, and Emperor Franz Josef of Austria.

Later, we found the dogs should have been on leads in the extensive English-style parkland gardens, although nobody seemed to worry. They ran happily on the vast fields of grass, shaded by magnificent mature trees. The buildings in the grounds, such as the Orchid House and the former stables and coach house, with its collection of eighty historic horse-drawn carriages, were closed.

Sometimes, the castle is called the Potocki Palace, after its final owners. Among Poland's most powerful families, the Potockis were connected through marriage to most of Europe's aristocracy, including the Habsburgs. Just before the Soviet army entered Poland and the outcome of WWII became clear, the last Lord of Łańcut, Alfred III Potocki, fled and abandoned his palace forever.

However, I found a previous incumbent, Stanisław Stadnicki, even more fascinating. Locals knew him as *Diabeł Łańcucki* – the Devil of Łańcut, for his 'colourful' behaviour.

Stadnicki could have inspired the 16th-Century version of *Nightmare Neighbours*. He robbed townspeople and, with his two-thousand-strong army of mercenaries, waged private wars on adjoining estates.

Tired of his anti-social exploits, Łukasz Opaliński, Governor of Leżajsk, and Duchess Anna Ostrogska set up an extreme Neighbourhood Watch scheme to sort him out. They merged their armies, set fire to his castle, then beheaded Stadnicki. On dark nights, legends say you can see his ghost riding a black horse.

Opaliński claimed to have, "Defeated the Devil and burned down Hell in Łańcut", but diabolical family habits die hard. Stadnicki's wife Anna became known as the 'Łańcut Devil-Woman', while his sons' behaviour earned them the title of the 'Łańcut Devil-Children'.

Never mind the darkness, the road, and the wasteland, we now had an additional ghostly reason to drive into town for dinner. Since we knew where it was, we returned to Restaurant Antico. Mark sampled pancakes, and I pointed at *gyros* on the menu and asked the waitress, "What's that?"

I never got an answer, but I did get a cheese-topped pork chop, with a few fried onions and peppers on the side. In Poland, I suppose that constitutes veggies.

We decided to move on the next morning, although like the Devil of Łańcut's last stand, we returned from dinner to find Caravan Kismet besieged and encircled by an army of neighbours. The only difference was that our blockade was composed of tents and motorhomes.

"That should make getting out tomorrow interesting." Mark said.

Quite how interesting, we could never have guessed.

30

A DE-CAMP BY COMMITTEE, ŁAŃCUT TO SANDOMIERZ

An Introduction to the Newton-Lambert Law and a CPC (Caravan Pushing Committee)

When Mark said, "That will make getting out tomorrow interesting," he had not been kidding.

The campsite had plenty of space, but Mark's comment referred to the French motorhome positioned directly in front of Caravan Kismet and the large tent to her left. With a fence and a ditch four feet deep to our right, we were hemmed in. Our only exit route was backwards, and that was anything but straightforward. We would need to reverse around a right angle on to a narrow bridge, while avoiding a tree, a hedge, the fence, and the ditch. However, Mark had a plan.

"I will just hitch, reverse past the tree, unhitch, spin the caravan through ninety degrees, re-hitch, and drive out."

Simples. Until, of course, the Helping Committee arrived.

The campsite owner, Eddie, insisted that we needed to push the caravan out.

"It will be fine," Mark told him. "I have a plan." But Eddie was immovable. He was a nice chap. A qualified lorry driver. And it was his site. What do you do?

I soon started to feel like William Wordsworth. All at once, I saw a crowd, but sadly, not a host of golden daffodils. It was a gathering of our stout French neighbour and a couple of burly Poles. The sight of a caravan being pushed was like a jelly-based picnic to a squadron of wasps. A shot at caravan pushing glory is always too much to resist, and I could tell our Frenchman was serious. He was wearing a T-shirt, so he didn't have sleeves to roll up, but he slid off his flip-flops. The Polish chaps came out of nowhere. I'd never even seen them around the campsite. The result was a trilingual CPC (Caravan Pushing Committee), operating in a babble of French, English, and Polish. It would never end well.

Of course, the number of opinions on what to do next was as diverse as the CPC. There was pushing, pulling, and twisting going on, all at the same time. At one point, I heard Mark enquire,

"So. What exactly are we doing?"

Mark also had to step in to prevent one Pole from hauling our 1.5 tonne caravan sideways using the lever that engages the ALKO stabiliser. As you might remember from Germany, the lever is emphatically not designed to be a handle. It activates the system that stops the caravan going into a deadly snake while being towed. If broken, would cause tremendous safety issues.

Heavy rain overnight meant that Caravan Kismet

soon hit a soft spot on the grass and sank. Only Mark would listen to the lone female voice,

"The wheel has sunk. It's stuck. There's no point trying to push."

This did not deter the CPC. Now, they had the caravan-pushing bit fully between their teeth. Like the Volga boatmen, they continued their heave ho. With the back end going nowhere, several strong shoves lifted Kismet's front end clear off the ground.

I appreciate I have ovaries, which affect my brain and mean I can't possibly know anything technical or scientific. However, by invoking the Law of Moments then Newton's Second Law, I calculated that half the weight of the caravan (0.75 tonnes) multiplied by the acceleration caused by gravity crashed on to one single, small point, i.e. the jockey wheel at the front of the caravan. While it's strong, it's possibly not that strong.

In fem-speak, imagine a one-legged elephant jumping up and down while wearing a single stiletto. My pretty pink conclusion, The Newton-Lambert Law is; "The weight of a caravan (or elephant) falling repeatedly on its jockey wheel (or stiletto heel) could be sufficient to cause breakage."

Somewhere amid the fray of trying to carry out a difficult manoeuvre while distracted by the need for crowd control, Mark sliced open his hand and began to bleed profusely.

It took some persuasion before the CPC got their hands off OUR caravan.

"I'm going to hitch up and reverse," Mark said firmly. "Don't stand behind the caravan, as I will now need to accelerate hard to get out of the hole."

The CPC scattered like a herd of sheep. In English and French, I did my best to shoo everyone out of the way. I recognised the elements congealing into the perfect scenario for an accident to happen. Of course, everyone knew better than a wee wifey how to direct Mark as he reversed Big Blue on to the hitch.

"I'm only listening to you, Jax," he confirmed, wisely.

"Merde. Attention. Arrêtez!" – "Sh**. Watch it. STOP!" yelled the Frenchman, suddenly waving his arms as he flew into a panic about Kismet's roof catching on a tree.

"It's fine, Mark, keep coming," I said calmly. "The tree is about three metres away. If the roof touches anything, it will be only the fine branches."

I cleared the crowd away from Kismet's rear then, with no tears, Mark carried out the original plan. He reversed Kismet then unhitched. The CPC was back on Kismet like locusts on a wheat field. I had to stop them from pushing Kismet further backwards into the hedge. One of them even started unscrewing the bracket that holds on the jockey wheel, the only thing holding up the front of the caravan.

"No – please don't push. We need room to turn. NO! LEAVE THAT ALONE!"

It was like dealing with a bunch of kids. "'ere mister. What does this do?" or a demented US President.

"Now, what will happen if I press this big red button?"

Once Mark had moved Big Blue out of the way, we twisted Kismet around, re-hitched, and Bob was our uncle. Our original plan, executed perfectly, without bloodshed, absolutely no need for a CPC – and if we'd done that in the first place, Eddie would not now have been crying over the crater in his carefully tended grass.

Thankfully, I remembered to double check for the wider ramifications of a CPC before we left. I made sure that the caravan was properly hitched; that its handbrake was off; and that the breakaway cable, electrics, and ALKO stabiliser were all connected.

CPC distraction and interference at inopportune moments often results in overlooking such essential safety details.

"Shall we check the lights?" I asked Mark.

"Let's do that once we're outside..." He'd had enough of hitching by committee.

Eddie's last word was,

"You should get a motor mover."

"Why?" we replied. "It would take up half our payload and drain the battery really quickly."

Plus, it would not have been any use at all in this situation. If the caravan is on ground flat enough for a motor mover to work, Mark and I can push it. And unlike some caravan owners, we ain't afraid to reverse. It's very rare to find ourselves in a position that we can't resolve between the two of us.

As we drove off, the pushing points of the caravan dripping with husbandly blood, we reminisced about CPCs past.

"Do you remember Romania, when the Caravan Pushing Committee left us with the back of the caravan hanging off?"

Oh, happy days – CPCs always end badly. My beloved and I had a well-rehearsed routine for hitching and manoeuvring, honed and used without incident for four years. Except when people interfere. I shall re-iterate the advice from Caravan Confucius; unless asked, please resist the urge to help.

Later, when we analysed the event, Mark and I vowed that our initial strategy should be to disperse a budding CPC forcefully, however kind and well-meaning they are, and however much offence it causes.

When you think about it, CPCs are quite rude. Not only do they think they know better than you, with your experience and well-oiled routine, they ignore your wishes when, as the owner of an expensive piece of kit, you decline their help but they join in anyway – and then cause damage to said expensive piece of kit.

We also agreed that should this fail, which it inevitably would, we needed to push down the ALKO lever, so it didn't present a temptation for someone to yank on and destroy.

Surprisingly, on our drive to Sandomierz, we experienced only one near-miss with a mad Polish driver. Had we not braked sharply, the car overtaking us would have ploughed into a queue of oncoming traffic. In Sandomierz, we overruled the satnav's peculiar directions and opted to stay on the main road. Our lack of faith forced us to execute a very tight U-turn on a narrow piece of road which passed a church. We had to mount the pavement to squeeze past a hearse and its funeral cortege.

Once we had pitched in the grounds of Karpiński Manor and I described what we would be having for dinner, Mark launched into a full mickey-take over our supply of tinned food, left over from lockdown. The low payload (weight carrying capacity) of the caravan meant we had to empty out heavy items, such as pans, crockery, and tins, every time we tow.

"I've made tuna pasta for dinner, which used up a few of those cans," I told him. "It's a bit of a bind carrying them in and out of the caravan every time we move. We still have some peas left."

"How many tins of peas are there?"

"Er, one," I admitted, but justified my position on peas by telling him,

"They are *Piselli Medi*, so they've come with us all the way from Italy."

In a faux Irish accent, Mark launched straight into both sides of a mock interview with me,

"So, Mrs. Lambert. What's your main memory of your tour of Poland?"

"Well, it's the peas, Eamon. We had this one tin that was with us *for ever*. We had to constantly get it in and out of the caravan. It was all a bit of a bind..."

Now c'mon Mark, that's just taking the peas.

31

THE DEVIL CHILDREN OF SANDOMIERZ

A Trip Around The Unlucky Alf of Polish Cities

From our campsite, it was a swift yet energetic walk into Sandomierz old town, up a steep flight of over one-hundred stone stairs.

The city is a medieval delight. Built on seven hills, some call it 'Poland's little Rome'.

To see the sights without crowds, we went in early for breakfast. As we stepped into the *Rynek* (market square), Mark and I exclaimed in unison,

"WOW!"

In the centre, the 14th-Century red brick Town Hall dominated the scene. It had a stunning crenellated *attic* (a decorative low wall around the rooftop) and an impressive white clock tower with a shapely Verdigris top. Characterful Baroque buildings bordered the square. Many were street cafés with sunshades and umbrellas, which tempted us in from the early morning sunshine.

Mark urged me to pick one, so I chose 2 Okna.

"Based on the music, I wouldn't have stopped here," Mark opined, referring to the strangulated modern jazz that accompanied our croissant and scrambled eggs. "But the coffee is one of the best of the trip."

In most historic cities we'd visited so far, gracious horse-drawn carriages conveyed tourists. Perhaps because of the hills, Sandomierz boasted an eclectic selection of electric cars, whose retro shapes and rainbow colours were straight from the cartoon series *Wacky Races*. Each was piloted by its very own Penelope Pitstop, sporting cascading locks and a pretty floral dress.

After breakfast, at two minutes to ten, the tourist office kicked me out,

"We don't open until 10 a.m."

"It's two-minutes-to, and the door was open. I only want a map."

"You must wait outside."

Two minutes and twelve seconds later, map in hand, Mark and I embarked on a lovely meander through the steep cobbled streets to admire the 120 historic buildings within the old town. Sandomierz was once a royal municipality on a par with Kraków and Wrocław. On a bluff above the confluence of the Vistula and San rivers, it was a staging post on important trade routes. Unfortunately, it seems to be the Unlucky Alf of Polish cities.

In the early medieval period, the Mongols, Tatars, and Lithuanians repeatedly sacked and burned down its wooden buildings. In the 14th century, Kazimierz the Great founded the basis of today's Sandomierz in stone, although Poland's turbulent history eventually crushed both its splendour and prosperity.

Hot on the heels of the invasion known as the Swedish Deluge in 1655 came a Hungarian incursion, then The Plague. Partition and annexation of the country followed the Great Fire in 1757. As a frontier town, Sandomierz lost its administrative importance and so its fortunes waned. WWI ravaged the city, although when Poland regained its independence, the authorities earmarked Sandomierz as the capital of the proposed Central Industrial Region. However, the onset of WWII halted this renaissance for good.

Our wanderings through this blissful backwater took us to Cathedral Hill, where the 14th-Century Gothic basilica is famed for its Byzantine murals.

Opposite the cathedral, the castle sits atop its own summit, which has been home to a stronghold since the 10th century. Kazimierz The Great built the stone fortress, which was much altered over the years. The biggest change came in 1656 when the retreating Swedes blew it up, leaving nothing standing but the west wing. The building limped on as a prison until 1959, but most of what's there today is a restoration that started in the 1960s.

An unusual feature of Sandomierz is what lies beneath. Go underground and you find a multi-storey labyrinth of subterranean passages. These were used by merchants as storage cellars, and by the population as a refuge in times of war. Legend mentions three tunnels which led from the castle, although these have never been found. In keeping with the Unlucky Alf theme, over time, many buildings collapsed into these vaults.

I do love an enigmatic underground. There is a visitor route through a 400 m section, but I was conscious of crowding in close confines. A flare up of coronavirus in Lower Silesia had hit the headlines. Although we were some distance away, it underlined the need for caution. In any case, once they finally let me in, the tourist information officer barked at me,

"Underground tours are Polish language only and no dogs allowed."

Near the 30 m (98 ft) high Opatów Gate, one of the few remaining parts of Kazimierz the Great's old fortifications, Mark and I spotted a nice-looking restaurant with an outdoor terrace. We strolled back in the evening, but every table was reserved.

Randomly, we selected a pavement café in the square. As we sat down, we asked for a beer, which was not forthcoming. After ten minutes or so, a waitress shoved a menu at us. She clearly considered her contract fulfilled by turning up for work. Anything else was an imposition to be marked with surly resentment.

After a further quarter of an hour, nothing had happened, other than repeated visits from a monster child intent on aggravating The Fab Four.

Despite the language barrier, we made it very clear we wanted him to go away, but he remained undeterred. His parents were oblivious. Like everybody else, they were glued to their mobile phones. Perhaps they were relieved at the peace, now that we were providing both childcare and entertainment. I wondered if their family tree led to the Devil Children of Łańcut, spawn of the Devil and Devil Woman, who had terrorised everyone at our previous destination.

It seemed unfair to admonish the dogs for barking when they were being provoked. The Devil Child of

Sandomierz prodded at Lani and distressed our sweet little girl to a point where she growled and snapped towards him. Later, in the square, she grumbled at another youngster who bent down to stroke her. This was something she had never done, and was certainly not behaviour we wanted to encourage. We had always been able to take The Pawsome Foursome anywhere to meet anyone and not worry.

Mark explained to the waitress why we were leaving. It was hard to pin down the level of indifference, but on a scale of couldn't give a f*** to couldn't give a flying one, she scored full marks. We denied her bonus points, though. Her level of disinterest was such that she didn't even seem grateful that by leaving, we'd saved her from having to serve.

By now, 2 Okna was full, so we settled on a wooden deck outside a traditional Polish fast-food place. They had laid out the picnic tables like an American Diner, with a corridor down the middle. Beer arrived within our fifteen-minute tolerance span, and the burgery-things-with-chips were tasty. The buzz of bonhomie around the square accompanied dinner, while a soft peachy sunset spread a deep blush across the red brick façade of the monumental Town Hall.

Ordering a second drink proved a challenge, but we gave up instantly when another flock of horror children appeared. Six parents squidged their vast bulk into the bench seats directly opposite us, ordered an ocean of alcohol, and abandoned their offspring to go feral. The little cherubs amused the entire restaurant with a thorough exploration of the acoustic effects achievable by stamping up and down on the wooden floor while yelling and screaming. They were very fair, and made sure to spread the joy by passing every table.

Since we'd finished our beer and found ourselves in the fortunate position of being unable to order another, we left.

When you've toured in France and Italy, where youngsters have manners and dine out like mini-adults, it's a shock to encounter juveniles doing a wall of death around a restaurant. As we wandered back, Mark observed,

"The only kids as badly behaved as the Polish are the British."

Ah. A small reminder of home.

We were sanguine and agreed; mostly, it had been a pleasant evening, spoiled by swarms of youths and a few mosquitos.

Unfortunately, this was a symptom of Sandomierz losing its 'hidden gem' status. It was unsurprising that a destination a couple of hours from Kraków and Lublin was gaining popularity, particularly with the pandemic-induced travel bans and trend towards staycations. The city also came on the radar as the location for a long-running Polish TV detective series, *Ojciec Mateusz* – Father Matthew.

There was plenty do in the area. Góry Pieprzowe – The Pepper Hills promised panoramic views over 'little Rome' and its rivers. Wąwóz Królowej Jadwigi – Queen Jadwig's Ravine is a gulley carved by rainwater and lined with tree roots. Sandomierz is also a rising star of Poland's winemaking scene. Further afield, a few people had recommended the two-hour drive to Zamość, the

'Polish Pearl of the Renaissance', set in beautiful, unspoilt nature.

But, crowded places in the height of tourist season are never our favourite and it was the weekend. Between the bugs, kids, coronavirus chasing our tail, and the number of unscheduled stops we'd already made, we decided to push on to Lublin.

Sandomierz is not a working town and is all a bit like a theme park, but Mark and I agreed that, if you can miss the crowds (and the Devil Children), it's well worth a visit.

PART III

THE GREAT ESCAPE

Map from Poland to the UK

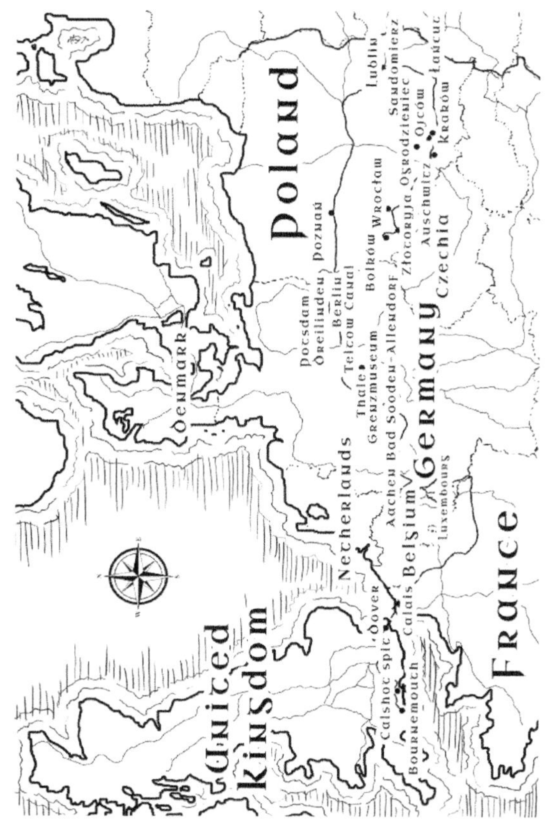

32

THE GREAT ESCAPE: LUBLIN TO POZNAŃ

Time finally runs out...

"It's not a matter of if, but when this driver will have an accident. I can pinpoint exactly the timing of this accident. It will happen just after his luck runs out."

This was one of Mark's early driving assessments as a young and feckless courier. I plagiarised it now to deliver judgement on the trucker, once I dared to uncover my eyes. Rounding a blind bend, we had come nose-to-nose with an articulated lorry, who had seized the day – and zero visibility – to pass a tractor.

For two hours and seventy-six miles, the scenery did not change. We did not escape the endless seas of barley, but driving in Poland is never dull. When we reached our destination, we had expended a further pair of our nine lives on impatient Polish truckers overtaking inappropriately.

Thankfully, nobody's luck ran out.

The outskirts of Lublin had promise. Through gaps in

the surrounding woodland, we glimpsed Zemborzyckie Reservoir, a huge shimmering lake. Mark had found a tiny campsite with only three pitches, set among the trees near the water's edge. Visions of walks and watery fun flashed before us. Excited, we immediately agreed,

"We'll stay at least a week."

Aleksi and Lena gave us a wonderful welcome. They made a tremendous fuss of our fur family and, to our immense relief, didn't help with pitching our hound cart. This showed great restraint, since getting into position in the tiny camping area was a fandangle of such mammoth proportions, it would normally prove irresistible to even the most reticent self-appointed CPC (Caravan Pushing Committee).

The manoeuvre required us to drive in; unhitch; hand-pivot Kismet through 180 degrees; re-hitch; then reverse up on to two tramlines of hard standing. It differed markedly from our experience at Łańcut. With no one 'helping', no blood was shed; nothing was broken; and in fewer than ten minutes, we were relaxing in the shade with a cuppa.

Sadly, a walk around the lake quickly tarnished its sheen. The nature of the litter led Mark to deduce,

"It's clearly a popular BB&B spot for city dwellers."

"What?"

"Beer, Barbeque, and Bonking."

We passed three rough sleepers, including a real-life Stig of the Dump, who lived in a shack made from twigs and plastic sheets. The conspicuous lack of bins or 'facilities' had dire consequences. I saw items a lady should never expect to confront again after the menopause, and there was minimal jeopardy on offer for a game of 'Poodunnit?' With no bears around, we knew only too well who had done what in the woods.

'No Swimming' signs showed the lake was off limits due to blooms of toxic cyanobacteria (blue-green algae). Keeping four pond-plunging pooches out of the water and away from the detritus in the trees did not make for a relaxing walk.

Antici-pointment is disillusionment in its bitterest form, and ours came with an added dilemma; we had too much time on our hands. It was still only the beginning of August, so in high season, we were confident our ultimate destination Hel, on Poland's north coast, would be crowded enough to live right up to its name.

Neither Mark nor I wanted to go near the revolting, polluted lake again. Although Lublin is 'The Gateway to the East', we were wary of crossing into nearby Belarus and Ukraine, since any sudden change to COVID rules could potentially bar us from re-entering the EU.

In addition, there was the small matter of the evolving conflict in Belarus, following the allegedly fraudulent re-election of its Kremlin-aligned dictator. On the positive side, we could visit Lublin and use the opportunity to see a few of the places we'd missed. Kazimierz Dolny and Zamość were only an hour away.

"We do need to do some jobs like laundry and shopping, and the campsite is a lovely, quiet place to relax for a while," I said. I had long since abandoned hope of a doctor's appointment.

Sometimes, our conversations resemble what you might expect to hear in a care home for the deaf and criminally insane. Mark muttered something unintelligible about a supermarket nearby.

"YOU SAW A COW FLAN?" I queried.

A trip to Kaufland will never be the same again.

Lublin is Eastern Poland's largest city and has twice been the country's capital, yet it is often overlooked as a destination. In 2007, it lost out to Wrocław in its bid to become the European Capital of Culture. Nevertheless, it has a vibrant arts scene and is known as 'The City of Festivals'.

To explore without the high-summer heat and crowds, we went in early. Next to the castle, Plac Zamkowy provided free parking. From there, it was an easy walk up into Plac Po Farze, which offered a panoramic view of the castle from the ruined stone outline of the old Parish Church, which had been demolished in the 19th century. The trademark regiments of tall, ornately painted town houses around the square were an immediate wow.

First things first, though. Our primary mission in any new place always involves a sugar hit, caffeine, and some time spent soaking up the ambience. The waitresses in the Trybunalska City Pub in the *rynek* (market square) were lovely. Without asking, they brought a bowl of water for the dogs and tended to our needs with effortless efficiency.

Heartbreak followed swiftly on the heels of this efficiency, though. The lady took our order so quickly I hadn't had time to fully peruse the menu. As I glanced further down, beyond the sweet treats we'd just ordered, I spotted an English Breakfast, available until 11.30 a.m. I was horrified. Few epicurian delights trump coffee and cake, but after an eighteen-month egg, bacon, and sausage drought, with the promise of beans, tomato and mushrooms (you can keep your hash browns) a Full English was the Holy Grail. Whether or not it came with proper brown sauce.

"Maybe we could join them again for breakfast tomorrow morning," I said to Mark, blissfully unaware of the sharks that lurked within the murky waters of our plans for the next twenty-four hours.

Further entertainment came in the form of a large chap opposite, with the tiniest white teacup dog. The café seating area was on a slightly raised wooden platform. His little fluff ball crept underneath, then refused to come out. Like a conjuror, the waitress produced a slice of ham as an incentive, but to no avail. The man interrupted his breakfast several times with attempts to coax her out, but she was having none of it. We dispatched Rosie and Lani as a welcoming committee. They elicited some barking from beneath the dais, but still no pup. Negotiations between Dog and Dogfather were ongoing when we paid our bill, but we saw him later and are happy to report them re-united.

For geometric pedants, which of course we are, Lublin's market square is actually an irregular trapezoid, with six narrow cobbled streets leading from it. The highly ornamented Renaissance town houses that surround it were built to replace wooden buildings destroyed in the fire of 1575. Over seventy percent of the buildings in the old town are original, and there is an ongoing programme of restoration. Some say the Blue House is the most beautiful. I rather liked the intricate patterns painted on the orangey-rust facade of Trybunalska, the setting for our failed Full English. The most haunting was definitely one which bore poster-sized black-and-white photographs of its former residents, who were killed in WWII.

The monumental Crown Tribunal/Old Town Hall building, which is now the Registry Office, dominates the centre of the trapezoid. Lublin's underground route starts in its vaults and takes you through the old wine cellars and prison. In 1637, the building hosted The Devil's Trial, one of Lublin's best known legends. The plot is much like Clint Eastwood's film, *Pale Rider,* without the six shooters, Stetsons, and spurs.

A wealthy nobleman, Kurdwanowski, robbed a poor widow and burned her out of her house because he had designs on her land. She took her case to the Crown Tribunal, but in keeping with local tradition, the not-so-nobleman had prepared his defence by bribing the judge and jury. When the court pronounced against her, the widow declared,

"If the Devil convicted me, it would have been a fairer trial."

That night, weeping tears of blood because human malice could out-evil even master badass Satan, The Almighty dispatched an unlikely God Squad to make amends. The posse, comprising Old Nick and a few horned demons, all sporting red robes instead of a distressed double-breasted overcoat and cowboy boots, set out to conduct a re-trial. If you have ever pondered the question, "The Devil, is he all bad?" Satan did offer the widow a fairer hearing than the judiciary and ordered Kurdwanowski to return her lands with compensation.

To underline his proclamation, Judge Satan slammed

his palm on to the table and scorched his hand print into the wood. The following day, the crooked adjudicators all broke their legs on the building's steps and their corrupt behaviour led to the dissolution of the Tribunal. The charred imprint of The Devil's Paw is on display in Lublin's Castle Museum.

We left the old town via the Kraków gate, *Brama Krakówska,* a gothic-style brick tower crowned with a shapely belfry and clock. *Brama Krakówska* is one of the few remains of the original medieval city walls and is a symbol of Lublin. A surprising musical medley serenaded us as we transitioned from old town to new. The eclectic repertoire included Ray Charles' *Hit the Road, Jack* and Abba's *Money, Money, Money*, but until you have heard Queen's *Bohemian Rhapsody* rendered on an accordion, Mamma Mia! You have never lived.

One of my favourite Gary Larson cartoons sums up everything you need to know about The Stomach Steinway. It depicts St. Peter at the gates of Heaven, separating saints from sinners. Those entering the Pearly Gates are given a harp. Those heading to Hades each get an accordion.

Imagine an eternity with that. Even without being out-evilled by humanity, it's enough to make Beelzebub quit dastardly deed making and become a principled judge in the Crown Tribunal. I can't help thinking that Freddie Mercury really meant to prelude Bohemian Rhapsody's guitar solo with the line,

"Beelzebub has a-ccordions put aside for meee, for meee, for MEEEEEE!"

The broad modern esplanade beyond led to Litewski Square and the multi-media fountain. At night, coloured lights illuminate the acres of water jets all shooting out of the pavement. On summer weekends, they project sound and light shows on to its liquid screen. During the day, it was more beige, the colour of the stone beneath, but provided a splendid solution to cooling off our hot dogs. Next to it, we found an oversized sign thoughtfully placed to remind amnesiacs where they were. It was the perfect location for The Fab Four to get their obligatory 'We Woz 'ere' postcard pic., with LUBLIN written in giant golden letters behind.

We walked back to Big Blue through the Grodzka Gate; the portal between the Christian centre and the Jewish quarter. I can't talk about Lublin without mentioning that it was renowned for religious tolerance and for over five hundred years, was home to one of the foremost Jewish communities in Europe. The Lublin Jews flourished after King Kazimierz Jagiellonczyk, one of The Great's descendants, granted them free trade in 1453. A third of Lublin's population was Jewish, and the city was world famous for its highly acclaimed *Chachmei Yeshiva Lublin* rabbinical academy.

Inevitably, this eminence led to horror under Nazi occupation. The dual carriageway that brought us into Lublin cuts across the former Jewish neighbourhood and the site of the Grand Synagogue, an architectural masterpiece built in 1567 to accommodate 3,000 worshippers. The Nazis re-purposed it to sort prisoners to send to death camps, then burned it to the ground. They also incinerated the contents of the Academy's library in the square. Eye witnesses say the books burned for twenty-four hours, and the Germans summoned a military band to drown out the distraught cries of the people as they watched the desecration of their history and culture.

With all the notoriety attached to places like Auschwitz, I was unaware that Lublin was really the epicentre of the Holocaust in Poland. It was the organisational headquarters of Operation Reinhard, Hitler's heinous programme of genocide, which aimed to murder the entire Jewish population of occupied Poland. Most of the clothes and valuables looted from the two million victims of the nearby death camps at Majdanek, Belzec, Treblinka, and Sobibór were sent to Lublin for consolidation and redistribution to Germany.

The Nazis usually hid their concentration camps to conceal their true purpose, but Majdanek is unusual, because although it is the second largest extermination camp, it stands blatantly on Lublin's outskirts. It is also one of the best preserved. So close to the border, a rapid advance by the Soviet Red Army liberated Majdanek months before Auschwitz. As such, they captured it intact, before its commander could destroy the evidence.

Estimates suggest that of Lublin's 43,000 Jews, only 230 survived the Holocaust.

Little wonder, then, that in Lublin, the nefarious nature of humanity caused God to cry tears of blood and the Devil to repent.

Near the Grodzka Gate, we passed beneath the life-sized sculpture of Jasza Mazur, 'The Magician of Lublin', walking a tightrope. Like the character who sought to escape his past in Nobel prizewinner Isaac Bashevis Singer's novel of the same name, our time had run out.

They say every cloud has a silver lining, although those that crowd on to our horizons are usually mushroom-shaped and lined with Polonium – an element discovered by the mother of radioactivity, Marie Salomea Skłodowska-Curie, and named after her home country.

We had deftly sidestepped the coronavirus outbreaks in Poland, but world events had finally caught up with us. As I read the evening news, I shared the bombshell with Mark,

"Apparently, France is 'bubbling with coronavirus cases and may be the next to come off the UK's safe travel list.'"

France was our route home. It was not just a question of health, we had a deadline. Big Blue's MOT safety test ran out in six weeks. Although there had been an MOT 'holiday' during the Britain's first coronavirus lockdown, it seemed unlikely that the DVLA (Driver and Vehicle Licensing Agency) would grant a grace period now if we got stuck abroad. No MOT meant invalid insurance. No insurance meant illegal to drive.

Also, with our house rented out and the government's Coronavirus Act meaning no chance of getting it back, we had no fixed abode where we could quarantine if we made it back to the UK from a red-listed country. Despite being effectively isolated in our caravan, we imagined campsites might not welcome guests from coronavirus hotspots, and like the cherry on the cake, exercising four dogs while isolating was the fissile neutron atop our mushroom cloud, primed and ready to detonate that shimmering polonium lining.

The Hel peninsula and Gdańsk on the north coast of Poland in September, when the crowds subsided, looked further away than ever. Our carefully laid plans to go to Hel in a hound cart had done exactly that.

"Let's leave Poland tomorrow and get a little closer to home," Mark said. "We might make it through France before the border closes down."

His quick route out of Poland would allow us to take in the former Luftwaffe prison Stalag Luft III. The prison camp for Allied airmen in Żagań is where the famous breakout fictionalised in the film *The Great Escape* took place, which seemed ironic in the circumstances. The enthralling sense of being immersed in history when you visit iconic sites is magical, but prudence dictated that we should make our own Great Escape as quickly as possible.

We were sorry to leave our lovely hosts but paid up and made an early start. They gave us bags of treats for the dogs and an English Lions flag. Even more shocking was our bill; just 60 Zł – about €12 – for two nights.

The intention was to break our journey about half way across the country near the palace at Nieborów, but that fissile neutron was teetering menacingly. As we pulled in, the campsite looked perfect; nestled in woodland, with a convivial café, and next to a petite military museum. Enquiries in the café revealed the campsite was closed, along with every other campsite in the area.

On the up side, a small non-nuclear silver lining shot out of this strato-cumulus, packing an Armstrong Siddely Viper jet engine.

Along with horses, the aforementioned Mr. Mercury, and TV Physicist Professor Brian Cox, aviation is one of my great loves. So, I was thrilled to get a photograph of Caravan Kismet in front of a PZL TS-11 Iskra – a Polish fighter training plane parked at the museum entrance.

If, like me, you also love a curious fact, Iskra is a gift

that keeps giving. It means 'Spark', which was the name of the Bolshevik underground newspaper produced by Lenin and Trotsky, among others, before they opened Pravda. The newspaper's motto was 'From a spark a fire will flare up', an epithet that can apply to many situations, including a global pandemic.

In the end, we traversed almost the entire country from the Ukrainian border to Germany in one day. Other than a distant view of Warsaw, there was literally nothing to see, so it was unsurprising that we did not encounter a single campsite between Nieborów and Poznań.

Poznań is one of Poland's oldest cities, but after our epic crossing, we had neither the time nor energy for sightseeing. All we wanted to do was eat, drink, and sleep. On that basis, I could live with the brick wall and industrial pipes that formed our view, but a banging rock festival in the park next door put paid to any thoughts of relaxation. The lake that looked so nice on the website was not unlike Zemborzyckie. There was unpleasant litter everywhere, including the trademark used sanitary items. The overpowering stench of a well-matured garbage truck hung in the air as we walked the dogs.

Tempting as it was to return to Posnania, the wonderfully named shopping centre we'd passed on the way in, for ease, we dined on site.

Vacillating between reception and the restaurant, we were told;

"Yes, the restaurant is open."

"No, we're shut."

"Yes, they're open."

"Okay, we're open but not doing food."

"Yes, they are doing food."

"Okay, you can have anything you want, so long as it's chicken and potato."

Over a beer and hard-won platter of reheated chicken and equally leathery potatoes, we reflected on our experience of Poland. Mark said,

"I wouldn't really recommend Central Poland for a road trip. There are some nice bits, but they are small, sometimes disappointing, and miles apart. The scenery is all just the same – there are no pretty villages or castles on hills. It's just miles of flat arable land, although I think places like Italy, France, and Romania, have spoiled us. There, even the boring bits in between the main sights are *magnifico.*

"With hindsight, I would have spent much more time in Kraków and the surrounding area, taking in Ojców and the salt mines. We've missed some fab places in the north and south, but the coast near Gdańsk will be packed this time of year, and I always intended to tie in the Tatra national park in the south with a visit to Slovakia."

We agreed we'd both had enough of the rudeness and dangerous, aggressive driving, but in Poland's defence, I added,

"Touring in a pandemic and the constant re-routing has added a lot of stress. We've had to keep our eye on the news, which is inevitably depressing. Then with all the mishaps, we've been in an almost constant state of anxiety.

"Plus, it's high season. Touristy places anywhere are awful in high season. We've missed loads of our planned destinations, which looked really nice, and usually, we meet and chat with people. We've hardly met or spoken to anyone here. There's much more of a language barrier

– there are so few English speakers – but I think people are keeping themselves to themselves much more because of COVID."

As usual, Mark summed it up perfectly.

"It's been a slightly awkward first meeting, but Poland would still make it to a second date."

We raised our glasses and finished our beer.

The following day, we would be in Berlin.

33

CHECKPOINT BRAVO, BERLIN AND A BOAR

If you go down in the woods today, you're in for a BIG surprise...

Sitting in the sun, overlooking tranquil waters, I wondered why I felt so out of sorts.

Our plans were constantly up in the air. Usually, that's a fun part of our nomad lifestyle; pursuing a recommendation here, or a must-see there. Recently, it had been more about infection spikes here and quarantine imposed there. Usually, we keep up with the headlines via satirical comedy shows on the radio. Sadly, while travelling in a pandemic, keeping abreast of the 'real' news had become a necessary evil.

The day before, we'd chased across almost the entire width of Poland, from Lublin to Poznań, because we felt the need to get closer to home, in case the borders closed. We had been looking forward to some windsurfing in Brittany, to make up for missing out on Poland's north coast, but with COVID-19 infections rising in France, that was not a given. In coronavirus times, uncertainty was the new certainty.

However, we found the positive side of being forced to watch the news. Had we not, we would have missed the cheeringly insane video of a middle-aged Berlin naturist giving chase to a wild boar, which had snatched a carrier bag containing his laptop, and made off with it.

Our home was City Camp Süd, in the Dreilinden woodland, close to Potsdam. We pitched right on the banks of the Teltow Canal, with a restful outlook towards the woods on the far bank. The utilitarian concrete buildings that housed the reception area and a three-storey watchtower in the centre of the campsite presented an immediate hint that the place had a past, but we could not have guessed at the extraordinary secret history we would stumble upon during our stay.

Following Germany's unconditional surrender in May 1945, the victorious Allied powers took over the country's governance. The Potsdam Agreement between the US, UK, and USSR divided the country into four administrative zones. The western areas came under the capitalist auspices of the Americans, British and French, and the eastern zone was ceded to the communist Soviet Union.

Berlin, once Germany's capital, was 110 km *inside* the Soviet bloc. It, too, was split into the same four administrative sectors, leaving West Berlin as an Allied outpost, surrounded completely by Soviet-controlled East Germany.

We knew the Teltow Canal, which ran between West Berlin and Potsdam in the former GDR (German Democratic Republic), marked the boundary between East and West Berlin. Only three decades earlier, our mere presence in this restricted location would have made us GDR border troops, staring across the water from East to West Berlin. What would have been our HQ building now housed the camp's hotel and reception.

Abandoned infrastructure is always spooky. We thought nothing of it when we launched our SUPs and paddled past the graffiti-covered footings of an old bridge, long since demolished.

On our first walk with our pooches, a sentry box confronted us on the path a few hundred yards from the campsite. It was near a garden gate, so however strange, we assumed it was decorative – in the same way some Brits make a statement with a red telephone box on their driveway. Further on, we came upon an incongruously huge bridge across the *Teltowkanal*.

This was no quaint stone arch that you'd expect to find on the Leeds-Liverpool canal. It was the width of Heathrow's number one runway. Its tarmac was crumbling and overgrown. We searched for other clues and found three flag poles, something that resembled a central reservation, and a rusting field telephone. It was unquestionably a place of some importance, but we had no idea what.

I made a beeline for an information board nearby, but it gave no hints about the bridge. Instead, it revealed that from 1961 when the Soviets built the Berlin Wall to seal East Berlin from the West, and 1989 when it fell, 136 people lost their lives in attempts to flee across it from East to West Germany.

During a global pandemic, we have learned the hard way that behind every impersonal death statistic lies a deeply human story. The sign shed light on one of these.

On June 15th 1965, West German businessman Herman Döbler and 21-year-old Elke Märtens had taken to the water for pleasure, as we had on our SUPs earlier that afternoon. June 15th was a similar carefree summer's day. Aboard Herman's motorboat, they set out from Wannsee and turned into the *Teltowkanal* at Kohlhasen Bridge. The East/West border was not clearly marked, although a full-width barrier blocked the waterway near the derelict bridge we'd just discovered. Unknown to Elke and Herman, however, the actual border was 100 m (330 ft) before the barrier.

Two border guards saw the boat stray into East German territory. One opened fire. Even though Elke immediately turned the vessel, four carefully aimed bullets connected with Herman's head and torso. He was dead before the boat reached the West Berlin bank. A bullet grazed Elke's head. She was badly injured, but survived.

Twenty-eight years later, in 1993, the guard who fired the fatal shots was brought to trial. He testified that Elke and Herman "provoked" him and that, "I decided to use my weapon to annihilate the border violators." The court convicted him of pre-meditated murder.

A faded map on the information board showed the route they took. The hairs on the back of my neck stood up as I studied it and shared my chilling conclusion with Mark,

"They must have been shot from the watchtower on the campsite."

A broad grassy ride swept through the forest directly away from the bridge, much wider than a firebreak.

"I think this was once a road – look at the raised banks on either side," I said to Mark.

A little further on, another large bridge, decorated with colourful graffiti, spanned the ride.

"That's a motorway bridge," I exclaimed. It seemed so out of place, abandoned in the middle of a dense forest.

The graffiti made me wonder whether it could be part of the Berlin Wall infrastructure. A few blocks of painted masonry had fallen down. Mark picked one up.

"What are you going to do with that?" I asked.

"Don't you think it will be cool to have a section of the Berlin Wall as a caravan levelling block?"

"Wow," I said. "YES!"

It took conversations with friends, fellow campers, and some dedicated internet research to piece together the dark history of the place.

The best-known border crossing between East and West Berlin was Checkpoint C, more famously called Checkpoint Charlie, if you pronounce the C using the NATO Phonetic Alphabet.

Yet, where there's a Charlie, there must also be an Alpha and Bravo. The derelict *Reichsautobahnbrücke* canal bridge we'd stumbled upon was the original location of the Allied Checkpoint Bravo.

In the American Sector at Dreilinden, Checkpoint Bravo accessed one of only three prescribed transit routes that crossed East German territory to access West Berlin from West Germany. Although less well known, it was possibly more important than Checkpoint Charlie, since it was the main motorway route. A journalist friend also told me,

"I may be wrong, but there's a bridge over that canal where they did all the spy swaps. The one I saw in films was like a small version of the Tyne bridge."

Old photos suggested that might have been the demolished bridge we'd paddled past that afternoon. The Glienicke Bridge, which crosses the Haval River in Potsdam, is the famous 'Bridge of Spies' featured in Steven Spielberg's film of the same name.

The ride we'd followed was the route of the AVUS motorway (*Automobil-Verkehrs-und Übungsstraße* – Automobile Traffic and Training Road). It connected Checkpoint Bravo in West Berlin's Dreilinden to the Drewitz entrance into East Germany, a few miles further along. The Germans knew the crossing as *Grenzübergangsstelle Drewitz-Dreilinden.*

Guards timed traffic as it passed between the Dreilinen and Drewitz checkpoints, and there were severe penalties for hesitation or deviation. Almost exactly the same rules as BBC Radio 4's comedy game show *Just A Minute,* where panellists have to speak for a minute without repetition, hesitation or deviation. I'm not sure about repetition. I said, I'm not sure about repetition (see what I did there?) but unlike the late, great Nicholas Parsons, who hosted *Just A Minute* for fifty years, GDR border guards were not famed for their sense of humour.

Until 1998, the AVUS also had form as a motor racing circuit. When not in use for motorsport, it provided the most direct *Autobahn* route between West Berlin and West Germany, but because it was built prior to WWII and partition, it snaked in and out of GDR territory. To enhance security, the authorities re-routed it in 1969 and moved the checkpoint.

What remains of its successor, Checkpoint Bravo II – The Sequel, is now mostly lost beneath the Europarc Dreilinden industrial estate, through which we passed on our approach to the campsite. It encompassed a vast area, although much of it had been parking to accommodate vehicles awaiting cumbersome border checks and paperwork – similar to the M20 in Kent post Brexit. The surviving part of Bravo II resembles a bright red motorway service station and is still visible from the *Autobahn* A115 – we saw it subsequently on our way into Berlin. In one of its nearby watchtowers, there is a small Checkpoint Bravo Museum, but that was another victim of COVID closure.

Although the receptionist said she knew nothing of City Camp Süd's past, she handed over a key to let us look inside the campsite's GÜSt (*Grenzübergangsstelle* – border crossing point) watchtower. It contained a few signs, several pairs of jackboots and other relics, along with the smell of old Bakelite and a palpably sobering atmosphere.

Our neighbours, puppy parents of Mocha, had confirmed that the fatal shots fired at Herman did indeed come from the campground.

Unknown to us, our doggie walk had joined a section of the *Berliner Mauerweg* – a 160 km (99 mile) commemorative trail that follows the outline of the Berlin Wall. The placard we'd seen about Elke and Herman was one of twenty-nine along the way, placed to commemorate those killed.

In 2012, the city auctioned off the 3.7-acre plot that comprised the original Checkpoint Bravo. A mystery buyer secured it with a single bid of the minimum asking price, €45,000. The anonymous owner is prohibited from building commercial or rental properties there, but what the future holds for this haunting historic site is unknown.

Yet, can you believe that uncovering an enormous chunk of A-Class Cold War history is not the big surprise I promised you down in the woods?

To appease my photo-phobic husband, I had not taken my camera on our first walk, thinking there would be nothing much to see. Obviously, this meant I had to drag him around the circuit again to bag all the photographs I'd missed. Close to the graffiti-covered motorway bridge, we heard a kerfuffle in the woodland. The Terrible Two, Rosie and Lani, shot into the trees, presumably on the scent of a bird or something. Moments later, they shot back out at the sort of velocity you'd associate with being fired from a cannon. Yelping and yipping, they both had their tails straight up in the air.

In keeping with the day's spirit of discovery, I reflected silently, *Ah. Now I understand the origin of the term 'high tailing it'.*

The midsection of four sturdy brown legs materialised in the scrubby space beneath the forest proper. As I looked more closely, I thought,

Is that a Rottweiler? You'd think such a big dog would have someone with it, but I can't see a soul.

Back at the caravan, Mark revealed his parallel ponderings, "The shape in the trees attached to the legs suddenly became clear, like when you stare at one of those magic eye pictures. That was when I yelled,

'It's a wild boar!'"

If you ever think your day's work is hard, consider Kenya's Dorobo people. They 'hunt' by psyching out lions to steal part of their kill. Their technique is to stroll slowly and deliberately towards a pride of apex predators at the moment they are consumed by a feeding frenzy. The Dorobo's only defence is to make themselves seem bigger by walking side by side. I can't vouch for the boar's thought process, but as the human-boar staring contest unfolded (our pack of throat-tearing guard dogs was nowhere to be seen) it thankfully reconsidered its charge.

Confronted by the terrifying vision of Mark and I gawping, I mean channelling our Jedi mind tricks, it remained on the treeline and opted not to break cover.

Later, the advice I read on *How To Survive A Boar Attack* came straight from the GÜSt Border Guard Manual; 'Shoot it, preferably in the head'.

Not much help if you're unarmed and in the open.

Running is not an option. Your average boar can out-sprint and out-hurdle Jesse Owens, especially over rough ground. A three-foot fence is no barrier to a boar, and they can clamber out of a six-foot pit. Yet despite their suiform superpowers, cloven hooves have disadvantages. In the absence of 'a car or boulder at least five feet high' upon which to seek refuge, apparently our best bet would have been to shin up a conifer. The top tip offered if you're ever gored by a charging *Wildschwein* is to play dead. Don't move a muscle or you risk a second assault.

We're 'glass half full' people, even though the base of our receptacle is generally awash with naval mines, box jellyfish, and baby piranhas. Pigs can't fly, but wild boar can swim, so it would come as no surprise if we found a few porcine triathletes in there as well, clinking their tusks against our ice cubes.

What goes around comes around, and in the spirit of irony, we fed The Fab Four wild boar dog food for dinner.

But, even on the way back to the caravan, Mark and I had already put a positive spin on our wildlife encounter,

"Well. At least we weren't naked and it hadn't stolen our laptop."

34

A POTTER AROUND POTSDAM

We Try Sans Souci – Living Without A Care

One city. Sixteen palaces. Each with its own unique landscaped park surrounding it.

It's no wonder they call Potsdam 'Germany's Versailles'. It is a veritable fairy-tale kingdom, which embodies the Age of Enlightenment's ethos; 'A picturesque, pastoral dream to remind residents of their relationship with nature and reason'.

Not only that, it is also Europe's Hollywood. The famous Babelsburg Studios has turned out classic films for more than a century, claiming bragging rights as the world's oldest large-scale film studio. Its impressive list of credits includes everything from Fritz Lang's iconic 1927 film *Metropolis* to *The Bourne Ultimatum,* with Spielberg's Academy Award-winning *Bridge of Spies* thrown in. It would have been rude not to, with the actual bridge, *Glienicker Brücke,* just on the doorstep.

I knew none of this. I'd heard of Potsdam only

because of its pivotal role in recent history. This scenic satellite of Berlin hosted the court of the Kingdom of Prussia and was once home to Otto Von Bismarck's Second Reich; hence the plethora of palaces.

Potsdam is where WWI started and is where Adolf Hitler laid the first foundations of his dictatorship in a historic handshake with President Paul von Hindenburg. It is where WWII finished; where Japan was issued an ultimatum of 'surrender or destruction'; and where the post war balance of power was decided at the Potsdam Conference, which begat the Cold War.

None of this momentous history was evident as we drove through peaceful tree-lined suburbs to Frederick the Great's summer palace in Sanssouci park. The restored Sanssouci windmill dominated our approach. A giant stone and wooden structure with 12 m (40 ft) sails, it towers nearly 26 m (85 ft) into the air.

Frederick the Great, known as 'The Old Fritz', was King of Prussia from 1740 until his death in 1786. A legend claims that noise from the mill disturbed His Greatness, who offered to buy it. The tale alleges that when the miller refused, Big Fred threw his royal toys out of the pram and threatened to take the mill anyway, to which the miller replied,

"Of course, Your Majesty could do that – if it were not for the Supreme Court in Berlin," which translates as, "Stuff that in your pipe and smoke it, your Maj. Even you're not above the law."

Apparently, this never happened – and might just have been a bit of 'Hark at my benevolence for not shafting the prole!' spin by His Greatness. Allegedly, however, Frederick, 'The Philosopher of Potsdam', did once say, "A crown is merely a hat that lets rain in", which suggests a degree of humility.

Rumours say he rather liked the rustic charm of a windmill at his rural summer retreat. The name Sanssouci sums up the spirit of the place. It comes from the courtly French, *sans souci,* meaning 'without worries' and epitomised his ideal of living without a care.

When talking about the many Sanssouci palaces, the word opulent doesn't really cut it. I have never seen magnificence on such a scale. Imagine slightly more than a baker's dozen of Britain's grandest stately homes spirited into vast acres of immaculately manicured gardens, after a bit of gilding for good measure. Potsdam is a housing estate of palaces.

Although I was never a fan, my mischievous side couldn't help imagining Sanssouci as the setting for a highly upmarket version of *Brookside*, a defunct UK soap opera set in Liverpool's Croxteth estate. Perhaps in a new plot twist, the residents of Brookside Close could all win the Lottery and move to Potsdam. It would give great scope for their challenging and increasingly improbable story lines, such as the body under the patio at Number 10, and the mystery virus that struck in 1995 and forced them all into lockdown...

Parked near the windmill, our potter started at the main Sanssouci palace, a long, single-storey building painted in a joyful shade of primrose, with a verdigris cupola at its centre. It followed the Brontosaurus school of architecture; thin at one end, fatter in the middle, then thin again at the other end.

At the front of its colonnaded and statue-studded rococo façade, elegant terraced vineyards were a nod to

Old Fritz's rural theme, while at the base, the Great Fountain and lake mirrored the stepped splendour above.

From the lake, a wide avenue took us through less formal parkland, veined with waterways where we saw a heron fishing. Sadly, even though Frederick used to enjoy Sanssouci with his dogs, our pups had to stay on their leads, even in the bits that looked like pasture.

The gardens are famous for their fountains, although as the temperature soared into the mid-thirties, we made use of irrigation sprayers on our progress around the grounds to keep The Pawsome Foursome chilled.

Through the trees, the sun glinted on a golden figure floating aloft, wielding an umbrella. Not Mary Poppins. We had reached the Chinese House, an opulent parasol-topped pavilion. *Chinoiserie* – anything Chinese – was the height of baroque fashion.

Built in a trefoil (clover-leaf) shape around a circular centre, the Chinese House is a delicate mint green, surrounded by gilded pillars and statues of Chinese revellers eating, drinking and living the good life. The characters look a little less oriental than they might, since the sculptors apparently used local people as models.

We sat for a while in the honey-coloured shade of vines at Schloss Charlottenhof, where our water-loving Ruby was most put out that the lake was off limits, just because it was in front of a Neoclassical Roman villa.

Fast forward forty-odd years from Frederick the Great to Crown Prince Frederick William (who became King Fred Will IV), who had added Schloss Charlottenhof on the foundations of an old farmhouse. His dad, Fred Will III, gave him the real estate bordering Sanssouci for

Christmas in 1825; an imaginative gift, if a little difficult to wrap.

Charlottenhof takes its name from its former owner, Maria Charlotte von Gentzkow, although the heir to the throne called it 'Siam' (today's Thailand), which was considered the land of the free. He remodelled the grounds into English-style gardens that connect with the main Sanssouci parkland. Italophile Frederick William IV also designed the nearby Roman Baths, where we took advantage of a shell-shaped fountain to cool off The Fab Four once again, while no one was looking.

At the western side of the park, a mile-and-a-half from the Obelisk that marks the eastern boundary, Fabulous Freddie the Great constructed the 200-room *Neues Palais* (New Palace). He built it to celebrate Prussia's victory over the Habsburgs at the end of the Seven Years' War, which ceded Silesia (originally – and now once again – part of Poland) to Prussia.

In contrast to the modest ten-room refuge of Sanssouci, the New Palace was a formal venue to receive and entertain dignitaries. Almost a century and a half after Fred The Great's death, it became the principal residence of Queen Victoria's favourite grandson, Kaiser Wilhelm II of Prussia, and is where he signed the Declaration of War in 1914.

We returned from our potter via Fred Will IV's Orangery Palace, a 300-metre façade built in the style of the Uffizi in Florence. With buildings like this to his credit, no wonder they knew him as the 'romanticist on the throne'. The surrounding Paradise Garden is home to many exotic plants. The University of Potsdam still uses his Botanical Garden for teaching.

In much need of sustenance and shade, we stopped at the windmill for refreshment and after braving a lengthy queue, I tried my first iced coffee. It was the most disgusting thing I have ever tasted – just like a normal coffee that had gone cold: a sensation I remember all too well from the heady days of having four puppies in the house. Like many first-time parents, I never managed to drink a cuppa before it had gone stone cold.

As with Kraków, we needed much more than a day to see Potsdam properly.

We didn't touch the Babelsburg Park or the Cecilienhof Palace, where the Potsdam Conference took place from 17 July to 2 August 1945, which shaped the future of post war Europe. I would have liked to see the Garrison Church, where on The Day of Potsdam, 21st March 1933, the popular, newly elected right-wing Chancellor, Adolf Hitler, celebrated the re-opening of the Reichstag following a fire.

Hitler chose this date carefully to commemorate the inauguration of Imperial Germany's first Reichstag on the same day in 1871. Hitler shook hands with Reich President Paul von Hindenburg to seal the 'marriage of the old grandeur and new power'. The notoriety of the Day of Potsdam shimmers down through history, since it sowed the seeds of 1933's Enabling Act, which opened up Hitler's path to dictatorship.

The Enabling Act granted absolute authority to the Nazi Cabinet, who could then bypass the Reichstag, President von Hindenburg, and the Constitution. Then, in the Night of the Long Knives, they simply murdered those who opposed them, thus completing Germany's alarmingly swift slither down the snake from liberal democracy to authoritarian dictatorship.

Does this remind you of any other popular right-wing leaders? I won't even mention Trump, but former British PM, Boris Johnson, who reputedly models himself on Churchill, expelled all the moderates who opposed him from the Tory party, including Winston Churchill's grandson. He also caused discomfort by avoiding parliamentary scrutiny while wielding the extraordinary powers granted to his government through the very enabling Coronavirus Act 2020. This law also forced the media to toe the government line on coronavirus reporting. Then, among many other freedoms, his controversial Police, Crime, Sentencing, and Courts bill threatens the fundamental democratic right to peaceful protest.

But like *Brookside's* preposterous storyline about a killer plague taking over the world in 1995, we all know that could never happen.

History couldn't repeat itself, could it?

35

A FIGHT AT THE OPERA AND OTHER STARTLING TALES, BERLIN

A Manhunt, A Fight at the Opera, and Berlin's Answer to the Total Perspective Vortex

Travel throws up all kinds of odd and unexpected scenarios. Fixing caravan brakes and visiting vets and dentists in France. Sorting out a flat battery in the Czech Republic, and finding replacement tyres in Poland. All run-of-the-mill stuff to the perpetual nomad.

However, I never envisaged launching an international missing person hunt from Berlin.

At 6 a.m., when we received the phone call, we were already driving into the city to avoid stress and traffic.

"I'm thinking of taking loads of pills and alcohol and ending it all."

Our friend Stuart's cosy, self-contained life had shattered when his long-term partner had left. Shortly afterwards, he was diagnosed with an aggressive, incurable cancer and lost his mum, while in the process of relocating to a new and isolated locale just before the UK's first COVID-19 lockdown. Once there, he knew no one, had no support network, and was so terrified of catching coronavirus he refused to leave the house.

My response of, "Oh Stuart, please don't," was perhaps not the most profound, but it came from the heart. He's a beautiful, gentle soul; ill-equipped to cope with this world, and we love him.

I gestured at Mark to pull over, as the phone signal in Europe's leading industrial nation was unreliable, and we talked.

"I feel sick. I think the cancer's come back and I need to go to hospital. But I don't want to die alone in hospital."

I have never had to talk someone down from suicide. I did my best to listen and reassure him.

"But, Stuart, all your tests were clear. You're a walking miracle – you defied medical science. If you still had cancer, it would have shown up."

After an hour, he told me he felt better. I had said he could call us anytime, which he did just as we were trying to find the entrance to a car park in central Berlin. With me removed from the navigation equation, Mark somehow entered a tunnel and we ended up six miles from the city centre – almost as far out as the campsite – when our intention was simply to nip around the block and return to the *Parkplatz*.

Without the added worry of our friend in dire need, driving in Berlin was nerve-racking, mostly because of the kamikaze bicycles. They took and offered no quarter. Even when you're on a green light filter to the right, a cyclist might shoot up to go straight on, and seemingly has priority. The Teutonic abuse we received from one *Radfahrer* certainly suggests this is so. He was so determined not to apply the brakes, he would have broadsided our van deliberately had we not executed a swift reverse to get out of his way.

It was not the short, relaxed mosey into the capital we had planned. Despite climbing out of bed at 5.20 a.m., we didn't park up until 9.30.

I was starving and needed the loo, so we sat at what looked like a pavement café, with people tucking into hearty breakfasts. We realised too late it was a hotel. Mark ordered coffee and waited patiently for someone to bring a menu while I used the facilities. Thankfully, when we sought to secure breakfast, they got our order spectacularly wrong. I say thankfully because on perusal of the menu, a single American breakfast cost €32. Two would have blown our food budget for the week. Welcome to the city.

Breakfast, when it arrived, was a saucer bearing two eggs and two slivers of bacon, both cold, plus two glasses of lukewarm milk, masquerading as *caffe latte*.

"I ordered flat whites," Mark whispered.

Seemingly, coffee for two was a concept they could grasp, but supplying a brace of breakfasts for a pair of patrons was an extravagant leap of logic. We were relieved, because the bill for our meagre rations still came to €17; two nights' campsite fees in Poland.

London has Big Ben; Paris the Eiffel Tower; and Berlin, the Brandenburg Gate. We reached it past the tree-filled Tiergarten.

The monumental gate itself is massive and impressive, crowned with the Roman goddess Victoria in a *quadriga* (four-horse chariot), wielding a lance bearing the Prussian eagle. Napoleon Bonaparte once kidnapped the statue and sent Victoria to Paris, but she was restored to her proper place when Prussia got its own back and defeated him. They added the iron cross wreathed in oak leaves to her lance as a 'Yah, boo, sucks,' celebration of Prussia's triumph over France.

Yet what surrounds one side of the most iconic and Instagrammable shot of Berlin can only be described as a big old load of *Scheiße.*

The Allies bombed Pariser Platz to rubble during the war, but although the government restored the Brandenburg gate, what was once Berlin's grandest square is now modern, grey, and soulless. It is definitely not the backdrop of choice for most Brandenburg selfies.

As usual, Mark had forgotten to bring his carefully marked-up sightseeing map, so we went to the tourist information office. A sign on the door said it opened at 10 a.m. Since it was ten to, we waited. Nothing happened. Upon investigation, we noticed a further note claiming it didn't open until 10:30, so we wandered over to the Reichstag, Germany's seat of Government.

In Douglas Adams' *Hitchhiker's Guide to the Galaxy*, the ego-on-legs that is Zaphod Beeblebrox is the only person known to have survived the Total Perspective Vortex (TPC). The TPC is a horrifying form of torture. For an instant, it shows its victims a glimpse of themselves amid the enormity and vastness of the Universe. The realisation of their absolute and utter insignificance is so demoralising, they fall dead immediately.

Standing next to the Reichstag gave me that same sensation. It is a colossal, solid, and belligerent building that oozes power.

(The TPC actually exposed Beeblebrox to a computer-generated simulation, which showed HIM to be the most important thing in the universe. Besides allowing him to survive, this did not surprise him at all.)

Nearby, we got to the paved banks of the River Spree, where brass plaques marked the course of the Berlin wall. It was easy to see how the *Berliner Mauer* had just been plonked down, arbitrarily splitting neighbourhoods, streets, and families.

As I mentioned earlier, at the end of WWII in 1945, following the Potsdam Agreement, Germany was divided into East and West, while the city of Berlin was split into four zones. Allied powers occupied the three western sectors, while, like the rest of East Germany, East Berlin was under Soviet control. This left West Berlin a capitalist enclave amid communist East Germany.

A flow of refugees to the west prompted the East German government to erect the Inner German Border in 1952. This separated East and West Germany, although travel between East and West Berlin was still possible. Berlin became the leaky bucket through which East Germans could escape poverty and repression for the more affluent and liberal west. Estimates suggest 3.5 million of the brightest and best, almost 20 per cent of East Germany's population, defected.

Clearly, Joseph Stalin was not happy with this 'Brain Drain'. He needed professional people of working age to rebuild East Germany after the war. In addition, this stream of emigrants was an insult to the communist ideal. (I love the irony that building a wall to prevent people escaping his communist Nirvana was not.)

The situation reached a head on 13th August 1961.

Known as Barbed Wire Sunday, East German police and military closed the border between East and West Berlin at midnight. Through the early hours, they ripped up roads, installed mines, and erected barbed wire fences. Troops had orders to shoot defectors on sight.

By the morning, families were broken up, neighbourhoods divided, and those with jobs in the West were summarily unemployed.

Construction of the 155 km (96 miles) of 4 m (13 ft) high concrete wall to fortify the original barrier started two days later. There were actually two walls, separated by a barren corridor of land known as 'the death strip'. Booby trapped and mined, the death strip offered no cover for escapees and a clear line of fire for border guards, who were posted in 302 watch towers along its length.

The plaques we saw on the ground formed part of the *Berliner Mauerweg* we'd encountered at Dreilinden. Some bore the names of those killed as they tried to escape.

When they opened eventually, the tourist office charged Mark €1 for a map. Tourist maps have been free in every other city we've ever visited.

While Mark was negotiating terms with the tourist office, I contemplated the moving memorial to the Sinti and Roma in the Tiergarten. After visiting Romania, my understanding and respect for these wonderful but persecuted people has grown massively. Half a million Roma are among the forgotten victims of the Holocaust. The circular pool of black water reflected the sky. The memorial, which documents the timeline of the genocide, is in sight of the Reichstag.

I felt it was a grave reminder of how destructive nationalism can be, just as it is once again on the rise across Europe. During our recent transit of Poland, the news highlighted that some Polish towns had declared themselves LGBT-free zones, and Poland had recently withdrawn from the Istanbul Convention, an international treaty to prevent violence against women.

On our way to grab a coffee and some calories to top up our costly but insubstantial breakfast, we ran into Eric Clapton Man. Such conversations happen when you wander the city streets with four dogs.

"My favourite band is Cream," he announced as he admired The Pawsome Foursome. "My favourite guitarist is Clapton. I was going to see him in Antwerp, but it's cancelled until next year because of COVID."

I told him, "Mark is from near Ripley, where Clapton's mum ran the post office for many years."

"Ah, Ripley," he replied, misty eyed. He knew all about Ripley, a tiny village in Surrey. "I read about it in Clapton's biography."

On the Pariserplaza, an imposing row of embassies towered above us. We found a café where a woman with arms the size of hams, who looked like she'd been hit in the face with a spade, almost hurled coffee and croissanty-type things at me. Service comprised yelling at the stupid foreigner in German through a facemask. I knew asking for a flat white designer *Kaffee* was pushing my luck, but my polite request for *Milch* was misunderstood or disregarded, because the yelling spade-faced woman slammed two black filter coffees on the counter and turned her not insubstantial back on me.

Our wanderings took us through elegant boulevards

to Checkpoint Charlie, the most famous crossing point between East and West Berlin. It was the location of prisoner exchanges and daring escapes in cars, such as that of Heinz Meixner, who slid under the barrier in a convertible Austin Healey with the windscreen removed. It was also the site of a tank standoff over a visit to the opera that nearly sparked World War III.

The furore started on 22nd October 1961 when, on his way to the opera in East Berlin, US diplomat Allan Lightner refused to show his documents to East German border police.

The US did not formally recognise the East German state, so Lightner argued that only Soviet officials could inspect his papers. He maintained that showing them to the East Germans would not only be a tacit acknowledgement of sovereignty, it also undermined agreed permissions to cross the border. To strengthen his case, Lightner employed his full repertoire of diplomatic skills, and returned with jeeps and armed militia.

Then US General Lucius D. Clay weighed in to defend Allied rights "by force if necessary" and deployed ten M-48 tanks. Predictably, the East Germans replied with ten T-55 tanks. For sixteen hours on 27th October, the Fight at the Opera continued with tanks staring each other down across Checkpoint Charlie. The world stood on the brink of war until Khrushchev and Kennedy agreed to play nicely.

Since we had the pups with us, we didn't go inside the Checkpoint Charlie Museum building, but spent a while perusing the extensive open-air display. As with Potsdam, we'd seen only a fraction of what Berlin offers. However, as the temperature scorched its way into the mid-thirties (mid-nineties) once again, two beaten tourists couldn't summon the energy to see any more of the sights we'd marked on our forgotten map.

Cities are not normally our thing, but it was very moving to visit somewhere so darkly iconic, which has played such a huge role in modern history. I found the small things most sobering – like the Roma Sinti memorial, and running my fingers over nondescript bricks in a section of wall by the Reichstag. Rather than division, this piece of wall symbolised unity, and the beginning of the end of communism in Eastern Europe.

It came from a Gdańsk shipyard and was a section of the wall climbed by Lech Wałęsa on 14th August 1980, when he organised the strike that led to the formation of the *Solidarność* – Solidarity trade union. Popular at home and abroad, particularly in East Germany, the Solidarity movement paved the way for the democratisation of Poland, and helped set in motion events that would eventually lead to the fall of the Berlin Wall in 1989.

We had touched base with Stuart several times throughout the day, and he had seemed okay. However, at 4 a.m. the following morning, he phoned us.

We were fast asleep and by the time we leapt out of bed to grab the handset, the phone rang off. We called back immediately, but there was no answer.

We redialled a few more times, but he did not pick up. Despite our concern, we both eventually drifted back into sleep. As soon as we awoke, we tried to call again, before we were distracted by the day's tasks; to get out a caravan blocked in between an electricity post and a small campervan that had cosied up to our rear.

Throughout the day, Stuart's phone went straight to answerphone. By mid-afternoon, we called the local hospital in desperation to see if he had been admitted. He hadn't. Then, we felt we had no choice but to try the police.

I assure you that isn't easy when you're out of the country. British emergency numbers like 999 and 101 don't work from abroad, but we found the number for his local police station on the internet. When Mark rang, a recorded message instructed him to ring 101.

While Mark played telephone tag, trying to contact friends, relatives, and the police, I emailed the wonderful charity, Missing People, who replied immediately with lots of helpful advice.

Eventually, Mark spoke to a person. Despite explaining that someone considering suicide had gone missing, they passed us from pillar to post with no sense of urgency. When we actually reached a man who we'd been told could help, he said,

"You need to call 101."

Exasperated, Mark said, "As I explained, we're abroad and can't ring 101. Our friend could be lying dead on the floor."

At that point, the man agreed to send an ambulance to check on Stuart.

I had mixed feelings shortly afterwards, when Stuart finally called us back and demanded,

"Why on earth did you ring an ambulance?"

"You called us at 4 a.m. and we've not been able to contact you all day. After our conversation yesterday, you must understand we were really worried," Mark explained.

The reply was as unexpected as it was bright and breezy.

"Oh. I was tired because I'd been up all night. I turned off my phone so I could get some sleep."

Although I was delighted that Stuart was safe and well, I can't deny that a small part of me was channelling another Victoria. Not the Roman goddess of victory atop the Brandenburg Gate, but the grandmother of Kaiser Wilhelm II.

One was not amused.

36

WITCHES, WURST, AND WALPURGISNACHT

We Plot a Course through Campsite Politics, Travel Shaming, and 'The Worst Crisis in History'

Peter Ustinov said, "Love is an endless act of forgiveness." For Mark and me, living the dream had become an endless act of problem solving.

We had done our best. At the first hint that France was 'bubbling with coronavirus' and might lock down, we'd made a homeward dash from the Ukrainian border. Now, in Germany, we had run out of time.

The news reported,

... anyone arriving in the UK from France or the Netherlands after 04:00 BST on Saturday 15th August will be required to quarantine for 14 days.

With more than half a million British tourists in France, never mind the rest of Europe, Eurotunnel claimed to be *"pretty much booked"* and *"didn't have the capacity to get additional travellers back to the UK."*

Industry group, Airlines UK, described the move as *"a*

blow amid the worst crisis in its history" and to top it all, the French government promised *"reciprocal measures."*

Could the day get any better?

At the time, we were still co-ordinating an international manhunt for our missing friend Stuart. Our to-do list now required us to deal not only with German campsite bureaucracy, but returning a caravan and four dogs to the UK without entering Holland or France, plus enduring a new form of abuse known as 'Travel Shaming' when we pleaded for help and advice online. The anonymous trolls on the internet deemed all travel irresponsible. They expressed their summary judgements without bothering to gather facts, of course. Being unable to return home after being stranded abroad by circumstances beyond your control was not an adequate excuse.

Our campsite in Thale was the type where you feel the management would be a lot happier with no customers to interfere with a routine smooth enough to make baby oil jealous. Blocked in at our previous site, we arrived with minutes to spare. Reception closed between 1 p.m. and 3 p.m., but quite how forcibly closure was enforced, we didn't yet realise.

After a bit of a kerfuffle in German between the staff, which I roughly translated as, "There's a huge British caravan just driven in. Are we expecting it?" they awarded us pitch number 9. In coronavirus times, for once, we'd had the foresight to book. The receptionist barked out instructions,

"Caravan doors must all face one way. Car at the front of the pitch."

It was a sensible rule. The pitches were so small that if the doors faced each other, you would likely mount your neighbour as you exited your van, and that would definitely break social distancing rules. Plus, there was nowhere else to put the car.

However, I had to return to reception and explain that pitch number 9 was not an option. The receptionist poo poohed my claim of insufficient room to manoeuvre.

When I asked if we could have the empty pitch next door, she looked at me like I'd asked to barbeque her children, and replied, "Definitely not."

She took the trouble to walk over to our pitch in order to prove me wrong. Even though I mimed the path of the swing to demonstrate that our caravan tow-hitch would unavoidably clobber a nearby motorhome as we pushed it in, her appraisal of the problem was swift.

"Ah. No motor mover."

I really couldn't be bothered to argue yet again that a motor mover is useless when there simply isn't enough room to move.

"You should put the caravan on the other side of the pitch," she announced.

"We can't," I argued. "That requires a much tighter turn."

Once more, we proposed a radical solution. Was there any way we could claim the vacant but curiously *verboten* pitch number 8?

By now, we had the added pressure of a queue of traffic waiting to pass, as we had blocked the one-way access road around the campground.

After a prolonged rummage back at reception, she granted us special dispensation to occupy pitch number 8. Then, without a motor mover, Mark shattered all expectations but mine by reversing straight onto the two lines where the wheels were supposed to go, with the door facing in the correct direction.

The only problem now was that we needed supplies from the supermarket, but found ourselves imprisoned between the hours of 1 and 3 p.m. When I approached the receptionist at 13:05 and asked her to open the barrier, which she was standing right next to, she snapped, "It's lunchtime." turned her back and walked away.

There is a large theme park in Thale and, at the campsite, a clientele to match. The scent of vape hung heavy in the air, while screaming children tore along the pedestrian walkways on their bikes. Parents left them to it, stealing a moment to punctuate their puffs with vats of wine, and lakes of lager. We made our escape on foot.

The Harz Mountains in Saxony-Anhalt is the land of German fairy tales: a world of dark forests, gushing rivers, and mysterious peaks, shrouded in mist. Once, it was a spiritual centre of pagan worship.

With a population who toiled deep beneath the earth in silver mines, it was a fertile breeding ground for fables and legends. Jacob and Wilhelm, a pair of academic siblings, collected and published the area's rich folklore. They are better known as The Brothers Grimm.

While *Grimms' Fairy Tales* is available in over 100 languages and has kept The Disney Company in royalties since they released *Snow White* in 1937, a lesser-known body of work is the *Grimms' German Dictionary*. Their lexicon ended abruptly at *Frucht* (fruit), although as we saw in the Dr. Johnson episode of the BBC's historical sitcom *Blackadder III,* compiling a dictionary is a tough gig. After accidentally incinerating Dr. Johnson's manuscript, on pain of death, Rowan Atkinson's character vowed to re-write Johnson's masterpiece overnight.

He got as far as 'Aardvark'.

I have to say the town of Thale was more Grimms' Dictionary than Grimms' Fairy Tale. Neighbouring Quedlinburg and Wernigerode are so unbearably picturesque that Quedlinburg's centre, filled with Germany's best collection of around 2,000 creaky half-timbered buildings, is a UNESCO World Heritage site, and a destination on Saxony-Anhalt's scenic *Straße der Romanik* (Romanesque Road).

The jumble of cobbled streets and steeply gabled gingerbread houses that one might expect in a settlement that dates to the 10th century and claims the title *Thale sagenhaft* (Legendary Thale) was notably absent. There are a few historic buildings, but read any description of Thale and it fails to mention the town's ugly modern centre, and cuts straight to the outrageously spectacular natural surroundings.

Although home to an iron works since 1445, Thale's more recent claim to fame (and fortune) is Europe's oldest sheet steel enamel factory, which dates to 1831. Once, it was responsible for ten per cent of the world's production.

When they covered Edwin Starr's original, Liverpool band *Frankie Goes to Hollywood* answered the question 'War (What is it good for?)'

You might agree with Frankie and Starr's appraisal of *absolut nichts,* but Thale begs to differ. When you've had a manufacturing monopoly on steel helmets since 1934, war is extremely good for business.

With excellent railway connections, tourism was the

unlikely progeny of Thale's industrial heritage. The radon-rich Hubertus (Healing) Spring and the spectacular and legend-filled Bode Gorge attracted thousands of visitors each year, along with notable poets such as Goethe, Heine, and Quedlinburg boy, Klopstock.

The tourist information office in the train station was a slight misnomer. It had very little information for tourists, and could shed no light on the *Mythenweg* (myth trail), which I had to look up on the internet.

This is a trail of horse shoes embedded in pavements which guides you around the town, taking in statues of characters from Norse mythology, such as Sleipnir; Wotan's eight-legged horse. Certainly, Sleipnir could provide a plentiful supply of shoes to mark the way, although I remain none the wiser about the Norse connection to Thale.

We bought a walking map to peruse over lunch in the cute Anatolia Bistro next door, which was so dog friendly it even had a Mutts Only menu.

In Anatolia, my time had come. I felt compelled to sample a dish so close to Germany's heart that it was the subject of a novel and play. It has its own museum in Berlin, and the car maker *Volkswagen*'s butchery division produces seven million of them a year. I'm talking about Germany's national delicacy; *Currywurst*.

They credit Berlin's Herta Heuwer with inventing *Currywurst*. Given ketchup and curry powder by British soldiers, she thought, "I know. I'll stick that on a sausage."

My first taste of this bestselling street snack left me wondering.

Why had I never thought to combine curry sauce with a steamed sausage? It truly is the food of the gods.

After lunch, we followed a trail into the Bodetal. It passed through the unbelievably busy Funpark and a mini golf course, but when we departed the motorway-like *Goetheweg* and crossed to the rougher track to the left of the river, the dogs could run free.

The path rose steeply up the walls of the gorge, through a dank mossy forest that oozed primordial serenity. It was so lovely we walked for miles before deciding it would be rude to miss the top. With impeccable timing, a strap on my sandal broke.

A couple of lads descended past us. I think I inquired if it was far to the summit, *"Is est lang der Kopf?"*

They fired something at me in rapid German. My blank look encouraged them to speak more slowly. The only thing I understood was "900 metres."

I mimed 'up' or 'length' and they mimed back 'length', so we carried on. With a substandard sandal, a steep rocky ascent was preferable to a steep rocky descent, and I knew that if I made it, salvation awaited in the form of a cable car.

The summit was a revelation. Called the Hexentanzplatz (Witches Dance Floor), it was originally a place of Saxon pagan worship. The site's big moment comes once a year on 30th April, exactly six months after Halloween. Known as *Walpurgisnacht* (Walpurgis night), local witches mount their broomsticks and fly to the nearby Brocken, the highest peak in the Harz range, which is the backdrop of a famous scene in Goethe's *Faust.*

A black Poodle, actually the demon Mephistopheles in disguise, takes Faust to the Brocken's summit on *Walpurgisnacht* where, "Tonight, the mountain's mad with magic". There, in his own blood, Faust signs a pact with the Devil and trades his soul for infinite knowledge.

Once they have danced the snow off the Brocken, the diabolical company broomstick their way back to the Hexentanzplatz. There, they finish their Walpurgis celebration with wine, song, and a wedding between Old Nick and the most comely in the coven.

Christian Frank immigrants forbade these pagan practices and posted soldiers at the Hexentanzplatz to enforce the ban. Dressed as witches with blackened faces, the Saxons scared the guards so much they never came back. Ultimately, however, the Christians got their revenge. Publication of their witch-spotting guide; *Malleus Maleficarum* ('Hammer of Witches') in 1487 literally ignited centuries of witch hunts and persecution. As an example, in a single day in 1589, Quedlinburg burned 133 suspected witches.

The scene that greeted us at Hexentanzplatz was as chaotic as the wildest Walpurgis night. We found an entire village of souvenir shops selling witch-themed tourist knickknacks, one of Germany's oldest open-air theatres, diabolical sculptures, a hotel, a zoo, and the *Walpurgishalle* museum, with its exhibit of a stone used for human sacrifice. If your granny lacks a broomstick to get there, fear not. The cable car from the theme park feeds a constant stream of ice-cream-guzzling tourists to the Hexentanzplatz, while in Wernigerode, an old steam railway can puff you to the top of the Brocken.

And if you want more, a second cable car is ready to whisk you to the *Roßtrappe*, a granite outcrop opposite the Hexentanzplatz. There, flaxen-maned princess Brunhilde, betrothed to the Prince of Harz, escaped her forced marriage to Bodo, the giant, by stealing one of his two colossal war steeds. One horse was white as snow, with eyes like stars; the other was black as night, with eyes like lightning. Neither was My Little Pony, but no prizes for guessing which she chose.

In sight of the Brocken, her lover's mountain pad, she hit a dilemma that was a metaphor for the quandaries we'd endured throughout our travels. Faced with the wild abyss of the Bode Gorge, her starry-eyed steed hesitated, yet behind, the terrible black horse with Bodo on board thundered towards her over the Hexentanzplatz.

When she spurred him on, her mount soared like an eagle across the chasm, and left the imprint of his giant hoof in the rock on the far side.

Brunhilde didn't make it entirely unscathed: she lost her golden crown in the depths of the canyon. Bodo and his horse fell and were shattered on the rocks beneath. Bodo transformed into a hellish black hound, destined to guard Brunhilde's crown for eternity. The gorge and river are named after him.

Mind you, for a flaxen-maned princess with a broken sandal, the gondola was a welcome sight.

Considering everything that had gone wrong with our plans, I was starting to believe we had a hex on us. Unaware that the light-green cars have glass floors to grant passengers the full vertigo experience, the fact we descended in cabin number 13 did nothing to reassure me the gods were on our side. In my arms, poor little Lani trembled all the way down.

That evening, we pondered our options for getting home. Our return ferry at the port of Caen was impossible to reach without stopping in France.

We faced the same impasse as we had in June, when Italian lockdown ended while the UK lockdown was in full swing. With our house rented out, we had nowhere to quarantine and had no idea how to isolate with four dogs to exercise. After studying the regulations, we came up with two solutions;

1. **"A person who has not been in a banned country does not need to isolate even in the same household as someone who has."** It seemed ridiculous, but if I flew home from Germany, I could still walk the dogs and shop for supplies while Mark quarantined. However, common sense suggested that boarding a plane significantly increased my risk of contracting coronavirus, and if I did, we would both have to isolate and be back to square one.
2. **"Travel Corridor Exception – if you do not stop in a banned country, you do not have to quarantine."** We could reach the Channel Tunnel non-stop from Germany. It would cost about £80 to cancel our ferry booking, but remaining self-contained in our van and caravan would certainly be a safer bet than a plane to avoid infection.

I asked for advice on a forum that claimed to be non-judgemental and had, to date, been very supportive through the pandemic. It came as a shock to be Travel Shamed by the Admin, no less. It really hurt. She slapped me down with a,

"Jackie, the purpose of quarantine is to keep us all safe."

I thought I was trying to do that, despite being faced with regulations that completely contradicted all logic.

Perhaps Mark and I should never have sold our souls to a black half-bred Poodle and her three Cavapoodle familiars.

37

IT NEVER RAINS BUT IT PAWS, BAD SOODEN-ALLENDORF

'Germany hits highest coronavirus cases since April, with 1,707 new infections'

With quarantine imposed on travellers returning to Britain from France and the Netherlands, this newspaper headline caused us considerable disquiet.

We had already brought forward our return to the UK by a month. Our plan was to flee to Aachen, on the German/Dutch/Belgian border. From there, we could reach the Channel Tunnel non-stop through France and Holland. This 'Travel Corridor' exempted us from quarantine once we returned to the UK, but now, with the possibility that Germany might also be red-listed, we decided to head home immediately, lest border closures caught us out.

It was a scenic run to *Camping Oase Wahlhausen*, through the secret misty forests of the Harz national park. We almost reached the top of the highest peak, the

Brocken, then wound through spectacular countryside to the outskirts of the gorgeously half-timbered town of Bad Sooden-Allendorf.

"It's pretty, but it's not France," I joked.

Once again, we were right on the former East/West German border, spookily overlooked by a watchtower, although unlike Berlin, this one was not inside the campsite. The tower formed part of the *Grenzmuseum* – a border museum that was instantly elevated to my 'must see' list.

I walked the dogs up to the tower while Mark set up. He used our piece of the Berlin Wall to level the caravan. By the tower, I found a wooden statue of a woman stepping through a door to symbolise freedom. It's hard to comprehend what life was like in East Germany under Russian control.

I had been starving since 11:30 and when I returned, it was nearly 3 p.m., so we drove into town for a late lunch. The only place open was a kebab house, where we sat outside to consume a dry and unusual-tasting Doner presented in a ciabatta, rather than flatbread. We washed it down with a very welcome and somewhat more conventionally flavoured *Weissbier*.

The Fab Four attracted the attention of the couple at the next table. As she fussed over our pups, the lady said,

"I've just lost my dog. He was aged 14. He was with me all the time. It is very hard for me." I could have wept for her. I dread that day when it comes, and told her to help herself to puppy love.

A few phone calls interrupted our conversation.

"It's my daughter," she explained.

"Trouble?" we asked.

"Always."

She added, "I'm on my way to see my 96-year-old mother."

Her companion chipped in,

"I am Austrian," he said. "Her mum liked me immediately because Hitler was Austrian."

I was truly shocked.

I thought history had judged Hitler. In my reality, it is a truth universally acknowledged that he was a really bad guy. I could not comprehend that anyone could admire someone who had perpetrated such evil, and on such a grand scale, but of course, I am condemned to judge only through the lens of my own experience in the free and wealthy West.

The following morning, we rescheduled our Eurotunnel crossing, made a vet's appointment for the dogs to have their mandatory tapeworm treatment, then discovered that we'd forgotten something. It was the August Bank Holiday in the UK. Every campsite we tried to book was full.

Another problem to solve.

That afternoon, we walked to the *Grenzmuseum*. Although the route was partly shady, the weather was roasting. Poor little Rosie, who had been stung by a wasp at the campground, got zapped by an electric fence next to the footpath. Kai was lagging, presumably because of the heat. As we stopped to chat to a young chap who told us he lived on the mountain called the Messner, and had chosen this area for the nature, Kai flopped in the shade, then seemed reluctant to carry on.

When I looked more closely, I noticed his left eye was purple and swollen shut. I could see something stuck in the corner – it was a bee sting, still throbbing and pumping venom into our poor boy's face.

"We need to get him to the vet," I shouted to Mark.

We removed the sting carefully and poured on some cold water to offer some relief. Then Mark swept him up, and we ran back to the campsite. Since we had phoned for an appointment only that morning, we already knew where the vet was. We bundled the pups into Big Blue and drove there, hoping against hope that it wasn't closed on Wednesday afternoons. Thankfully, it was open, and the vet saw us straight away. She didn't speak English, so I stumbled through with my rudimentary German. She administered some cortisone gel, which immediately reduced the swelling. Kai came out of the surgery with his eye slightly open. We were so relieved.

"Five times a day today, then three times a day after that," I translated to Mark as she handed over the tube of gel.

As when Rosie was stung, our worst fear – that he would go into anaphylactic shock – didn't happen. Kai was sorry for himself, but didn't rub his eye too much. The vet re-examined him during our official appointment the next day and assured us there was no lasting damage to his cornea.

Emotionally, I felt like screaming into a void of despair, then throwing myself down and beating the floor like a toddler having a tantrum.

Studies show that if you believe you are lucky, you will be, because you tend to note and add weight to the fortunate things that happen to you. Likewise, if you believe you're unlucky, you dwell on misfortune.

Although I am foolishly optimistic by nature, the seemingly endless string of problems and mishaps was getting to me. This had certainly been our most challenging trip. We'd escaped Brexit only to find ourselves locked down in a global pandemic. We'd endured near-death experiences, health, and mechanical issues. Like any dogmother, it broke my heart that my beloved fur family was suffering. Besides Kai's ocular emergency, the pups all had upset tums from the oppressive heat and humidity, and although we had applied bicarbonate of soda to Rosie's wasp sting, her pained whimpers cut right through me.

Touring in a pandemic because we couldn't go home had also taken its toll. We'd had little interaction with people, and news of outbreaks and infection spikes had governed our every move. Then, my concerns about The Beast, the enormous truck we'd bought unseen, and our plans to drive her to Mongolia through an area of increasing political instability bubbled to the surface.

Mark and I had a heart to heart.

"I feel blighted. It seems like everything is going wrong," I said.

"But everything that has gone wrong did so in a really great way!" he replied. "On the first day, when the caravan was stuck on the hairpin in Italy, the workmen got us out in ten minutes, with hardly any damage. That could have been a real predicament. When it happened, I couldn't see any way out without trashing the caravan. On the road, you will inevitably face some problems. It's bad that it happened, but what's important is the resolution couldn't have worked out better.

"Yes, Kai had an emergency, but we'd already researched the vet for the pups' tapeworm treatment, so it wasn't as bad as it could have been. I'd say that actually, we're really lucky."

"But, what if the pups get bitten by snakes or stung by scorpions in places where there are no vets?" I replied.

"There aren't that many worrying things in Central Asia," he reassured me.

"But what if we made a mistake? What if the truck's too big?"

"It is undoubtedly too big, but we'll have fun with it. Nothing is ever exactly right. There's always a compromise. I'm looking forward to visiting Norway next year, and even if we only go to Morocco with The Beast, it will fare better than Caravan Kismet. I constantly worry about Kismet, even on slightly uneven roads. She is just not built for it. And I wouldn't trust Big Blue on another long trip."

Our van was definitely due for retirement. She had been a hard-working and faultlessly loyal travel companion, but was ready to go out to grass. Her eyes were rheumy and her rear suspension collapsing like the back legs of an old Alsatian. *(To mollycoddle her through her MOT, we had to polish her cloudy headlights with toothpaste and replace both rear leaf springs.)*

The following day, we set off for the *Grenzmuseum* in the cool early morning. No stings or zappings by electric fences. I found it quite moody and humbling to walk along the border, where stretches of the intimidating metal barrier were preserved. The occasional crucifix marked locations where citizens had lost their lives trying to beat division.

The East German regime copied the Nazis by concealing the death toll and destroying all records when it fell. There is little reliable evidence of numbers, identities, or circumstances regarding those killed trying to escape across the border.

Exhibits in the museum described everyday life in the GDR. During 'Operation Vermin', some 10,000 'politically unreliable' individuals were relocated forcibly at night. 'Operation Consolidation' bulldozed entire villages near the border. The authorities split up families, and threatened those who refused to move with violence.

I tried to imagine being dragged from your bed in the dark by thuggish officials, before seeing your home and sanctuary destroyed. Far from providing protection, the state kept its people in constant fear.

Compared to the rest of the Eastern Bloc, GDR living standards were high, although the population still suffered shortages. From an early age, they moulded and trained citizens in socialist ideology, and surveillance was widespread. In 1950, the regime introduced the *Ministerium für Staatssicherheit* (Ministry for State Security). Better known as the MfS or Stasi, the unit collaborated closely with the KGB, Russia's notorious security service. The Stasi claims the dubious crown of exceeding the reach of any secret police force in history, including the Nazi Gestapo.

In its 40-year existence, this 'shield and sword of the party' employed a quarter of a million personnel. It also enlisted an unofficial network of almost the same number of private individuals, who spied on their neighbours' lives. Every apartment block in the GDR had its own Stasi informer.

The Stasi was relentless in its pursuit of opponents, and did not shy away from blackmail, imprisonment, or assassination. They could call on the Russian military for backup, as they did when they brutally suppressed the People's Uprising in June 1953 using Soviet tanks.

They also employed an insidious programme of psychological harassment known as *Zersetzung,* which translates literally as 'biodegradation'. Targets might have their relationships and careers sabotaged, have unnecessary medical treatment administered deliberately, or be subjected to 'gaslighting' attacks. These were subtle disruptions, such as having their furniture or pictures moved in their absence. Such tactics caused the individual to question their sanity, which sometimes led to lasting mental illness and suicide.

In a pandemic year, we all had first-hand experience of how it feels to be separated from loved ones, to suffer shortages in the shops, and to have restrictions placed on liberties we had formerly taken for granted.

My thoughts strayed back to the grandmother who so admired Hitler. What if the Soviet regime in East Germany had been so unbearable that it made Nazi rule look like Nirvana? I pondered what she may have endured, particularly so close to the border. Perhaps her life *would* have been better if the *Führer* had won the war.

I wondered whether those bombarded with Nazi propaganda, then imprisoned behind the Iron Curtain, ever found out about atrocities such as the Holocaust, which only came to light after the war.

Shakespeare's Hamlet uttered the famous aphorism,

"There is nothing either good or bad, but thinking makes it so."

It was a poignant reminder that now and then, you need to question and recalibrate what you think you know for certain, and try to understand why someone could have a very different viewpoint when their life and experience are completely removed from your own.

It was a long drive to Aachen. We passed a place called Titz, which obviously cheered us both up, and Mark gloated about going such a distance without a wrong turn.

"There's still time," I said, and there was.

In a tunnel, the satnav lost its signal. We missed a turning and had to tow through the centre of Dusseldorf.

Places in the *Stellplatz Aachen* campground were available on a first-come-first-served basis. Although it was packed and popular, we drove straight into the only empty space on the site. The chap next door said,

"It must be your lucky day!"

"It makes a change," I grumbled to Mark. "After all the things that have gone wrong on this trip, it's about time something went in our favour."

Mark's reply surprised me. He looked directly at me and said,

"Every day's our lucky day."

And do you know what? When you think about it, he's right.

It was the end of an era, which fizzled out like a damp squib as we made another break for the border.

We crossed three countries in the pouring rain to reach Eurotunnel. As we filled out our online entry forms in Aachen, we had another piece of 'luck'. We realised we had spent the exact number of days in Germany required to invoke our 'Travel Corridor Exception'. UK customs allowed us to re-enter with no requirement for quarantine.

We overcame our Bank Holiday accommodation issues by scoring a winter seasonal membership at a private campground on Calshot Spit, overlooking Portsmouth, the Solent, and the Isle of Wight. Despite assurances that our new truck, The Beast, would be finished by July, then October, progress was slow. Even by year end, she was anything but ready.

Our tenant gave notice and moved out in October, so we went back 'in the brick'. There seemed little point paying to store Caravan Kismet when our intention was to move into The Beast as soon as she was converted. We said a sad goodbye to Kismet. She had been our home for four years, and had given us safe conduct through ten countries. A dealer with a waiting list of pandemic staycationers snapped her up. On their website, she showed up as 'Sold' the same day. I hope she's having an easier retirement.

The sale of our principal residence completed. Since we couldn't find a short-term rental that would accommodate four dogs, we were relieved when our buyer agreed to rent our home back to us on an informal month-by-month basis.

The UK locked down for a second time in November.

Once again, Mark pointed out how lucky we were to have got our house back with such impeccable timing.

Obviously, I had my first date with The Beast, the truck we'd bought unseen from the internet...

And that is how our new adventure begins.

A REQUEST – PLEASE SPARE ME A SENTENCE!

Thank you for buying my book. I hope you enjoyed it. All authors appreciate feedback – especially the good stuff – and rely on reviews and recommendations. As an independent author, I don't have the marketing might of a global publishing company behind me, so reviews are really important to help other readers find my books, and I read every one.

If this memoir has taught you something, given you a giggle, inspired you, taken you on a pleasing armchair journey – or anything else – please let others know. You don't have to write *War and Peace* – a single sentence on Amazon, Goodreads, and/or Bookbub would be just lovely.

If you leave a review, The Fab Four and I will be eternally grateful, and will also do a happy dance!

Today is Make An Author Happy Day!

I know. What a coincidence.

If you have already written a review and want to spread the love even further, please could you:

· Share your review on social media
· Tell a friend (or 50!) about my book
· Like a positive review, or mark it as 'helpful'
· Add my books to your 'To Be Read' shelf on Goodreads
· Like and share my blog and social media posts
· Ask your local bookshop and library to stock my books
· If you don't do it for me, do it for my fellow authors – we're all in the same boat

Go on. Make our day!

KEEP IN TOUCH

If you want to know when I release new books, here are a few ways to connect with me:

· Follow my blog: www.WorldWideWalkies.com
· Follow me on Amazon: author.to/JLambert
· Follow me on Goodreads: www.goodreads.com/author/show/18672478.Jacqueline_Lambert
· Follow me on Bookbub: www.bookbub.com/profile/jacqueline-lambert
· Like me on Facebook: www.facebook.com/JacquelineLambertAuthor

I am also a member of We Love Memoirs, the friendliest group on Facebook.

WLM connects readers and authors to discuss all kinds of memoirs, including travellers' 'tails' like this one. If memoirs, competitions or book giveaways are your thing, pop in and say 'Hi' there too!

ACKNOWLEDGMENTS

I would like to thank the following people:

Debbie Purse – for her wonderful book cover designs and for being an absolute joy to work with.

Caroline Smith – for friendship, company, and eagle-eyed editing.

Sophie Wallace – @SophieWallaceProofreading for support and advice beyond the call of duty, as well as ever perfect and painstaking proofing. Sophie is also the talent behind the delightful *Deerhound Rhodry* children's books. (Rhodry is the canine star of the BBC and HBO TV series *Gentleman Jack*.) Find her books on your local Amazon store at author.to/Rhodry

The 'B' Team – (Really an 'A' Team of Wonderful Beta Readers:) **Dawne Archer, Sue Bavey, Judith Benson, Julie Haigh, Rebecca Hislop, Eileen Huestis, Susan Jackson, Stephen Malins, Veronica Moore, Simon Michael Prior, Sabina Ostrowska, Anna Rashbrook, Alyson Sheldrake, Jane Smyth, and Lisa Rose Wright** for kindly reading my manuscript and offering their valuable feedback.

Vojin Kremic – for creating the wonderful maps to illustrate each section.

To My Readers Around the World – as authors, we bare our souls for your entertainment. Your kind words, reviews, and encouragement mean so much.

And of course, Mark, Kai, Rosie, Ruby and Lani for filling my everyday with unconditional love.

Dog Bless You All!

ABOUT THE AUTHOR

Photo: The author with Ruby in the lavender fields of Valensole

Jacqueline (Jackie) Lambert is an award-winning travel writer, adventure traveller, and blogger, who loves history and curious facts. B.C. (Before Canines) she hurtled, slid, submerged and threw herself off bits of every continent except Antarctica. With husband Mark, A.D. (After Dog), she became an Adventure Caravanner. Her aim: To Boldly Go Where No Van Has Gone Before.

Jackie has published six light-hearted memoirs about her travels since quitting work: *Fur Babies in France, Dog on the Rhine, Dogs 'n' Dracula, It Never Rains But It Paws, To Hel In A Hound Cart,* and *Pups on Piste.*

Her forthcoming books will chronicle her Brexit-busting plan to convert a 24.5-tonne army truck and drive to Mongolia.

BY THE SAME AUTHOR

"If you are an animal lover, you will love her books. If you like to travel, you will love her books. If you like to read memoirs, you will love her books." Dawne Archer, Author of Trekker Girl Morocco Bound.

Adventure Caravanning with Dogs Series

It's caravanning, but not as you know it...

Year 1 – Fur Babies in France – *From Wage Slaves to Living the Dream:* is the true story of a couple who accidentally bought their first caravan – then decided to give up work, rent out the house, and tour Europe full-time with their four dogs. This book follows their first year on wheels, which involved lots of breakages and a near-death experience on Day 1.

"Full of fun. Told with excitement, vibrancy, and humour." Julie Haigh, Goodreads Librarian and Top 1,000 Amazon reviewer.

"Well written, full of bounce and fun." Valerie Poore, Marvellous Memoirs: Reviews and links

Dog on the Rhine – *From Rat Race to Road Trip:* Now, with a little caravanning experience under their belts, the crew gets a bit more adventurous and cross Germany, before going on a brief bark around Bohemia and the Balkans (the Czech Republic, Slovenia and Croatia). But lest they mislead you into thinking that Livin' the Dream is all sunshine and rainbows, they return home to a huge Fidose of reality...

"An inspirational travelogue." Windyoneuk on Amazon.co.uk

"Makes me want to take my dog, buy a caravan, and go traveling." Chris on Goodreads

Dogs 'n' Dracula – *A Road Trip Through Romania:* Told they would be robbed, scammed, kidnapped by gypsies, eaten by bears or attacked by wild dogs and wolves, if they managed to avoid the floods, riots – and vampires – the team Boldly Goes Where No Van Has Gone Before. Join them as they explore Europe's largest wilderness, adopt a street dog, and tow a caravan across the Carpathian Mountains on one of the world's most dangerous roads.

WINNER: Chill With A Book Premier Readers' Award, 2022

FINALIST: Romania Insider Awards for Best Promotion of Romania Abroad, 2019

"Armchair travel delight." Frances Hampson on Amazon.com

"A delightful book about the nomad lifestyle." Sharon Geitz, Gum Trees and Galaxies blog

It Never Rains but it Paws – *A Road Trip Through Politics And A Pandemic:* Five years after giving up work to travel full-time, Jackie and Mark race against time to leave the UK before Britain exits the EU. If Brexit happens, their four precious pups will lose their pet passports and will be unable to travel. But Brexit isn't their only obstacle. How do they cope when, a few months into their trip, the pandemic leaves them trapped in the epicentre of Europe's No.1 coronavirus hotspot?

"Her nimble writing rivals Bill Bryson and Paul Theroux." Liisa W. on Amazon.com

"A very light-hearted and enjoyable read." Alison Williams Author, Alison Williams Writing

To Hel in a Hound Cart – *Journey To The Centre Of Europe:* "Go to Hel!" The local wasn't being rude. She was describing Hel, Poland, well known for its fine beaches and windsurfing. Released from coronavirus lockdown, Jackie and Mark pack themselves and their four Cavapoo pups into their 'hound cart' (RV), but are unsure where their wanderlust might take them. Their adventures soon start stacking up. Dodging precipitous cliff-side roads, political unrest, and a global pandemic, will they go to Hel in a Hound Cart, or will that be what happens to their plans?

"Exuberant, sparkling with wit, insights, and well-researched historical facts... it's laugh-out-loud, poignant and superbly written." Fi Kidd, Overland Adventurer

"Her irrepressible sense of irreverent humour and quest for knowledge once more shine through." Sue Bavey, Author of Lucky Jack (1894-2000)

Adventure Travel with Dogs Series

Pups on Piste – *A Ski Season in Italy:* Jackie, Mark, and their canine crew spend three months in Monte Rosa, a little-known ski resort tucked under the second highest peak in Western Europe. It also happens to be in the world's Top 5 off-piste ski destinations. With parables from on piste and off, our snowmads get lost, stranded – and are told by an instructor, "Don't miss the turn or you'll go over a cliff."

"Highly recommended for dog lovers, ski enthusiasts, and adventure travellers." Louise Capper, Waggy Tales Book & Dog Blog.

"Excellent reference book! Jackie's story telling and informative approach has not only relieved me of some of my anxieties (about a planned trip) but really inspired me! Most interesting is that it's a thoroughly good read by a very eloquent writer." Hannah James – Winterised.com Motorhome Skiing

Anthologies

Travel Stories Series and Box Set

Itchy Feet: Tales of travel and adventure: Come with us as we take an epic journey out of Africa, through the Indonesian jungle and raft the Zambezi. Ride a Harley through France and Spain and find out what makes someone a perpetual nomad. Itchy Feet was released to a string of five-star reviews. A free photo album accompanies each book in the Travel Stories series.

"An excellent choice for lovers of travel and adventure stories. It's one to dip in and out of or immerse oneself in. Either way, it's a thoroughly entertaining read." Beth Haslam, Vine Voice Reviewer and Author of the Fat Dogs and French Estates series

Wish You Were Here: Holiday Memories: Whether it is a childhood 'bucket and spade' family holiday, the 'once-in-a-lifetime' dream destination, your first trip abroad, or the city where you first fell in love, we all have that one holiday that stands out in our minds. The award-winning and top travel memoir authors in this anthology bring out their postcards and photo albums and invite you to join them as they reminisce about their travels. Maybe they will inspire you to book your next holiday too!

"From Paris to Galapagos – from the comfort of our armchair – you'll wish you were there too." Jules Brown, Author of the Born to Travel Series: Tales from a Travel Writer's Life.

The Travel Stories Box Set: with 17 (yes – *seventeen*) bonus chapters, including *A Honeymoon Horror Story* by yours truly, that's nearly a whole extra book!

Robert Fear Anthologies

40 Life Changing Events, 2022 edition: 25 writers share events that have changed their lives. Some of these stories are tragic, others full of joy, but they all encapsulate tenacity, resilience, and self-belief. This fascinating compilation will encourage you to pause and reflect, with tales that offer much needed motivation and inspiration in these challenging times.

"From a letter to a past lover to the Namibian desert, dogs and thieves, there is a wealth of experiences to enjoy." Fabulouschrissie on Amazon.com

50 Intriguing Personal Insights, 2023 edition: In this anthology of real-life stories, twenty-nine writers share fifty fascinating experiences about themselves or those close to them. Take a break from your busy schedule and immerse yourself in this remarkable book. Discover how pivotal moments have affected their lives in unpredictable ways. You will feel stimulated by their honesty and take away a sense of intrigue and fulfilment.

"Another great collection. You can read it all in one – or it's perfect for dipping in and out of, a few stories at a time." Julie Haigh, Amazon Top 1,000 reviewer.

Follow this link to find all of Jacqueline's books on your local Amazon store: author.to/JLambert

APPENDIX 1

Recipe – Jackie's Baked 'Prussic Acid' Cheesecake

Ingredients:

- 75g (3oz) butter
- 110g (4oz) digestive biscuits, crushed
- 50g (2oz) amaretti biscuits, crushed
- 3 drops almond essence
- 170g (6oz) tub cottage cheese
- 250g (9oz) tub ricotta cheese
- 75g (3oz) caster sugar
- 25g (1oz) cornflour
- 1 lemon, grated rind
- 150ml (5 fl oz) sour cream
- 2 eggs, separated
- 75g (3oz) sultanas

Method:

1. Melt the butter in a pan and stir in the crushed

biscuits and almond essence. Press into the base of a deep 20cm (8″) dish.

2. Blend together both cheeses, add the sugar, cornflour, lemon rind, sour cream and egg yolks.

3. Whisk the egg whites until stiff, then fold into the cheese mixture with the sultanas. Pour the filling over the biscuit base.

4. Bake at 180°C, 350°F, Gas Mark 4 for 40-45 minutes, until set and golden brown. Cool, then chill well.

5. Serve dusted lightly with icing sugar, decorated with lemon slices and with cream if you like.

6. Await flattering comments from Uncle Norman.

Printed in Great Britain
by Amazon

12604537R00192